PERSPECTIVES ON INDIAN ENGLISH LITERATURE

Edited by
VINOD KUMAR MAHESHWARI

ATLANTIC PUBLISHERS AND DISTRIBUTORS

Published by
ATLANTIC PUBLISHERS AND DISTRIBUTORS
B-2, Vishal Enclave, Opp. Rajouri Garden, New Delhi-27
Phones : 5413460, 5429987

Sales Office
4215/1, Ansari Road, Darya Ganj, New Delhi-110 002
Phones : 3273880, 3285873, 3280451
Fax : 91-11-3285873
web : www.atlanticbooks.com
e-mail : info@atlanticbooks.com

ISBN 81-269-0093-8

Typeset at
APD Computer Graphics, Delhi

Printed in India at
Nice Printing Press, Delhi

PREFACE

At the very outset of the Preface to this volume, one must acknowledge the pioneering role played by Prof. K.R. Srinivasa Iyengar through his well-known classic, *Indian Writing in English*. The very fact that in most of the Indian universities, Indo-Anglian Literature has been taken as a subject at the Post-Graduate studies and research shows its literary and academic importance at the international level; and it is hoped that in times to come, the Indian writings in English would gain deeper roots in the cultural subsoil of emerging India. More and more young students and teachers engaged in higher studies would get interested in knowing about the writings of Indian writers in English in different literary genres : Prose, Fiction, Criticism, Poetry and Drama. Keeping this view in mind, an humble attempt is being made through the publication of the present volume — which is essentially a volume of critical evaluations of the works of some important Indian Writers. Eminent teachers and scholars from different parts of the country have framed critical articles on the contemporary Indian Writers in English.

The authors specially focused upon in this volume are : Malgonkar, Sarojini Naidu, Kamala Markandaya, Mulk Raj Anand, R.K. Narayan, Arundhati Roy, Nayantara Sehgal, Anita Desai and Kamala Das.

In addition to these, there are also some other critical articles included in this volume on *Perspectives on Indian English Literature*. Taken together, all these research articles are expected to enkindle keener interest among scholars and students of English literature in India; and it is hoped that there would come out more and more fruitful studies on life and literature by Indian writers and critics in English. They have an onerous responsibility to share because of the complexity of Indian life, which is getting transformed very fast under the impact of forces from all over the world since Independence.

Electronic devices have specially given a great boost to these cultural changes. And as the country, along with the rest of the world, is in a melting pot, Indian academicians and scholars should rise to the occasion and seize this opportunity by giving utterance to these changes as they have come to affect almost every man and woman in this 1-billion sub-continent. There is, indeed, a pull of tradition with its amazingly complicated caste-system and social practices; and there is also an hour-to-hour impingement by forces from overseas with different outlook and cultural values. It is hoped that the budding and established writers in English would take into account the cultural implications of these global changes. Despite the passing note of despair and frustration, one need not be blown off one's feet. One should remember Sri Aurobindo's far-sighted words in terms of his *Magnum Opus, The Life Divine* that India has a divine mission to fulfil. Sri Aurobindo wrote in English language; and so, other Indian writers writing in English should share his prophetic feelings by committing themselves, totally, in a truthful manner, to understand Indian life with its glorious past caught in the maelstorm of world-wide changes. William Faulkner at one stage stated that human heart has its own agonies and it is the moral responsibility of an artist to give utterance to them after chiselling them in the crucible of his creative mind. In this way, much of the garbage and debris associated with the crude Indian caste system would submerge as the creative genius of India has been able to establish the principles of true secularism, as the *rishis* and sages of the *Upanishads* had visualised. For the benefit of contemporary generation the same has been re-uttered by Shri Aurobindo in *The Life Divine*.

Thus, I would like to conclude these prefatory observations with the hope that the present volume on *Perspectives on Indian English Literature* would prove a milestone and give further impetus to scholarly pursuits in India.

I am grateful to all my teachers, well-wishers and members of my family under whose blessings and guidance I have been able to bring out this volume.

Finally, I record my gratitude to Dr. K.R. Gupta, Managing Director of M/s Atlantic Publishers and Distributors, New Delhi, who by his own work, advice and example, both aided the inception of this volume and encouraged its completion.

V.K. MAHESHWARI
Editor

CONTENTS

1

Malgonkar's Art of Characterisation

—*P.N. Sinha*

Malgonkar is one of those few Indo-Anglian novelists who show how well an English literary form can be adapted to develop Indian themes and how effectively the English language can be used to express and convey Indian sensibility. True, he does not act on the observation of C.D. Narasimhaiah who has said : Indian fiction in English can, it seems to me, make headway by continuing the Raja Rao line....[1] Malgonkar does not follow the Raja Rao line. Amar says about him, "His approach to the novel is radically different from that of Raja Rao."[2]

Malgonkar scrupulously keeps away from Raja Rao's metaphysical speculations. Still, he has definitely made a mark for himself in Indo-English fiction. In fact, he presents a study in contrast with all 'the big three' — Raja Rao, Mulk Raj Anand and R.K. Narayan — in Indo-English fiction. Malgonkar's inclination is neither towards the life of the downtrodden in the Indian society (as Anand's) nor towards the middle class life in the fictional world of Malgudi (as R.K. Narayan's) and not even towards the other wordliness (metaphysical world) of Raja Rao. He stands rather apart from other Indo-English novelists and shows a strong historical sense in portraying the important phases of the Indian national movement right from 1857 to 1949 in his novels. A.N. Dwivedi says, "It is not the psychological, sociological or anthropological themes that attract Malgonkar but the historical one."[3]

Malgonkar holds historicized attitude to life. Even when he describes his contemporary society, he looks at it historically. He pin-points the historical forces and conflicts that lie behind the contemporary life. His novels give a historical understanding for the problems of contemporary society. His historical novels are an artistic expression of an historicized attitude to life. A.N. Dwivedi has rightly said, "Malgonkar is one of those Indo-English novelists who have shown a keen awareness of Indian tradition and her hoary history."[4]

Where R.K. Narayan is democratic in the choice of his subject-matter and displays a deep sense of compassion for the middle class people in the Indian society, Malgonkar is aristocratic and committed to conservative values. He borrows his major characters from the upper strata of the Indian society. The major characters in his novels are military officers, princes, ministers, lords and big businessmen. Amar says about him, "His concern is not so much with the average and the democratic...."[5]

Malgonkar's portrayal of the upper strata of the society has been mistaken for his indifference towards the lower strata of the Indian society. Amar says, "Those who seek glimpses into the depths of Indian poverty or the degradation of its down-trodden masses would be utterly disappointed with Malgonkar."[6] V.S. Naipaul goes one step farther and says that Indo-Anglian novelists are 'withdrawn' from the social life of Indian and cites *The Princes*, one of the novels of Malgonkar, to prove his contention. He says, "Withdrawal, denial, confusion of values : these are vague words. We need more direct evidence; and a little, I feel, is provided by a recent Indian novel, *The Princes*, by Manohar Malgonkar."[7]

Much of the misunderstanding (misconception) about Malgonkar is because of our indifference towards his objective as a novelist. The fact to be born in mind is that Malgonkar is a historical novelist. As a historical novelist, he is primarily concerned with the portrayal of historical events and more particularly, the historical conflicts which characterize a definite period in the recent history of India. Apart from portraying the historic movement of 1857 in *The Devil's Wind*, he portrays the racial, ideological and communal conflicts and their impact on the social and private life of individuals in his novels. The manifestation of these conflicts gets fuller and vivid expression only in the upper strata of society. The very nature of the conflicts which he seeks to portray conditions his selection of characters and the section of society. For a historical novelist, the portrayal of historical forces and conflicts is more significant than the portrayal of a particular section of society. That is why, perhaps, Malgonkar says, "The social life of millions of Indians centres round the dustbins of great cities. Granted. But mine doesn't...."[8]

The significant point about a historical novelist is not that he portrays the society from 'above' or 'below.' His success as a historical novelist is to be judged on the extent to which he succeeds in portraying the characteristic features of social life at a definite period. Lukacs says, "The overwhelming majority of Scott's, Pushkin's and Tolstoy's heroes come from the upper sections of society, and yet the life and destiny of the whole people are reflected in the events of their lives."[9]

Besides, Malgonkar is a true artist. He does not venture beyond the field of his own experience except in *The Devil's Wind*. His own army service and princely ancestry brought him into close contact with the upper class of people. His insistence on the authenticity of felt experience keeps him within the confines of direct involvement. Rajagopalachari says, "He is one of those few writers who gain the stamp of unmistakable authenticity by transmuting felt experience into art."[10]

Malgonkar's own diverse experiences in the fields of big-game hunting, civil service, army, business and politics have helped him "catch the color of life,"[11] especially of the upper strata. Malgonkar writes novels on the self-experienced history of India (except in *The Devil's Wind*). In all his novels he presents "a subtle blend of the historical and personal themes."[12] To present contemporary history in fictional mode is deeply rooted in the Indian tradition. Long before Malgonkar in the first half of the seventh century A.D., Banabhatta had portrayed his contemporary history in his famous novel Harsa-carita, which is known as Akhyayika in Sanskrit literature. Like Bana, Malgonkar presents in fictional terms the central drama of contemporary history. Malgonkar is fully aware of his native tradition. He adopts and adapts it to suit his own purpose. "He shows a deep awareness of his cultural heritage and national history."[13]

Malgonkar believes that real persons are not suitable for treatment in novels. As people are rather colourless in their real life. If one of their aspects is worthy of putting into a novel, their other aspects are equally unsuitable for treatment in novels. That is why Malgonkar does not use real people in his novels. He says, "I think most novelists will never admit that they have used real people in their novels.... Certainly as a character you cannot put a real person into a book."[14] But his fictional characters are based on real people. Dayanand says about his characters, "The characters are modelled on real people and incidents closely resemble real events."[15]

He takes "the physical features from one, the peculiarities from another and character from some one else"[16] and puts them into a single fictional character and creates composite personalities in his novels.

Hiroji and Abhayraj in *The Princes* are not historical persons but creatures of Malgonkar's imagination. What Malgonkar has done is to take the authenticated facts of the State of Devas Senior, its Maharaja, and his son, and camouflage them through the transforming power of novelistic imagination. Commenting on the process of turning a real person into a fictional one in *The Princes*, Malgonkar says,

"I thought they were sufficiently camouflaged for you not to think of them as real persons. They are actually composite personalities, you know, there is no real person."[17]

He camouflages his characters by disguising the voice or size of the real persons. The reshaping of fact into fiction can be clarified by pointing to some examples from his novels. Dayanand says, "Malgonkar transformed His Highness Sir Tukoji Rao III; K.C.S.I., Maharaja of Dewas State Senior into His Highness Sir Hiroji, the Fourth, K.C.S.I., Maharaja of Begwad, and his son Maharaja Vikram Sinha Rao, later called Chhatrapati Shahaji, into Abhayraj, Bedar III."[18]

He transforms the real persons so much that in his hands facts become fiction. Even then his characters are life-like and convincing. He is a true artist. He is genuinely interested in creating live characters. His prime concern is 'how to make a fictional person into a real person.'[19] He gets inspiration from Marquand, an American author. Marquand has said somewhere that the creative author is the closest thing to God on this earth because "he creates characters which to many are actually real people."[20] Malgonkar is inspired by Marquand to create live characters in his novels. He knows that human beings are not simple by nature. That is why he creates composite personalities and breathes "the air of reality"[21] into his fictional characters.

It is by the technique of camouflage that Malgonkar successfully creates what Henry James has called "the illusion of life."[22] The Maharaja of Begwad, Abhayraj, Henry Winton, Kiran, Devi Dayal, Gian — all the composite portraits who take their cue from Malgonkar's personal knowledge of various princes, soldiers, British officers and Anglo-Indians. However, in *The Devil's Wind*, he adds some of the charms of fictional character to the historical personage of Nana Saheb. But what he says about Nana Saheb is also true about all his characters, "I treat him as a human being...a rather mixed up human being, like most of us are."[23] All his characters are a compound of good and bad.

In fact, Malgonkar's art of characterisation is based on the Indian conception of human nature. According to Indian conception, human nature is an amalgam of three 'Gunas' (attributes) : 'Sattva, Raja and Tama.'[24] These 'Gunas' are mixed up in different proportions with the predominance of one over the other in an individual. An individual's nature is determined by the predominance of any one of the three 'Gunas.' But the predominance of one 'Guna' is never final. According to Indian conception the predominance of one Guna is both variable and alterable. With the change in circumstances and acquisition of experiences, the predominance of one 'Guna' gives way to another. It may be altered even by conscious efforts. That is why, human beings are complex by nature and undergo changes in their approach and attitude.

Malgonkar represents and illustrates the role of history in individual's life by means of his character. He illustrates by means of his characters that 'the roots of the present lay in the past.'[25] Malgonkar seems to share the view of Jawaharlal Nehru : "All that we are and that we have comes from the past."[26]

Lt. Col. Kiran Garud's loyalty to the army code (*Distant Drum*) is the product of his British training in the Indian army. Henry Winton's indifference (*Combat of Shadows*) to the Indians is the product of his upbringing in the British tradition. Abhayraj's initial opposition to his father's ideas in *The Princes* is the manifestation of his education in Public schools. Gian's initial belief in truth and non-violence in *A Bend in the Ganges* shows the impact of Gandhian philosophy. Nana Saheb's antagonism (*The Devil's Wind*) to the British rule in India is determined by the British cruelty and ruthlessness in India.

One significant point about Malgonkar is that he endeavours to portray the historical conflicts and their impact on the life, behaviour, thought and action of people by means of his characters. With the help of his characters, he demonstrates that historical circumstances and conflicts existed in precisely such and such way. His characters represent historical forces both in their thought and action.

Lt. Col. Kiran Garud in *Distant Drum* represents the concept of individual's potentiality which contradicts the then current concept of racial superiority. The concept of racial superiority was often extended by the British for the continuation of the British rule in India. Henry Winton (*Combat of Shadows*) is blind with racial arrogance and represents the British tendency of looking down upon the Indians. Malgonkar presents him as a true representative of the British race in an ironical way. The Maharaja Hiroji and even Prince Abhayraj, a little later in his life in *The Princes*, represent conservative values. Gian and Debi Dayal in *A Bend in the Ganges* represent the ideological conflict between violence and non-violence which was a characteristic feature of the life in 1930s and '40s in India. Nana Saheb in *The Devil's Wind* represents the then people's aspiration for freedom. Lala Vishnu Saran Dev (*Distant Drum*), Yugal Kishore (*Combat of Shadows*) and Kanakchand (The Princes) represent the prevalent corruption in the political life of his country just before and after Independence.

This is not to suggest that Malgonkar has created only types or flat characters in the novels. The fact is that he has created both types and individuals in his novels. The observation of A.N. Dwivedi is quite relevant in this connection. A.N. Dwivedi says, "Malgonkar's characters include both types and individuals of the first category are the army men and the courtiers, the loyal ministers and the opportunistic leaders, the courtesans and the harlots, the prisoners and the businessmen; and of the second are Lt. Col. Kiran Garud, Henry Winton, Debi-dayal, Gian Talwar, Abhayraj and Nana Saheb."[27]

Of all the characters in Malgonkar's novels, the portraits of the Indian political leaders belong to the category of flat characters. They have been constructed round a single idea and their nature can be summed up in a single sentence. They pose to be nationalist but they are selfish, corrupt and vindictive at heart. They recur in his different novels.

Malgonkar is aware of the corruption that has crept into the social and political life of his time. He has personal experience of the pulls and pressure, corruption and immorality that are in operation at every level of our social and political life. His hatred and prejudice against political leaders in India get better expression through the mouth of Henry Winton (*Combat of Shadows*). He says to Jugal Kishore, "God help India if people like you are to be elected to assemblies."[28] Malgonkar illustrates the prevalent corruption and degeneration in social and political life of his time with the character of political leaders.

Lala Vishnu Saran Dev (*Distant Drum*) is Malgonkar's first portrait of the upstart politician who has made his appearance on the Indian political scene during the country's struggle for freedom. He wants the army 'Shamiana' for a political show and gets Lt. Col. Kiran Garud transferred when he does not oblige him. He misuses his political power against an honest and loyal officer. Jugal Kishore (*Combat of Shadows*) is crooked, corrupt and quite immoral. He offers his niece Gauri to Henry Winton as a mistress in exchange for a job for her. Amar says about him, "Jugal Kishore, 'dangerous, cunning and vindictive,' is one of Malgonkar's recurrent images of the Indian politician."[29]

Even Kanakchand (*The Princes*) is no better. He is submissive and servile in the beginning but turns sour and twisted in later life. He becomes vindictive. He says to Abhayraj, "I want revenge."[30] All the portraits of the political leaders are concrete illustration of Malgonkar's prejudices against them and the prevalent corruption in the political life of his time. Amar says, "Portraits of the emergent politician — Lala Vishnu Saran Dev, Jugal Kishore and Kanakchand — are too consistently typical to leave us in much doubt as to what he thinks of them."[31]

Malgonkar is dissatisfied with the quality of political life of his time. He believes that there is no place for an honest man in the political life of his time. He fights the general elections to the Parliament twice but loses it only because of his honesty. John Morris says about him, "He would not have made a successful politician since he is completely honest and also an idealist. Politicians in India tend to be more corrupt than in other countries."[32]

Malgonkar communicates his personal experience of political life with the help of his characters. One discovers a fine blending of personal experience and history in the very presentation of political leaders as flat characters.

The creation of flat characters is not the indication of failure on Malgonkar's part to realize the complexities of the ordinary human mind, as it is generally believed. In fact the presentation of political leaders as flat characters in his novels is deliberate and has a definite purpose. It serves the artistic purpose of reflecting the typical traits of political leaders of his time. He sounds a satiric note against the popular leaders of his time by presenting them in the form of flat characters. It is the part of the genius of Malgonkar that he uses types and caricatures for a definite purpose. Besides, he individualises his types.

All the major characters, particularly the protagonists in Malgonkar's novels are round characters. They grow wiser and maturer in course of time. They undergo a change in their attitude in course of gaining experiences.

Lt. Col. Kiran Garud (*Distant Drum*) who proves his loyalty to the army code by refusing to lend 'the Shamiana' for 'a political show' even at the cost of his transfer from the regiment, fails to resist the call of old friendship with General Abdul Jamal who was fighting from the side of Pakistan. Without caring a bit for the army code of conduct and his career, he drinks shampagne with the Pakistani General on the Kashmir front. He boasts of sacrificing even his sweetheart Bina Sonal for his professional future but succumbs to the dictates of sensual pleasure and spends the night with Margot Medley, the wife of his brother-officer. But he learns by his mistakes and grows maturer.

Henry Winton (*Combat of Shadows*) who is proud and conscious of his racial superiority, often lapses into cowardice. He pales into insignificance before the 'Combat of Shadow'. Amar says about Winton's story, "It culminates in the hero's apocalyptic realization of the 'moment of truth.' "[33]

Prince Abhayraj in *The Princes* is critical of his father's conservative ideas and tyrannical behaviour during the early part of his life. But he succumbs to the dead weight of the previous tradition and becomes a true representative of his father's ideas and ideals. He is transformed by his experiences. Dayanand says, "*The Princes* is also the initiation story of Abhay, his growth from boy to man."[34]

Gian Talwar (*A Bend in the Ganges*) begins as a disciple of Gandhi and believes in truth and non-violence. But he realises the inadequacy of non-violence after the murder of his brother. He discards non-violence and kills Vishnu Dutt, the murderer of his brother. He develops relationship with Debi Dayal's sister Sundari on the basis of a series of lies. Both Gian and Debi Dayal who fight for the freedom of the country in their own way, withdraw themselves from political life and seek fulfilment in domestic bliss towards the end.

Nana Saheb (*The Devil's Wind*) who was fired by the glittering dream of freedom, was also addicted to pleasure and sex. He fights for the freedom of his country but at the end he takes refuge in the domestic bliss with Eliza Wheeler. Thus, we see that all his major characters undergo a change in their attitude and vibrate with life. Rajagopalachari says, "Malgonkar's characters in fact do not subscribe themselves to any rigid code."[35]

In this respect Malgonkar presents a study in contrast with R.K. Narayan. The major characters of R.K. Narayan do not change even though they undergo experience that would normally result in change. Uma Parmeswaran says about Narayan's characters, "Vasu remains a villain until death and beyond it, Margayya the financial expert, Raju the guide and Mr. Sampath remains rogues; Krishnan the English teacher and Chandran the bachelor of arts remain romantic."[36] Only in the earliest two novels and in the last do the main characters change within the novel.

Malgonkar is a mature novelist. He allows his characters reveal themselves through their speech and action. His novels are packed with action and drama. His characters reveal themselves in their interaction with a series of events and incidents. Malgonkar's characters and incidents are so inter-dependent in fiction that his technique exemplifies Henry James's comment that character is 'the determination of incident' and incident, 'the illustration of character.'[37]

Malgonkar does not identify himself with his characters. Despite the first person narrative in *The Princes* and *The Devil's Wind*, the novels are autobiographical in method, not in substance. Abhayraj is not Malgonkar. About the story of Nana Saheb, Malgonkar says, "This, then, is Nana's story as I believe he might have written it himself."[38]

Even in *Distant Drum* where he describes his own experiences of the army life in Indian and the Burma War in which he participated, he does not identify himself with Lt. Col. Kiran Garud, the protagonist in the novel. Lt. Col. Kiran Garud does not leave the army in spite of being offered a highly lucrative job by the old General Ropey Booker. Whereas Col. Malgonkar himself left the army because he found the 'army life a little repressive.' Rajagopalachari has rightly said, "Though he insists on 'felt experience,' he maintains discrete aesthetic distance in the delineation of characters."[39]

Malgonkar is impartial both in the interpretation of events and in the delineation of characters. Despite his own army service and princely ancestry he shows no favour to army officers and princes in his novels. With artist's characteristic detachment, he exposes their pretension and false vanity in his novels. One may not agree with Meenakshi Mukherjee who says, "Malgonkar completely withholds his sympathy from all the characters who are not "rich and well-born" or do not share the British public school virtues."[40]

Lt. Col. Kiran Garud, Henry Winton and Abhayraj are product of public school. But Malgonkar shows no favour to them in delineating their character. On the contrary, he exposes the inadequacy of public school values in the complex human situation. They suffer from the same human weakness, as one discovers in a common man.

Even in the portrayal of women characters, Malgonkar is chiefly guided by historical sense. The very selection and portrayal of women characters is strictly in tune with the temper and psychology of the time. He has portrayed women in different forms — concubine, beloved and wife — in his novels. But there is uniformity in their attitude towards life and sex and also in the role which they play in the life of men in the society. A.N. Dwivedi says, "Obviously, women play second fiddle to men in the works of Malgonkar, whose world is manifestly a world of men."[41]

The introduction of concubines in his novels has no other relevance than to reveal the historical condition and position of the women in the feudal society of India. More specifically, it reveals the characteristic feature of the life of the Indian princes and their attitude towards life and women. The princes, relaxed and permissive, did not crack down on sexual expression before marriage. James Y. Dayanand says about the princes, "They had a custom of providing young men with healthy concubines."[42]

The Maharaja in *The Princes* was presented with his first concubine, Bibibai, on his sixteenth birthday. Later on he took two more concubines. Prince Abhayraj was present with Zarina, a young concubine, at the age of nineteen. Nana Saheb in *The Devil's Wind* was initiated into the world of sex and happiness only through his concubines, Champa and Azijan.

As he had a mysterious curse about his marriage. The attitude of the princes towards marriage was prosaic. The Maharaja in *The Princes* lectures solvenly on marriage, "It is not a private, purely personal matter at all, but an affair of the state."[43]

The attitude of the princes towards their wives was no better. The wives were looked upon as a piece of furniture to be displayed on public occasions. The princes were indifferent to their feelings. They often behaved cruelly with them. The Maharaja in *The Princes* kicked his wife on the very first night of their marriage. She was cast on the dust heap in the full bloom of youth with all her womanly desires still unslaked. She never knew what it was to be 'a complete women.'[44] She has strong resentment against the cruelty of her husband. She prefers the state of "a woman of the streets"[45] to the status of "a Maharani in Darkness."[46]

Kashi-bai, the third wife of Nana Saheb in *The Devil's Wind* had no better tale to tell us. She was obedient, dutiful and above all, serviceable. But Nana abstains from all physical relations with her. True, he had a mysterious curse about his marriage. But then, he had no right to play with the life of an innocent girl. Kashi was a live girl. She was not a doll to play with. She says, "I was never a Peshwa wife — I was a child widow."[47] She was a virgin even after twelve years of her marriage with Nana.

Even the attitude of the people of upper strata towards women is no better in Malgonkar's novels. They look upon them as 'a pleasure giving commodity.' A.N. Dwivedi says about his women character, "As for women, they mostly appear as symbols of sex and comfort, be they queens (like the mother and wife of Abhayraj in *The Princes* and Kashi in *The Devil's Wind*) or plebians (like Sundari in *A Bend in the Ganges,* Ruby and Jean in *Combat of Shadows,* and Miss Bina in *Distant Drum*)."[48]

Lt. Col. Kiṛan Garud in *Distant Drum* loves Bina Sonal, perhaps, because 'the way, her nose wrinkkles when she laughs'. He says to Bina, 'I am terribly in love with you,'[49] but he is not willing to sacrifice his career for her. He says to Bina's father, "My career to me is more important than anything else — more important than your daughter."[50]

Henry Winton (*Combat of Shadows*) meets Ruby Miranda, an Anglo-Indian girl, and is at once struck by her good looks. He is moved by his lust for her "eyes of the real Chandani Chowk whore, black and gold."[51] He is a man of lust without love. He seeks sensual fulfilment and pays her a hundred rupees a month of the Company's money for his private pleasure. Even Abhayraj in *The Princes* loves Minie Bradley, an English girl for her earthly sensuousness. For him, Minnie is an object of lust and not of love. His approach is cold and business-like. He loves her more because he is initiated into the searching, revealing and intimate experience of sex. Amar says, "There is, of course, plenty of sex in his novels."[52]

If we look at the women characters in his novels from man's point of view, they do not fare better either. He has created women characters of different origins — Indian, Anglo-Indian and the English — in his novels. But all of them resemble one another in respect of their attitude to life and sex. They seem to have a craze for leading a full-blooded life of sex. The wives in general in his novels appear infidel to their husbands. Margot Medley, the beautiful wife of Lt. Col. Bob Medley in *Distant Drum* spends the night with Lt. Col. Kiran Garud and does not repent on it. She says, "No one can help these things...they just happen to one."[53]

Henry Winton (*Combat of Shadows*) discovers his English wife, Jean, locked in the arms of Eddie, her Anglo-Indian lover. The Maharani in *The Princes* elopes with her Muslim lover Abdulla Jan, an ordinary Police officer of the palace. Kashibai (*The Devil's Wind*) betrayed her husband when he most needed her. She says, "I want to be in the glitter of a great King's Court, not in a hermitage."[54] "That is why, perhaps," Amar says, "the women tend to run into limited and easily identifiable types."[55]

One significant point about Malgonkar is that he does not distinguish Indian women from the Anglo-Indian and the English women in his novels. The Indian women in his novels do not correspond to the Indian conception of ideal womanhood. It may be said that he ignores the fact that the western society is based on a "totally different conception of man-woman relationship from ours."[56] Even then one discovers uniformity in the thinking of all women characters. True, the Maharani and Kashi-bai are 'abandoned wives' But their idea of changing husband is not conducive to the spirit of Indian culture. Whatever may be the justification, but their action cannot be approved of in the light of Indian culture. What Amar says about Gauri who is a woman of easy morals in *Combat of Shadows,* may be said about other Indian women in his novels. Amar says, "Malgonkar's women characters have never been fully credible and Gauri is no exception.... We find hardly anything about her which is truly and representatively Indian."[57]

In the delineation of Indian women, Malgonkar presents a study in contrast with A.S.P. Ayyar in Indo-Anglian literature. Ayyar's women characters reflect Indian culture both in their thought and action. Uma Parameswaran says, "Almost every women in *Baladitya* is a paragon of virtue, jealous of her honour, bounteous in compassion, unselfish and dutiful."[58] Malgonkar does not distinguish the Indian women from the Western women in thought and action. Meenakshi Mukherjee says, "Each writer has to make his own definition of what is for him the West and what is East."[59]

Despite the fact that Malgonkar does not particularise the Indian women, it would be wrong to infer that Malgonkar is ignorant of or indifferent to the Indian conception of womanhood. The fact to remember is that Malgonkar is a historical novelist. As a historical novelist, he is primarily concerned with the social features and trends of thought in his contemporary society. A.S.P. Ayyar depicts the ancient India in his novels whereas Malgonkar seems to suggest the impact of western culture on the modern India, particularly on the women of upper strata. Meenakshi Mukherjee says, "The impact of the West has created certain cultural problems and crises in values in all parts of India."[60] The Indian woman in Malgonkar's novels may not appear credible in the light of Indian culture. But if one views them in the modern context, they represent a fact of history.

Another significant point about Malgonkar's art of characterisation is that he distinguishes his characters by means of language. He knows that Indians speaking in English have certain characteristic modes of expression. He does try to achieve authenticity in tone and expression of his character. One may not agree with Meenakshi Mukherjee who says that writers like Santha Ram Rau. Kamala Markandaya and Manohar Malgonkar "have generally hypassed the linguistic and stylistic problems inherent in the Indo-Anglian situation."[61]

No writer of importance can bypass the problem of his medium and yet succeed in writing a good book. Malgonkar has met the challenge of his foreign medium squarely and bent it to serve his own purpose. An examination of the different speech styles that Malgonkar employs in his very first novel from the British army officers to that of the betel chewing politician, Vishnu Saran Dev, would show the core and accuracy with which these have been observed and recorded. Lala Vishnu Saran Dev talks to Lt. Col. Kiran in a peculiarly Indian tone : "I yam the Chairman aaf the District Caangrus Committee...."[62] Here Malgonkar reveals the Indianness and illiteracy of the character and distinguishes him from the rest of the characters by his mode of expression. Meenakshi Mukherjee says, "Particularising of character is an indication of a novelist's skill and part of the means of doing it is through subtle nuances of language.[63]

Like Mulk Raj Anand, he changes the spelling of the words to indicate the half-educated position of Indian political leaders and to give an Indian touch to the speech — as 'aan' for 'on,' 'yaas' for 'yes,' 'faar' for 'for,' 'ishport' for 'sport,' and 'gownment' for 'government.'[64]

Bernard Shaw has also made use of the artistic device of particularising character by distorting the spelling of the English words in his play *Candida.* He distinguishes Burgess who is illiterate from Morell who is an intellectual and religious guide of the people. Burgess says to Morell, "When I gev you arsh words in my natral disappointment, you turned my daughter again me."[65] Malgonkar is not as inventive as Raja Rao or as vernacular as Mulk Raj Anand, but he does give a touch of Indianness to his characters by making them use Hindi words in their English. He makes use of Hindi words such as 'izzat,' 'ulloo,' Arri,' 'maara' (*Distant Drum*), 'Sansar,' 'Toba,' 'Arre' (*A Bend in the Ganges*), 'Zidd,' (*Combat of Shadows*), 'Dada,' and 'Shabash' in *The Princes*. Malgonkar makes further subtle distinction between 'tu' and 'aap' (in place of you) in *A Bend in The Ganges*, which is relevant in the Indian context. The use of 'thou' in place of 'tu' would not achieve the same effect. Shakti Batra says, "Exclamations of surprise, wonder and joy, such as 'Toba, Toba,' 'Shabash', 'Hai, Hai,' 'Harey Ram,' 'Arre,' 'Hai Allah,' 'Yaah' and 'thu' add to the overall realism and authenticity of characters."[66]

Malgonkar certainly recaptures the real speech of British officers in the Indian Army or that of hardcore hunters and half-educated political leaders. It is no wonder, then, that the novelist's linguistic excellence made a correspondent of the Times Literary Supplement once writes that a "new Malgonkar in a piccadilly bookstall puts the seal on British achievement."[67]

Malgonkar is a consummate craftsman. He makes use of all possible devices to create life-like characters. We find his characters emerging in flesh and blood, affirming their identity in their interaction with events. Malgonkar's obvious love of plot, story and action in the novel has not impaired his sense of characterisation. M. Rajagopalachari says, "Malgonkar pits his characters against the backdrop of dramatic action and lets them grow as authentic individuals."[68] One cannot agree with

Shakti Batra who says, "Malgonkar's account takes the form of a cool, impersonal debate among the characters; it looks like a scientific analysis of the situation rather than something which emerges out of the characters themselves and their convictions."[69]

Malgonkar analyses his characters and events with a bit of detachment characteristic of a historian. But his success lies in individualising his characters. He individualises even his flat characters. He catches and portrays the sudden and unexpected variation in his character's attitude and approach. He says, "I revel in incident, in improbabilities in unexpected twists...."[70] Even then the thought and action of his characters appear quite convincing. The 'unexpected twist' only reveals Malgonkar's awareness of the complexity of human nature.

Malgonkar is a consummate artist. He makes use of all possible devices to create life-like characters. We find his characters emerging in flesh and blood, affirming their identity in their interaction with events. Malgonkar's obvious love of plot, story and action in the novel has not impaired his sense of characterization. Rajagopalachari says, "Malgonkar pits his characters against the backdrop of dramatic action and lets them grow as authentic individuals."[71] His characters live freely and display all their strength and weaknesses in the struggle of life. Marshall A. Best has rightly said that he knows "how to stretch the readers' willing suspension of disbelief for the sake of a dramatic confrontation."[72]

NOTES AND REFERENCES

1. C.D. Narasimhaiah, "Raja Rao's Kanthapura : An Analysis," *Critical Essays on Indian Writing in English,* edited by M.K. Naik, The Macmillan Co. of India Ltd., Madras, 1977, p. 270.
2. G.S. Amar, *Manohar Malgonkar,* Arnold Publishers (I) Pvt. Ltd., New Delhi, 1973, p. 9.
3. A.N. Dwivedi, "The Historian as Novelist : Manohar Malgonkar," *Perspectives on Indian Fiction in English,* edited by M.K. Naik, Abhinav Publications, New Delhi, 1985, p. 145.

4. *Ibid.*, p. 148.
5. G.S. Amar, *op. cit.*, p. 13.
6. *Ibid.*, p. 13.
7. V.S. Naipaul, *An Area of Darkness,* Andre Deutsch Ltd., London, 1964, p. 66.
8. Marshall A. Best, "Malgonkar, Manohar (Dattatray)," *Contemporary Novelists,* edited by Janes Vinson, St. Janes Press, Ltd., London, 1976, p. 879.
9. George Lukacs, *The Historical Novel,* Beacon Press, Boston, 1963, p. 284.
10. M. Rajagopalachari, *The Novels of Manohar Malgonkar*, Prestige Books, New Delhi, 1989, p. 11.
11. Henry James, "The Art of Fiction," *American Poetry and Prose,* edited by Norman, Faerster-Houghton Mifflin Company, Boston, 1962, p. 1169.
12. G.S. Amar, *op. cit.*, p. 133.
13. A.N. Dwivedi, "The Historian as Novelist : Manohar Malgonkar," *op. cit.*, p. 147.
14. James Y. Dayanand, *Manohar Malgonkar, op. cit.*, pp. 94-95.
15. *Ibid.*, p. 89.
16. *Ibid.*, p. 95.
17. M. Rajagopalachari, *The Novels of Manohar Malgonkar, op. cit.*, p. 16.
18. James Y. Dayanand, *Manohar Malgonkar, op. cit.*, p. 96.
19. M. Rajagopalachari, *The Novels of Manohar Malgonkar, op. cit.*, p. 20.
20. James Y. Dayanand, *op. cit.*, p. 95.
21. Henry James, "The Art of Fiction," *op. cit.*, p. 1164.
22. *Ibid.*, p. 1164.
23. M. Rajagopalachari, *op. cit.*, p. 69.
24. "Sattva, Raja and Tama — these Gunas, born of Prakriti, bind the imperishable spirit to the body, O mighty-armed." 5, *Srimad Bhagavt Gita,* Fourteenth Chapter, By Swami Ramsukhdas, Gita Press, Gorakhpur, First Edition, p. 620.
25. Jawaharlal Nehru, *The Discovery of India,* Meredian Books Ltd., London, 1956, p. 9.
26. *Ibid.*, p. 6.

27. A.N. Dwivedi, "The Historian as Novelist : Manohar Malgonkar," *op. cit.*, p. 146.
28. Manohar Malgonkar, *Combat of Shadows,* Harnish Hamilton, 1962, p. 109.
29. G.S. Amar, *Manohar Malgonkar, op. cit.*, p. 63.
30. Manohar Malgonkar, *The Princes*, Hind Pocket Books, Delhi, 1970, p. 300.
31. G.S. Amar, *op. cit.*, p. 96.
32. John Morris, *Eating the Indian Air*, Hamish Hamilton, London, 1968, p. 143.
33. G.S. Amar, *op. cit.*, p. 39.
34. James Y. Dayanand, *Manohar Malgonkar, op. cit.*, p. 97.
35. M. Rajagopalachari, *The Novels of Manohar Malgonkar,* Prestige Books, New Delhi, 1989, p. 13.
36. Uma Parameswaran, *A Study of Representative Indo-English Novelists,* Vikas Publishing House Pvt. Ltd., New Delhi, 1976, p. 51.
37. Henry James, "The Art of Fiction," *op. cit.*, p. 1165.
38. Malgonkar, "Author's Note," *The Devil's Wind,* Penguin Books Pvt. Ltd., New Delhi, 1988, p. x.
39. M. Rajagopalachari, *The Novels of Manohar Malgonkar, op. cit.*, p. 9.
40. Meenakshi Mukherjee, *The Twice Born Fiction,* Arnold-Heinemann Publishers (India) Pvt. Ltd., 1974.
41. A.N. Dwivedi, "The Historian as Novelist : Manohar Malgonkar," *op. cit.*, p. 146.
42. James Y. Dayanand, *Manohar Malgonkar, op. cit.*, p. 102.
43. Manohar Malgonkar, *The Princes, op. cit.*, p. 166.
44. *Ibid.,* p. 320.
45. *Ibid.,* p. 320.
46. *Ibid.,* p. 320.
47. Manohar Malgonkar, *The Devil's Wind,* Penguin Books (India) Pvt. Ltd., 1988, p. 271.
48. A.N. Dwivedi, *op. cit.*, 5.146.
49. Manohar Malgonkar, *Distant Drum,* Orient Paperbacks Pvt. Ltd., New Delhi, 1974, p. 191.
50. *Ibid.,* p. 207.
51. Manohar Malgonkar, *Combat of Shadows, op. cit.*, p. 19.

52. G.S. Amar, *op. cit.*, p. 146.
53. Manohar Magonkar, *Distant Drum, op. cit.*, p. 35.
54. Manohar Malgonkar, *The Devil's Wind, op. cit.*, p. 271.
55. G.S. Amar, Manohar Malgonkar, *op. cit.*, p. 146.
56. R.K. Narayan.
57. G.S. Amar, *op. cit.*, p. 65.
58. Uma Parameswaran, *op. cit.*, p. 34.
59. Meenakshi Mukherjee, *op. cit.*, p. 72.
60. *Ibid.*, p. 27.
61. Meenakshi Mukherjee, *The Twice Born Fiction,* Arnold-Heinemann Publishers (India) Pvt. Ltd., New Delhi, 1974, p. 170.
62. Manohar Malgonkar, *Distant Drum, op. cit.*, p. 59.
63. Meenakshi Mukherjee, *The Twice Born Fiction, op. cit.*, p. 169.
64. Manohar Malgonkar, *Distant Drum, op. cit.*, p. 61.
65. Bernard Shaw, *Candida* Orient Longman (P) Ltd., Calcutta, 1960, p. 14.
66. Shakti Batra, "Two Partition Novels," *Indian Literature,* Vol. 18, July-Sept., 1975, p. 91.
67. *The Times Literary Supplement*, October 22, 1964, p. 966.
68. M. Rajagopalachari, *op. cit.*, p. 84.
69. Shakti Batra, "Two Partition Novels", *op. cit.*, p. 97.
70. Manohar Malgonkar, "Purdah and Caste marks," *op. cit.*, p. 491.
71. M. Rajagopalachari, *op. cit.*, p. 84.
72. Marshall A. Best, *Contemporary Novelists,* edited by James Winson, St. James Press Ltd., London, 1976, p. 880.

2

The Ideology of Space in *Fire on the Mountain*

—Rama Kundu

"There is not even silence in the mountains"

—The Waste Land

For a period of more than two centuries space in English literature had epitomised — perhaps more sharply than any other item — the binaries of the colonial situation. Space was often perceived in imperial literature in terms of the binaries of home and frontier, centre and periphery, metropolis and the 'native,' which found their corollaries in racial and cultural binaries, with the imperial/white centre obviously holding (and upholding too) the 'correct' standards in ethics, law, art and every other aspect of social-political-cultural life. In the postcolonial era the psychocartography was ironically reinscribed from the colonized's perspective, and the binaries were reversed. But they remained binaries all the same. Only "cartography turned a cartwheel" with decolonisation."[1] Since then the Empire has been writing back to the imperial centre not only in terms of consciousness, concepts, perceptions, but also in particular, of specific spaces. These spaces could be some lush green Caribbean island across the 'wide Sargasso Sea' (Rhys),[2] a village by the forest in the heart of Ibo (Achebe),[3] the lake region of Canada (Atwood),[4] or the desert of Australia (White).[5] Postcolonial fiction especially has often been *geografictione,* using geographical identity-marks as a device for post-colonial deprogramming of the colonizer's psycho-cartographic programming.

Again, to the diasporic perception the image of space has continued to figure as a site of intersection between the place *where* one has got lost and the place *which* one has lost; the inaccessible lost place which was home once but has now been reduced to a dot on the map, and as such, has been shifted from empirical reality to the region of nostalgic memory. Thus space epitomises for the diasporic writer a prison on the one hand, and an impossible longing for a mirror on the other, which, to use Rushdie's beautiful image, has broken, with some of its pieces being irretrievably lost.

The Indian scenario offers interesting instances of these varied phrases and trends in the discourse on space. Way back in the nineteenth century — H.D. Arnold's *Oakfield* (1863), P.M. Taylor's *Confessions of a Thug* (1838) — through the early twentieth century — Forster, Kipling, Orwell — right into the late twentieth century — Ruth Prawar Jabvala — India as empirical space(s) has manifested to the European imagination the 'Other,' with its irressistible lure and threat, with its baffling enigma and fascination. The landscape — be it mountains or plain, desert or forest — proved to be an elusive and, not unfrequently, dangerous attraction.

During the early phase of postcolonialism one finds a self-conscious assertion in the writings of Indian authors who introduced carefully built constructs in order to epitomise the Indian space in microcosms, like 'Malgudi' or 'Kanthapura,' for example. It was their own lovable loved space despite its inadequacies. It was a proud, rather emphatic, way of inscribing one's own space. The expatriate Indian writers' tributary, nostalgic, myth-oriented poetry and prose in the post-independence decades — including Ramanujan, Parthasarathy, Ezekiel, for example — only further affirmed the same assertion that 'this is *my home* which was *your exile;* this *my centre* which was *your periphery.*'

Besides these typical postcolonial treatments of space the discourse has reached a new plateau in the last decades of the millennium in the writings of two successive generations of Indian women writers as they search for a space of 'her' own — as a woman and as an individual. This falls in pattern with the slow but steady emergence of women in various walks of life since independence. The journey has been an uphill one in the context of a society which is still largely governed by patriarchal ideologies and norms; and the women writers in the last three decades have been giving voice to their aspirations and ordeals as well as the anguish and frustration of the previous generations — their mothers and grandmothers. One of the many ways of expressing this consciousness is voicing the longing for a space of 'her' own, or the anguish at failing to find one. In the fiction of the 'Big Three' in the pre-Independence days space often served as scaffolding for social and political ideologies. The importance of 'Kanthapura' or 'Malgudi' to the affective and experiential modalities of culture was apparent. But Indian women writers since the 'seventies have inscribed the Indian landscape with new meanings, signs and signals. To quote the concluding sentence of Mary Conde's essay "Women Inscribing the Indian Landscape,"

> "Lacking the titillating consciousness of writing fiction-driven fiction about an imperial possession, Indian women writers inscribe Indian landscape with moral criticism, sadness, entrapment — or simply dreariness" (141).

Actually, however, it has been all this and much more. Devina, the heiress in Sujata Sabni's *Silent Whispers* (1996) 'buys' a vista; the sea.

> "She loved to stand there for hours, just watching the sea, and its chameleon moods. Turbulent, calm, mischievous or mature, playful, angry, constantly changing yet always the same. This heartbreakingly

> beautiful vista had been the clinching factor in her decision to buy the flat" (23).

Everybody is not so lucky. Thus Ammu in *The God of Small Things* has to live a cramped life both before and after her marriage and divorce; she has nowhere to go, nor does she have a space of her own to 'be' and 'become' in any of the houses of her father, husband or brother. When she rebels against this denial she is crushed. It is only in the wild garden that she gets a breather. Significantly it is a wild overgrown garden, and not the beautifully clipped and trimmed garden of *Nurjahan,* which epitomises prison and enslavement.[6] Githa Hariharan's story-tellers in *When Dreams Travel* (1999)[7], suffocated by the palace, which has no windows but only solid stone walls, prefer the freedom of a shanty in a desert tract, because it is open, even if dreary. In Shashi Deshpande's novels one comes across women who have been forced to spend their entire lives in a corner of an old house, — a claustrophobic space though a sprawling structure — without any privacy, any scope to indulge in creativity or thoughts of individual being and becoming.

On the other hand, in Anita Desai's *Fire on the Mountain* (1977) one finds a superb expression of the woman's dream of a space of her own. Here the author allows her protagonist the expanse of a mountain. From the very start the most noticeable aspect of the novel is its sense of geographical space. The hillstation report of Kasauli, to which Nanda Kaul, the elegant widow of the Vice-Chancellor, retires in her old age is a real empirical space and at the same time it is apparently emblematic of Nanda's protest and assertion, the penultimate act of assertion that she has made at the fag-end of her life, regarding her need of 'a room of one's own'. It seems to be a contrast to the male spaces she had lived in in the past, which were occupied and controlled by her father or husband. Coming here "on the ridge of the mountain" she has reached "the place...she had wanted and prepared for all her life" (3).

It gives her "a great, cool flowering of relief" (3) and she wants "no one and nothing else" (3).

Paradoxically, however, with the death of Ila at the end it appears that even this space has been abrogated by forces of violence and chauvinism. One also learns at the end that coming to the mountain was not Nanda's own choice, that this was but the appropriate closure to her inwardly barren life, though after settling down here she had persuaded herself to believe that she had at last found her real home, her goal and fulfilment.

The author's elaborate projection of the mountain as a geographic location and a fictional space consistently underscores an ambiguity, — a similar ambiguity that underlies Nanda's posture of self-assurance and her innate uncertainty, her firmness and hesitation, her withdrawal from, and reaching out to, life. The organization of the fictional space is obvious here; it operates as a structuring principle. It does not scaffold a political-social ideology, but relates to a feminine consciousness which is essentially ambiguous in its ambivalences between assertion and hesitancies, stark truth and the lure of fantasies.

The way the mountain has been made vivid with its varied sights, its wide range of sounds, its smell, its occasional dust-storms, long spells of rain, sudden flowers bursting out after a night of rain, its flora and fauna, its wind and fire is really fascinating. One can, as it were, share Nanda's cool solace in this mountain reclusion. At the same time the mountain is not envisioned as an idyllic place. The threats of disharmony cruelty, violence are also there, and cannot be ignored. The other carefully weaves a network of details to bring out this duality.

Isolation and remoteness add to the distinction of this mountain. It is necessarily not within easy reach of mundane life on the plains. One can wind up to Carignano, Nanda's house on the top, only with difficulty. It also takes long to come up from the plain as it is far far away from the big cities. Yet painful memories of the other life, spent in the big cities, remembrances of other locations where Tara suffer, where Nanda had suffered, float back *en route* the protagonist's consciousness down memory lane.

The mountain is bare both literally and metaphorically. It is not a typical Indian landscape which should normally contain one temple at least. No myths are attached to it. Nor do political waves or busy commerce reach this farflung place. The only evidence of industrial operation is the medicine factory down the hills which is supposed to squeeze, crush, maul animals in order to make medicine. Neither is there a fine soothing useful river as is so common with Indian landscapes in literature, but only the ravine and the gorge receiving the factory waste.

The mountain is unambiguously clearly located. But the locationing itself sends ambiguous signals. It is a concrete, perceptible, specific place whose boundaries are drawn with care to indicate two opposite features of the naturescape. From Carignano, Nanda's home on the ridge it is an immense expanse. "In every direction there was a sweeping view — to the north of the mountains, to the south, of the plains" (4). But whereas the north-facing windows open "onto the blue waves of the Himalayas flowing out and up to the line of ice and snow sketched upon the sky" (4), the south-facing ones "looked down the plunging cliff to the plain stretching out, flat and sere, to the blurred horizon" (4). Thus, the mountain seems to suggest an aspiration towards the infinite expanse and altitude at one end, and a decline to a dull vista of the plains on the other.

Nanda prefers the knoll, the topmost point of her garden where the wind is "keenest and the view widest" (4). But there too she cannot avoid spotting the postman coming up from the plains, carrying news from the other world down there. She finds the view of the hilltop from her veranda to be "more comforting" than the other view from the back windows "of the cliff plunging seven thousand feet down to the Punjab plains" (13). This seems to be symptomatic of the ambiguity of her mental situation, her defiance and her longings, her stoic strained withdrawal, and her imaginative and wishful structuring of the past. She looks fascinated at the elusive gold and violet, (27) light and space of the peaks where "hills melted into sky, sky into snows, snows into air" (28); still she would often go round to the back of the house and gaze "down the gorge with its gashes of red earth, its rocks and gullies and sharply spiked agaves, to the Pujab plains — a silver haze in the summer heat — stretching out to a dim yellow horizon" (17). At such moments she also synchronically looks down "over all those years she had survived and borne" (17). And she sees them not bare and shining as the plains below, but "like the gorge, cluttered, choked and blackened with the heads of children and grandchildren, servants and guests, all restlessly surging, clamouring about her" (17). Here is a subtle suggestion that in spite of her apparent withdrawal from the plains and from her past life there, she still carries these other spaces within her consciousness; later she would weave her fiction, — "memory-making" (123), around these spaces.

After a rain one can get a glimpse of the extraordinary expanse of the scene. "Away in the north the rock-scarred snow range glittered. To the south many hundreds of miles of the plain were visible, streaked with streams and pitted with bright pools of rain" (87). Raka's resentment is blown away as she scrambles up to the top and sees before her "a breadth of space, a vast sweeping depth" (61). The author describes the scene as "an ancient scroll" unrolled at her feet.

> "To the north, the soft, downy hills flowed, wave upon wave, gold and blue and violet and indigo, like the sea" (61).

But the other end of the hill, which obsesses Raka, offers a contrast to this serene beauty :

> "...the lip of the cliff and the sudden drop down the red, rock-spattered ravine to the plain that lay

> stretched out and heavy, the dusty pelt of a yellow animal panting in the sun" (41).

It is also hot in contrast to the cool north. From the plains the heat comes up to assault the cool of the mountain.

> "The plain below opened wide its yellow mouth and it was its oven breath that billowed up the mountainside..." (48).

The suggestion of an ugly animal writhing in heat is appropriately accompanied by the image of a demonic creature — "a square dragon" (42) which, to Raka, "seemed to dominate the landscape" (42). It is the factory with its enormous concrete walls. It is also the "central dagger" (48) evoking the violence and disharmony of the act of 'piercing.' "The chimneys piercing the white sky, lashed about with black whips of smoke" (49). Raka sniffs the air and smells cinder, serum, chloroform, spirit, — things which are supposed to be anachronistic in an idyllic pastoral. It is the shabby, seedy assault of the industry on the mountains :

> "Sharp chimneys thrust out cushions and scarves of smoke *on the milky blue of the afternoon sky* (italics mine)."

Perfectly in tune with this polluting presence

> "chutes emerging from its back wall seemed built to disgorge factory waste into the ravine and immediately below them were small, squat structures that looked like brick kilns amongst the spiked, curved blades of the giant agaves that were, besides the pines, the only vegetation of that *blighted gorge*" (42) (Italics mine).

In addition to this disturbing presence on the mountainscape the reader is also reminded that "the army is everywhere" (57), and "too many tourists" (57) scratching names and dates on trees, which stand out "as incongruous and obtrusive as the barbed wire" (57) or the "frightening" instrument up the hill that looks like an atomic reactor or "some such scientific monstrosity" (57). Nanda finds it "a shame." Nanda feels uneasy and bitter. "Too many tourists. Too much army. How they are ruining this — this quiet place.... It really is — is saddening" (57). An unmistakably Eliotian echo :

> "There is not even silence in the mountains...
> There is not even solitude in the mountains."

The beauty of Dagshai and Sabathu, looking like "handful of pebbles gleaming on golden hilltops" (43) may be exquisite, but still it cannot obliterate the "daggers" or the smoke of the factory "piercing" the sky and "blighting" the ridge. Carignano, on the hilltop, may be safe, but down the hillside dangers await one. The way is full of hazards for a lonely old woman (139). At the end Ila is finished by a black shape detatching itself from the jagged pile of the rocks, "that last rock between her and the hamlet" (142) and *springing soundlessly* upon her. The mountain ceases to be a "heaven-haven" at this point and comes closer to the scene of predatory violence.

The mountain is largely barren and steep along the upper mall. The steep path makes people automatically bend forward excepting Nanda who self-consciously keeps erect (11). It is part of the Kasauli range, the author points out, whose "chief virtue" is "its barrenness," its "starkness" (4). The author carefully brings out its austere aspect. Nanda and Raka, the great grandmother and the great granddaughter walk together along "the sere, silent hillsides on which boulders seemed to have been arrested in downward motion and nothing grew on the pine-needle-spread earth but a few tangles of wild respberries, hairy with thorn, and contorted agave" (57). Carignano, Nanda's 'own' house (the only one) at last, stands on the "bleached ridge" (5) with its "orderly austerity" (91). Raka likes it; but she is more drawn by "the ravaged, destroyed and barren spaces in Kasauli...the ravine where yellow snakes slept under grey rocks and agaves growing out of the dust and rubble, the skeletal pines that rattled in the wind, the wind-levelled hill-tops..." (91). The echoes from *The Waste Land* are too obvious to be missed :

> "What are the roots that clutch, what branches grow
> Out of this stony rubbish?"
>
> Or
>
> "The dead tree gives no shelter, the cricket no relief"
>
> and
>
> "Dead mountain mouth of carious teeth that cannot spit."

The vegetation life in the mountain is in tune with this barrenness. Pine and cicada, — again like *The Waste Land*[8] — are the plants of this rock, and Nanda finds them appropriate and acceptable. The very opening sentence evokes the fragrance and resonance of pines and cicadas as Nanda Kaul pauses under them. They seem to throw around her a sort of protective shelter. There are some fine touches suggesting her oneness with these mournful trees. As she feels annoyed at the sight of the approaching postman who may be bringing messages from the world she wants to have no connection with, she steps backwards into the garden and "the wind suddenly billowed up and threw the pine branches about as though to curtain her" (8). Nanda fancies herself merging with the pine trees and being mistaken for one. "Grey," "tall," "thin," in her silk sari that makes "sweeping, shivering sound" (4), she is, as it were, another pine-tree, and she yearns "to be a tree, no more and no less" (4). "She would be a charred tree-trunk in the forest" (23). Here the reader is reminded of *Surfacing* the Canadian novel, — published in 1972 were Atwood's female protagonist withdraws from the city to the country, finally beyond the lake into the forest and there she attains a similar perception : "I lean against a tree. I am the tree leaning" (181).

The pines have a sort of beauty too which Nanda can perceive. As Nanda waits for Raka to arrive, the peace of her mind is "ruffled". Synchronically "on the knoll and the gate the wind *ruffled* (emphasis added) the pineneedles so that they glistened silver in the sunlight"(36).

Besides the pine and cicada there are the "thorny snatchful(s) of respberries" (5) the truant school boy looks for; the clumps of Iris at Carignano had "finished blooming" (4). At the same time it may be noted that the chestnut tree at the foot of the hill is "leafy" (4); the signboard of Carignano is nailed onto this tree. On the northside the wall of Nanda's house is "washed by the blue shadows of the low, dense apricot trees" (5). In the deserted burnt house on the hill there are only dry pabbles. But Nanda knows better and tells Raka :

> "It looks dreadful...but one shower of rain will bring out hundreds of flowers — lilies, dahlias that the old woman had planted" (57).

By the shady veranda of Nanda's house pots of geraniums and fuchsias bloomed unimpaired by the sun (13). In the morning after the first rain Raka wakes up to find "hosts of wild zephyranthes that had come up in the night" (88). Damp lilies have also come out, though damp lilies in the milk-jug on the table look rather like Raka's mother, ill in a nursing home, under a pink blanket (89). In spite of the pervasive barrenness, starkness the hills have obviously their rare patches of colour.

As the pine is the chief plant of this mountain, the eagle is the fauna of this space which is made of light and air. Carignano has a sweeping view in every direction with an occasional eagle swimming through the clear unobstructed mass of light air (4). As Nanda waits for Raka's arrival — rather annoyed — an eagle sweeps into ken a thousand feet below, "its wings outspread, gliding on currents of air without once moving its greart muscular wings which remained in repose, in control. She had wished, it occurred to her, to imitate that eagle — gliding with eyes closed" (19). Raka too feels in the same way towards the eagles. As she scrambles to the top of the Monkey Point it is for her a moment of ecstasy. She is sure "if the let go...she would fly, fly off the hill-top and down, down on currents of air, like the eagles that circled slowly, regally below her" (61). In the coppery light of June evenings the child watches "the eagles soar and glide soundlessly in the gorge and out over the plains" (76).

It is perhaps natural that the two freedom-loving lonely souls should seek to imitate the high-soaring eagle. But the eagle is also a predatory bird; its circling, soaring, gliding are punctuated by its hunt for prey. Similarly the vulture's circling indicates rot, dead flesh. Significantly vultures are also a common feature of this mountainscape. Raka, on her lonely prowlings on the hills, sees "in the sky, huge vultures circled lazily, *stealthily* (emphasis added), on currents of air, prowling for game" (43). Once the child is scared. As she slides down on her habitual course in the direction of the factory suddenly she sees a vulture.

> "A vulture had moved its claws up a little, shrugged its massive shoulders, stretched out its rubber-hose neck and belched. The child started. Then walked backwards, away from the tree. Turning around abruptly, she dropped on all fours and came scrambling up the hill so fast..." (73).

It does not seem to be a very safe world for the child; though she moves around unharmed there are potential threats all the time. Once on her lonely exploration of the hill Raka comes upon "a great, thick, yellow snake poured in rings upon itself, basking on the sunned top of a flat rock," — her first view of "a loose soft sackful of snakes" (49). Even before this she had glimpses of "the tips of snakes' tails parting the cracks of rocks" and "slit eyes watching" her from shade, had heard the "slither of scales" upon the ground (49).

There are varieties of birds, animals, reptiles, insects on the mountain. It seems to be less a world of humans than of other creatures; and references to these creatures of the mountain are often disturbing, carrying suggestions of ferocity, cruelty, violence, or rot. Even smaller creatures seem to be part of the pattern. Immediately Nanda flings away an apricot, "a bright hoopoe," attracted by the flight and flash, "*struck down* at it and *tore* at its bright flesh" (4); as it feeds the nestlings their "screams were shrill and could madden" (4). Sitting in the shade of her veranda Nanda gazes at a pair of bulbuls quarrelling, falling in a flurry of feathers to the ground; they "stirred up a small frenzy of dust, then shot off in opposite directions, scolding and abusing till a twist of a worm distracted them" (13). When apricots run out the hoopoe has to make up "by catching moths in mid-air and dragging worms out of the earth" (65). This is a compulsion on its part. A similar compulsion prompts the herd of goats in the deserted ravine, "nibbling at the sparse thorns and nettles with rubber-lipped greed and nervous avarice" (73). Not the idyllic picture of a pastoral.

However, there are a few fine strokes suggesting an idyllic pastoral peace and beauty. As Nanda, rather annoyed at the arrival of a letter, looks intently at the vast uninterrupted expanse, "a large white and yellow butterfly crossed over, disturbing her concentration" (13). Or as she leans over the gate of Carignano, her eyes resting on the hillsides mauve and violent, "cattle browsed homewards to small hidden hamlets in the valleys, all grew softer and greyer" (in tune with her graceful ageing (28). Later, during their evening walk together, Nanda watches Raka scrambling up the hill :

> "Unseeing, she almost ran into a goat, then a kid, then a whole herd that came springing down, leapt over her back and flew like birds, landing at Nanda Kaul's feet and tripping nimbly homewards, the small goatsherd casually whistling and sauntering after them" (60).

The "woollen hills" (65) is a fine expression evoking the scanty grassy coat as well as the coat of a sheep envisioning the mountain as a flock of sheep. The pastoral connotations of sheep and shephered hardly need to be stressed.

But there are also the "wild horde" of black-faced *langurs* who are not meek at all, — "those fierce, lithebpanthers of the monkey world, more feline than simian" (58). There are the jackals and dogs. Ram Lal confidentially tells Raka about "the ghosts of people who have died of dog-bite and snake-bite" and "roam on the hillsides" (44). The old man warns the child about the ravine. "See those chutes? They empty the bones and ashes of dead animals down into the ravine" (44). These are animals used for test and subsequently thrown away; apparently the target of the vultures. Ram Lal continues his eerie report : "Jackals come at night to chew the bones. Then they go mad and bite the village dogs. The mad dogs run around, biting people.... It isn't safe, hear?" (44). Inside the safety of the room Raka "met a spider that groomed its hairs in a corner, saw lizard's eyes blinking out of a dark groove" (41).

Like a living being the mountain has its own smells and sounds. Some sounds of the mountain originate from the fauna, some from the trees, and some in the wind. Humans appear redundant in the scheme. The very opening sentence evokes the "sibilance" of the pines and the "fiddling" of cicadas.

> "Nanda Kaul paused under the pine trees to take in their scented sibilance and listen to the cicadas fiddling invisibly under the mesh of pine needles" (3).

At once the mountain becomes vocal and vivid. This is the appropriate music of the place, and not the club music which seems incongruous and vulgar on the hills. For the lonely old woman in the old empty house "there were only the cicadas to be heard, a sound so even and so insubstantial that it seemed to emerge from the earth itself...a scent of pine-needles made audible" (13). They are the tireless players in a ceaseless orchestra. Rala, stealthily entering the empty clubhouse on a hot summer afternoon feels, "all Kasauli slept except for the cicadas that sawed and fiddled without stop" (43). All Nanda wants at this fag end of her life is "the sound of the cicadas and the pines" (19). The music of the withered rose-creeper is also acceptable to her, which is "an exhausted mass of grey creaks and groans" (17). Does she find an extension of herself in it? Towards the end when the two old ladies talk in the empty garden cicadas "audibly sizzled" under the sun (103). Raka seemed to move about "in a kind of dream, set to the sound of cicadas and the wind in the pines" (64). Not that the sound is sweet or pleasant; the old lady and the child stand gazing at the withering flowers under which "a cicada shrilled and whirred frenziedly" (73). Still it is the mountain's own sound, and part of its aloof, rugged grandeur, like the sound of the keen mountain wind. Just as from the hilltop the hills look like seawaves, the sound of the wind too, "rushing up through the pines and then receding was the *sound of the sea*" (61).

This is the sound of the place at its superb. But there are also other sounds — not so grand or harmonious, and sometimes even disturbing in their evocations. When the wind comes in the form of a dust storm it can be terrible, and its terror is brought out in terms of a powerful auditory image. Raka herself "a bird fallen out of its nest, a nest fallen out of a tree" (50) sees a storm-tossed bird.

> "A white hen was lifted into the air and tossed past the window in a frantic, fluttery arc, its squawks snatched out of its beak and shattered like glass" (53).

Jackals howl at night (44). While hiding behind the clubhall in the night of revelry Raka is scared; she remembers the painful scene of her mother being abused by her drunken father. The memory of her mother crying merges into the actual sound of a jackal howling in the ravine. The desolation, fear and pain of the shattered child is finely brought out by means of the sound.

> "Ahead of her, no longer on the ground but at some distance now, her mother was crying. Then it was a jackal crying...." (72).

As Raka scrambles uphill, she starts "small avalanches of pebbles and loud, clanking ones of empty tins. She disturbed the crickets[9] and made them raise their voices in alarm. Like a chorus singing and singing at the back of a stage" (49). They sing in a difficult tongue she had not met before in the big cities of the world. The child is baffled and exasperated. "It was complicated, shrill, incessant and Raka shook and shook her head to get the buzz out" (50). Again, as Nanda and Raka walk homewards in the gathering darkness, the "great silence" is "*rent* (emphasis added) now and then by the clear, ringing call of some invisible bird that defied night" (62).

There are a few instances of soft sounds. For example, Nanda weaves her stories to Raka but keeps her eyes averted where the rooks "cawed" and afterwards the owls began to call softly, experimentally (99). One fine touch early in the novel seems proleptic. On the eve of Raka's arrival Nanda feels annoyed and disturbed. She remembers that she wanted to be only like the eagle, the lonely high-soaring bird.

> "Then a cuckoo called, quite close, here in her garden, very softly, very musically, but definitely calling — she recognized its domestic voice" (19). And she acquiesces.

On the other hand the sounds Raka imagines amidst an "eerie" soundlessness are disturbing. As the child looks at the distant forest fire from her window

> "Holding her ear to the cold pane closely, she thought she heard the cries of animals and birds burning in that fire. But when she removed her ear from the pane she heard only the crepitation of silence. Once, the soft hooting of an owl" (75).

The soft hooting of the night-bird mingles into the eerie silence of the night instead of dispelling it.

One of the most remarkable icons of the mountain is its forest-fire which may burst out anywhere unpredictably, bring devastation in its trail and leave scars long afterwards which seem beyond healing. From the beginning through carefully accumulated suggestions the reader is prepared for the final fire-ritual. At the start it is a series of references to/reports of previous fires. Then there is an actual fire, though still seen from a distance. At the end Raka herself sets the forest on fire. Early in the novel one gets a proleptic hint. Three pine trees stand at the gate of Carignano "in their exaggerated attitudes as of *men going up in flames,* with their arms outstetched, *charred* too (emphasis added) about the trunks" (12) — a reminder of an earlier fire. Sighting Nanda, grey and faintly stirring under them, the postman "felt something ominous hover in the heavy summer light" (12).

During the dust storm Ram Lal is worried, because "this is how forest fires do start. I can't tell you how many forest fires we see each year in Kasauli" (53); the many burnt trees and houses bear evidence. Ram Lal tells Raka the story of the burnt cottage on the hilltop, where the resident "an English Mem" had gone mad after failing to rescue her cat from the fire.[10] Later a proleptic touch is added to the story as Nanda relates it to Raka.

> "Up on the hill there, Raka, you will see the burnt black shell of a house. It was burnt down in a terrible forest fire.... An old lady lived there alone and they say she went mad and was put away. Poor woman, I wonder if she would not have preferred to die in the fire" (57).

One may note that at the end Nanda's death is synchronised with the forest fire, started by Raka.

The images and relics of fire seem to fascinate Raka. She imagines herself to be a pine tree in flames. She stealthily visits the burnt house. Here "she raised herself onto the tips of her toes — tall, tall as a pine — stretched out her arms till the felt...she was alight, ablaze" (91). She climbs over the ruins and standsstill in the "scorched, empty" room (90) listening to the murmuring silence and the demented birds that "beckoned Raka on to a land where there was no sound, only silence, no light, only shade, and skeletons kept in beds of ash on which the footprints of jackals flowered in grey" (90).[11] As Raka sees her first forest fire she is excited at the scene of the silent, swift, threatening blaze; she is "obsessed" (75). The novel closes with the sound, flame and smoke of a spreading fire.

> "Down in the ravine, the flames spat and crackled around the dry wood and through the dry grass, and black smoke spiralled over the mountain" (146).

The reader may recall the prairie novels of Canada; there too fire is used, often with symbolic overtones as a typical natural calamity, unpredictable, uncontrollable, overpowering.

Again, when the rain comes it is also like a kind of climax after the high wind "whining" through the pine trees all afternoon and the clouds gathering like "a great polar bear crouching" and "what rain! The house shook, the roof crackled, long raindrops slanted in" (81). Nanda Kaul begins her "memory-making" stories during the rain, "raising her voice above the drumming of the rain on the roof and the booming and echoing of thunder in the hills that followed the rain like hunting horns" (86).

Carignano, Nanda's *own* house on the ridge of the mountain is a space within the space. The mountain enfolds the house with its sounds, views, smells, its storms, rain; still, being a house it retains a degree of seclusion and distinction from the rest of the landscape. Like the Mall the house too has a colonial history when it had been inhabited by a series of lonely old women. Nanda has not tried to alter it; she has allowed it to be just as it was, still she loves the place as the only house of *her own.* She has a special feeling for this house. Even when she invents stories about the houses of her father and husband "Carignano she had kept clean, true, open for the wind to blow through" (104). She also feels that Raka would be the only true inheritor of Carignano (80).[12]

At the same time Nanda Kaul knows that Raka belonged to the mountain, the outer space, rather than the house. "Raka no more needed, or wanted, a house than a jackal did, or a cicada" (103). She perceives with perfect clarity the semblance and the difference between Raka and herself *vis-a-vis* the mountain. Both want "only one thing — to be left alone and pursue her own secret life amongst the rocks and pines of Kasauli" (48). At the same time Nanda is conscious of the difference in their respective responses to this space to which, willy-nilly, both have come for shelter.

> "If Nanda Kaul was a recluse out of vengeance for a long life of duty and obligation, her great grand-daughter was a recluse by nature, by instinct. She had not arrived at this condition by a long route of rejection and sacrifice — she was born to it, simply" (48).

She appreciates and admires the child for being what she herself could not be.

The difference between them is the difference between two generations of women on either sides of a century regarding the outlook on a 'space' of theirs. However, it is their common attachment to the mountain that makes them true blood relations, makes the child true inheritor of her (great-grand) mother's garden in the Alice Walker sense.[13] At the same time these two lonely recluse — one women and one girl child, one rejected and ravaged by life, the other 'a bird fallen from a nest fallen from a tree,' one longing to be a pine on the hill, the other burrowing like an insect into it, enable us to grasp the meanings/suggestions of the mountain as space, as sign, as trope in the context of the novel.

The dream geography of a mountain stands for an idealised position in the traditional pagan, European and oriental concepts. The Greeks placed the abode of their gods on the Olympian mount. The Christian imagination founded the Paradise on a mount. The high profile gods of the Hindu pantheon are supposed to haunt the Indian mountains. To the traditional Indian imagination the mountain has been a spiritual space, especially the Himalayas which is called *Devatatma*. It is also the recluse of monks and ascetics who abandon the material world, and the route to *Mahaprasthanam,* supposedly leading to Heaven.

To the European/English romantic imagination mountain was a common image for the detachment/aloofness/sweeping view of the poet. After the war people sought the mountains as shelter or sanatoria for the 'magic'[14] of healing. In the British colonial writings about India references to Indian mountains often measured them against English landscape which was taken as the norm. The lure and threat that epitomised India as the 'Other', seemes to acquire intensified manifestation in its hills and mountains. Forster's Marabar Hills (*A Passage to India*), for example, are the region of 'mystery'/'muddle' offering neither solace, nor peace, nor detachment. Kipling articulates a similar sense of awe at the reductive mystery of the great grey hills which make one feel dwarfed and insignificant (*The Heart of a Maid,* 1890).

In *Journey to Ithaca,* a later novel of Desai, people, including two Italians, end up at the higher regions of the Himalayas in course of their search for peace and spiritual fulfilment. But in *Fire on the Mountain* introduces an unusual mountain space with no myth or conventional adages attached to it. It is a real place of the free wind roaring, booming through the hills, of dust storm that rage and tear the rocks, of rain, thunder, of prolonged aridity and devastating forest fires, of snow-white peaks, of red-yellow gorge blighted by factory-waste. Still Desai projects it in such a way that the mountain itself becomes a trope. Though Nanda is reminded of Hopkins's "Heaven-haven" she does not mythicise her "haven"; she knows it is "a place" (58). Indeed the author gives no mythicised, or fantasised or imaginary geography as such the geographical location to the colonial past. But real geography has been made to imbibe imaginative meanings, as it is made to come alive by means of exquisite imaginative touches.

Thus, the place appears to be a parallel to Nanda's physical isolation. The fictionalised mountain emerges as a site that symbolically implies her predicament and also her dream of a world of her own. Kasauli also becomes symptomatic of the desire of women to exist without constriction/limitation. As Mary Daly observes at the beginning of her book *Gyn/Ecology* "patriarchy appears to be everywhere. Even outer space and the future have been colonised" (1). Women writers across the world today have been constructing worlds of isolation as escape from this patriarchal domination. Canadian writer Aritha Van Herk's *Places far from Ellesmere* (1990) is a typical example where she envisions an escape into a far-flung island along with Tolstoy's Anna Karenina. But whereas Van Herk's isolated island epitomises unambiguous self-assurance and assertion of the woman, the mountain of Desai seems to offer an ambiguous signal. Perhaps this amiguity is necessarily embedded in the very nature of the space she has chosen. An island can be isolated and autonomous. But a mountain is not autonomous in that sense. The distant snowy peaks are the inaccessible utopia. At the other end the mountain slopes down into the mundane hamlets where brutal death soundlessly springs upon Ila Das from behind the dark rock. So it does not necessarily follow that the self-actualising journey of a woman reaches its goal in the mountain, though for Nanda it is the end of the road, "privacy achieved only at the very end of her life" (36), and for Raka who had always seemed to lack the ticket to social life (52) the "best" home (91).

The basic paradox highlighted by the geography of the story is that in spite of all the longings one cannot occupy a bounded or enclosed cultural space. True, the human society remains largely invisible; true, the world seems remote from here like Herk's island from where "the world exists in some enigmatic novel far beyond" (121). Still the fact remains that it is an eroded hill that has received the beatings of the weather; the purity of the hill wind is threatened by the factory; its smoke lashes the white sky; its smell of chemicals fills the air; it is haunted by violence. Even Carignano, Nanda's 'glass palace,' on the ridge is invaded by the outer world, as suggested by the postman at the beginning and by the telephone at the end.

Fire on the Mountain may be categorised as 'geografictione' to use the term coined by Aritha Van Herk, an Italian-Canadian word, to denote a species of narration which combines geography with fiction, creates its own geography as it creates its own specific narrative space. *Fire on the Mountain* represents this trend in fiction, which, instead of using place as backdrop, reinterprets it and reinscribes it with fresh meanings.

The traditional male/colonial way of seeing a place was as a "virgin" woman, a female to be conquered and possessed. Nanda and Raka do not try to possess the place. They just want to get merged like a tree or an insect.

For the perceptive reader the configuration and etching of Kasauli in Desai's novel is resonant with intertextual echoes, among which echoes from *The Waste Land* in particular — the pine and cicada, the crickets, the ruined house (even to the cawing bird on its roof), the barren rocks, the wrecked solitude — are unmistakable. But it seems significant that whereas Eliot's waste land was blessed at the end by thunder and rain, here the story finally comes to a halt at a richly ambiguous open ending with the strong forest fire quickly spreading across the mountain.

Desai's treatment of mountain as space in an emblem of her *ecriture feminine* and thus offers the possibility of fresh, varied, contrary and multiple interpretations.

NOTES

1. "Those three-hundred-odd years of European exploration, conquest colonization and empire...established a lasting psycho-cartography of their own, positioning Europe and the Atlantic as fount and centre, and all the rest of the vastness of creation as outlying and peripheral, and created for the purpose of serving servicing the centre...." (Nayantara Sahgal, "The Myth Reincarnated," *Journal of Commonwealth Literature,* XXX, i, 1995).
2. Jean Rhys in her novel *Wide Sargasso Sea* (1966) uses Sargasso as an emblem of the geographical-political-cultural-colonial divide between England and the Caribbean island.
3. Achebe, C., *Things Fall Apart.*
4. Atwood, M., *Surfacing* "I am a place" (181).
5. White, P., *Voss.*
6. "Birds in gilt cages" (26) : "Little slave girls ran about" (135) (Jyoti Jafa, *Nurjahan,* New Delhi : Lotus, 1994).
7. In *When Dreams Travel* (1999) Githa Hariharan rewrites the *Arabian Nights;* new stories are narrated here by Sahrzad's sister and a slave girl.
8. "If there were the sound of water only
   Not the cicada...
   But sound of water over a rock
   Where the hermit-thrush sings in the pine trees" (11. 351-55).
9. "Where the dead tree gives no shelter, the cricket no relief" (*The Waste Land*).
10. Echo of *Wide Sargasso Sea*; Annette went mad after failing to rescue 'Coco,' the pet parrot, and her little son during the Coulibri fire.
11. One is struck by the resemblance between this passage and the following lines from *The Waste Land* :

    "In this decayed hole among the mountains...
    Over the tumbled graves...
    There is the empty chapel, only the wind's home.
    It has no windows, and the door swings,
    Dry bones can harm no one.
    Only a cock stood on the rooftree
    Co co rico co co rico...." (11. 385-92)
12. An echo of Forster's *Howard's End*; Mrs. Wilcox wanted to bequeathe Howard's End to Margaret whom she had recognized as the true spiritual inheritor to her very special house.

13. Alice Walker in her essay, "In Search of Our Mothers' Gardens" (1983) explores the situation of women in traditional culture and celebrates the achievements and resiliency of women in history.
14. Thomas Mann, *The Magic Mountain.*

WORKS CITED

Atwood, M., *Surfacing* (1972) London : Virago Ltd., 1980.

Conde, Mary, "Women Inscribing the Indian Landscape," *The Atlantic Review,* I : 2, 2000.

Daly, Mary, *Gyn/Ecology.* London : The Women's Press, 1987.

Desai, A., *Fire on the Mountain.* London : Penguin Book, 1977.

Eliot, T.S., *The Waste, Land* in *Collected Poems.* London : Faber & Faber, 1963.

Herk, Aritha Van, *Places Far From Ellesmere.* Red Deer Alberta : Red Deer College Press, 1990.

Sabni, Sujata, *Silent Whispers.* New Delhi : Har-Anand, 1996.

3

A Critical Estimate of Sarojini Naidu's Folk Songs in *The Golden Threshold*

—Ashok Kumar Bachchan

Sarojini Naidu started composing verses at an early age. Her poems, written in her teens, were published by her father under the title *Songs*. *The Golden Threshold* brought about a sensation among the English speaking people. *The Golden Threshold* has three sections : Folk songs, Songs of music and Poems. The first section consists of twelve poems, the second six poems and the third twenty two poems.

The Palanquin Bearers begins with a typical traditional picture of palanquin bearers, which deals with the common sight of the whole of India during the 19th and early 20th century. One can come across the palanquin bearers in remote Indian villages even nowadays also. They generally carry a bride to her husband's house usually in *the palke.* They usually sing songs in rhythmic harmony with their footsteps.

The setting of the poem is romantic and impressive in more than one way. The theme and imagery are fused so artistically that they seem to be two inseparable parts. Sarojini Naidu communicates her poetic ideas with her sparkling and suggestive imagery. The stream of poetry and imagery do not flow side by side, they rather coalesce into each other. The coalition of poetry and imagery in Sarojini Naidu's poetry lends universal appeal to them. The song sung by the palanquin bearers describes the basic human emotions and it is so impressive that the mind of the bride is under complete control. Her mind is hypnotized and in the body is naturally swaying like a flower in the melodious tunes of music created by the singers. The poet presents a fine combination of the abstract and the concrete. The song of the palanquin bearers is so hypnotizing that it creates a kind of romantic wind with strange effects on the listeners. The bride is overwhelmed in a kind of ecstasy and she seems to be a bird on the foam of a stream. She is again compared to a laugh from the 'lips of a dream.' The charming world of romance which the poet creates reminds one of the romantic creations of William Wordsworth who also presents a fine fusion of romance and realism in his poetic creations. P.B. Shelley is deficient in this art of fusing romance with reality. At times Sarojini Naidu communicates her sense so consummately that she reminds one of the excellent poetic art of John Keats.

Imagination has been used marvelously and with great gusto. The bride is going to meet her love. The memory of her parental home is still alive with tears in her eyes. The mixed feeling of an Indian bride who experiences both the pangs of separation as well as hopes for life and happiness is beautifully expressed in the poem.

Sarojini Naidu sings songs of eternity and timelessness, love and life and death. The poem *Wandering Singers* is reminiscent of William Wordsworth's *The Solitary Reaper*. The poem breathes an air of buoyancy, carefreeness, abandon and release. The wandering singers are gay, but not concerned with the present or the future, they cherish no hopes, no dreams. Nothing in the world binds them — neither home nor family, nor love, nor comfort, nor space. 'All men are our kindred, the world is our home.'[1] For them, there is no direction, no destination; they move freely like the winds. But at the same time, they move freely like the winds. But at the same time, they sing of uprooted cities, of dead women, of the old battles, and kings, and of simple and sorrowful things which are decidedly the timeless themes.

Indian Weavers is a symbolical poem based on a common Indian scene. Weavers can be seen anywhere in India weaving cloth on handlooms in different coloured patterns. The poem is in a question-answer form. The three stanzas of the poem suggest the three stages of man's journey of life : birth, youth and death. The first two lines in each stanza forms a question and the last two the answer. The questions asked at three different hours of a day also symbolize the three different stages of man's life with its associated pleasure and pain. The poet is much inspired by man's journey of life from birth to death. She watches the weavers weaving their yarn, and is led to the mystery of life, love and death. The poem begins with a flesh of thought. The break of the day is the harbinger of new hope, new promise and new faith. The garment is gay and colourful, for the birth of a child brings a great joy to the parents. The poem takes a symbolical turn. It is the Fates weaving the web of human life, and the fates is almost a universal mythological belief The weavers remind us of the three fates or sisters of Greek mythology. The weaver stands for the supreme creator who weaves the yarn of human life in mingled pattern of pleasure and pain. The impact of the Hindu thought, the conception of Hindu trinity — of Brahma, Vishnu and Shiva — is powerful on her mind. The poem gives a convincing proof of her deep awareness and understanding of her tradition. The weavers are Brahma, Vishnu and Shiva wearing the web of human life. The first stanza is assigned to Brahma, the patron, deity of birth. He is associated with lotus which blossoms at the break of day. One can imagine Brahma, the God of creation, sitting on a lotus emerging out of the blue seas aptly recalling the blue colour of the halcyon wings. The weavers weave a gay garment, blue as the wing of a halcyon wild, the robe for a new-born child.

The second stanza presents the second stage of man's life. This is the stage of youth, the stage of fulfilment of hopes and aspirations. It is at this stage that man craves for his identity for pleasures and longs for a partner to realize the dream of life. It is quite appropriate that the weavers should weave against the background of night. Nightfall is the hour of joy for which the newly-married couples eagerly wait. The peacock's purple and green plumes agree well with the Queen's bright marriage-veils and also suggest life's colour and magnificence. Vishnu stands for youth, is associated with colour, gaiety and adventure. He is the God of prosperity and splendour; the purple and green plumes of peacock suggest beautifully all the colour and magnificence associated with Vishnu and also with the youth of man's life.

The third stanza, set in the moonlight chill, suggests symbolically the last stage of man's journey of life. The weavers 'solemn and still' are weaving 'a dead man's funeral shroud' (p. 5). The chill moonlight is reminiscent of the chilly night in Coleridge's *Christabel.* As man has experienced his share of pleasure and pain, he desires for peace and rest. Shiva comes forward and relieves him of worldly pain and misery. Shiva is the God of death and destruction who destroys all that is meaningless and dead in life and prepares the soul for receiving new life. 'Solemn and still' in the 'moonlight chill' is Shiva smeared with ashes. Moonlight draws attention to Shiva for he wears the crescent moon in his mattresses. 'The white feather' and 'white cloud' suggest death and also evoke the idea of snowy Himalayas, the abode of Shiva. The three Gods are engaged eternally with their tasks of creation, maintenance and annihilation.

Indian Weavers achieves an allegorical dimension without any deliberate philosophical gravity or technical policy. Dastoor, impressed by the poem, observes : 'we are made to realize that the web of our life is of a mingled yarn, grave and gay together.'[2] Prof. C.D. Narsimhaiah, no great admirer of Sarojini, is highly impressed by the poem. He observes :

> Here in twelve lines, is an elliptical allusive and symbolic representation of life's journey from birth

> to death.... It is not merely a competent poem, but a very distinguished one for Sarojini, because the poet here is in full possession of rare gifts — a profound awareness of her own tradition, admirable poise, economy, and an ear and eye for striking rhythm, image and symbol, all used to fine advantage to make the poem most evocative.[3]

Coromandel Fishers depicts the happy busy life of fishers, 'the sons of the sea,' who gets out with the morning light to catch fish. Man and Nature work together for human sustenance. There is a perfect harmony between fishers and their environment which ensures professional success, prosperity and gladness. The three stanzas of the poem set three vivid scenes from a professional day of the fisherman : sunrise, sunset and full moon. The first stanza depicts the stir of activity at sunrise which brings freshness and promise for the whole day. The mood of nature at down blends well with the fishermen's reverential attitude towards their crafts and tools. The attachment and faith towards the sea is described skillfully in the imagery of a child sleeping quietly in the loving arms of his mother.

The second stanza describes the busy and strenuous life of the fisherman on the sea. The lines are packed with action, effort and movement. Man-nature relationship gets thicker; nature becomes a vital part of fisherman's existence in the world. The sea is our mother, the waves are our comrades all. The fishermen respond to the call of the sea. The man-nature relationship is extended further to man-nature-god relationship. Sea-god appears to bless the sons of the sea and grant them prosperity and joy.

In the third and final stanza, the fishermen return to the shore in a mood of contentment with the fruit of their day's labour. They are back to their resort in the 'shade of coconut glade' (p. 6). They enjoy the fullness of life on the moon-lit sands with the familiar music of the waves. The poet presents a realistic picture of an Indian evening at the seashore.

The fishermen's joy and fulfilment after a day's professional success is beautifully expressed in the earth's joy and fulfilment in a full-moon night. Sarojini Naidu discovers in the call of the sea something more significant than the fishermen's mere dependence on it for their living. The call of the distant sea allures the fishermen too. This poem is as typically Indian in setting, tone and temperament as John Masefield's *Sea-fever* in English.

The poem *The Snake Charmer* presents a charming as-well as an authentic scene of human life. The real charm of the poem lies in the mystical presentation of the art of the charmer who invites the snake to come to him promising that he should feed it on milk and wild red honey. The poet vividly recreates the romantic atmosphere of sweet and delicate perfume which attracts a snake. The charmer treats his pet as his fiance and bride to be wooed with love and enthusiasm. He creates a new world and attributes significance and meaning with his professional magic. The poem has an intense natural beauty like romantic poetry where we come across beautiful flowers which present natural piety of the Romantic poets. The poem also opens with an intense perfume of *Keora and Jasmine*.

In the last stanza we find the snake charmer in deep love as well as a professional attachment with his pet. The snake emerges from its hideout in nature or from its citadel rushes like a glittering bride of 'silver-breasted moon beam of desire' (p. 8). The charmer identifies himself with his pet. The snake becomes a bride of his 'mellifluous wooing' (p. 8). He woos his bride with love.

There is no sense of terror, here, for in Indian myths and legends serpents are never looked upon with horror. In the west, they are supposed to be the embodiments of evil and cruelty, but here in India, we have the conception of *Vasuki*. *Vasuki* offered himself as a rope when the gods and demons undertook the strenuous task of churning the ocean. Serpents, like the other creatures, also lend their services to the welfare of man. They are attributed spiritual sanctity and worshipped on the eve of *Nagapanchami.* The snake appears as a lovely glittering bride and not as a frightening deadly object. This poem shows a typical Indian's positive attitude towards the snake.

Sarojini Naidu has wide sympathy for the passions and pursuits of her fellowmen. She shows sympathy not only for human beings but also for birds, animals and insects. Many of her poems are inspired by her sympathy for the sufferer and downtrodden. *Corn Grinders* is a pathetic song which accords well with corn grinders' sad predicament in which the villagers try to break the monotony of their strenuous life by chants and songs. It is a genuine folk song in form and spirit. We find abundant use of birds and animals in the Greek tragedy. Here also animals and birds are assigned the roles of human beings. The poem beautifully reflects the sorrow and grief of life, the ache of parting and the pain of loneliness. It abounds in death pictures.

In this poem, the little mouse, the little deer and the bride bewail the death of their respective partners. The first two lines in each stanza pose a question while the remaining lines evoke the answer. The poem reveals a poet's, nay a woman's tender heart which incompasses even the animal world. It opens with the agonizing notes of a mouse whose lord is dead, caught in a 'baited snare.' The pangs of separation are unbearable. The lot of the little mouse is pathetic in absence of her beloved partner. In the second stanza the grief-stricken little deer, whose partner is ruthlessly killed by a hunter, laments the death of her lover who has met with the hunter's arrow when 'at fall of eventide he went/To drink beside the river-head' (p. 9).

The concluding stanza depicts the unbearable grief of a bewailing, bride whose lover has just died. The little bride weeps while the whole world is asleep. She breaks down in intense agony :

Alas! alas! my lord is dead!
A! who will stay these hungry tears (p. 10).

The pathos reaches its height. The bride is waiting through 'the want of famished years (p. 10), for her ultimate union in death with her lover. The sadness and sorrow that life brings and the ache of parting and the pain of loneliness, are revealed with transparent compassion and spontaneous feeling which characterize the folk song.

Village Song is cast in the form of a dialogue between a mother and her child. A conversational diction has been maintained throughout the poem. The mother talks to the child bride whom fairies call insistently. She is too young to have fascination for 'bridal songs' and 'sandal scented leisure' (p. 11). The mother is trying to stop her child from going to the call of fairies whereas the child is not responding to her mother. The mother wants to make her convince about the worldly surroundings by creating a lovely atmosphere of her lover and she says : 'would you grieve the lover who is riding forth to wed you?' (p. 11). In spite of the remembrance of the lover she is not ready to stay and very eagerly declares : 'Mother mine, to the wild forest I am going' (p. 11).

The child, fascinated by nature's unspeakable beauty and balmy solitude, finds practically no interest in the trivial luxuries of life. The lure of the forest call is simply irresistible to her.

The fairies form an integral part of the poem. The poem has grave notes. The poet is fully aware of the intricacies of human life, its mixed fabric of pleasure and pain but nature's magical mirth holds her in a spell.

The last stanza shows distinctly Shelley's thought in his (Shelley's) oft-quoted lines :

> We look before and after,
> And pine for what is not.
> Our sincerest laughter
> with some pain is fraught;
> Our sweetest songs are those
> that tell of saddest thought.[4]

It is a superb lyric with its rhythmic movement, lucidity of diction and spontaneity of expression.

Sarojini Naidu shows feminine urge and partiality for colour and brightness. Colour inspires her to weave out exotic patterns of beauty and delight. In the poem *In praise of Henna* she beautifully captures the common folk scene of young Indian women colouring their palms and feet with henna leaves. Really, henna leaves are an essential item for an Indian bride and young girls. The women can be seen in the countryside, gathering fresh green leaves of henna tree for colouring their palms and feet. The poet sets the scene with 'the red, the red of the henna-tree' (p. 13) so essential an item for 'lily-like fingers and feet' (p. 13). The scene becomes vivid and appealing with concrete and visual images.

Harvest Hymn deals with one of the oldest Indian themes. It reminds one of India's medic heritage. It is a song of praise offered to different deities — Surya (the sun), Varun (the lord of the Rainbow), Prithvi (Earth), Om (Lord of the Universe), and Brahma (the lord of Creation). It is a choral song, sung by men's voices, then by the women's voices, and finally by all voices. It vividly creates the joyous atmosphere of the Indian countryside at the harvesting time. The happy peasants invoke different deities to please them at their prosperous crops. Varuna is addressed as the 'lord of the rainbow, lord of the harvest' (p. 14). The poem is a kind of thanks giving to the lord of rain and harvest. The men sing in chorus to invoke the lord who is great, beneficent and omnipotent. Brahma, the supreme creator is worshipped in the last stanza.

Indian Love-song expresses the deep-rooted love of man and woman. The lover and the beloved present their deep feelings of love in a very romantic way. Both imagine many natural flowers which can feel their heart with beauty. The beloved is as true to the lover as the serpent is to the calling voice of flutes. The poem clearly indicates love feelings of the lover and the beloved towards each other. Both are responding to the call of their love. It is a fine example of

Indian love based on sincerity, devotion and attraction towards each other.

Cradle-song is a kind of lullaby to a young little child — 'a little lovely dream' to it. It is one such lullaby sung by a doting mother to send her baby to sleep, who lies in the cradle and goes to sleep there as the lullaby is sung. Sarojini Naidu has captured here the sweet melody of the Indian lullaby.

In the first stanza the mother tells the baby that she has brought a bright beautiful dream, bright as the dew. She has brought it from the groves of fragrant spice-trees, across fields of rice and streams in which lotus flowers grow.

In the second stanza the mother tells the baby that wild fire-flies dance round the neem trees which is called 'fairy,' for in the Indian folk tradition it is supposed to be haunted by fairies. She has stolen the lonely dream from the trunk of poppy plants, and it should send him to sleep.

Lastly the mother kisses the child affectionately and thus passes the lovely dream, so to say, on its eyes. As the child goes to sleep, she wishes it good night and prays that it may have a sweet lovely dream in its sleep. For example, she wishes that it should dream that the stars are shining round it with their golden light. 'Cradle song' is a melodious lullaby and as such it is bound to be unsubstantial and romantic. Sarojini Naidu has related the human to the cosmic. Both the forces bless the child with sound sleep and sweet dreams.

Suttee is a pathetic poem which deals with the sad predicament of an Indian widow whose husband has just died. The poem brings to focus one of the prevailing social stigmas of the country in the 19th century, against which Ram Mohan Roy raised his strong voice. It was the prevailing custom for the wife to burn herself on the funeral pyre of her husband even though she was young and hesitant. This evil has not been sentimentalized by the poet in her poem rather it highlights the intensity and height of 'love and sacrifice in which an Indian widow throws herself into her husband's funeral pyre. The stress in the poem is not on the social evil or custom but on the unfathomable sense of sacrifice that an Indian women alone can show. Instead of condemning barbaric practice she is moved by the sense of devotion that the Indian woman shows for her husband through her act of immolation. In her admiration for the intense love, death is considered less painful than separation.

In the first stanza the wife describes her departed husband as the lamp of her life, extinguishedly death's cold breath and cries out 'Love, must I dwell in the living dark?' (p. 18). In the second stanza she refers to her husband as the tree of her life, crushed to the roots under Death's cruel foot and asks : 'shall the blossom live when the tree is dead?' (p. 18). In the last stanza she calls him life of her life. The widow proves her love by saying that she and her husband are one spirit in two bodies, and that when the soul is gone, the body can hardly survive. 'Suttee' means a virtuous woman or a faithful wife. Her immolation is a symbol of love and sacrifice and this idea is difficult for the western writers to understand.

Sarojini Naidu neither glorifies nor sentimentalizes the custom of suttee in this poem. She worked throughout her life for the welfare and uplift of Indian women. In her first major speech on women's role in the national movement, she says :

> when your honour strikes, when you need torchbearers in the darkness, standard bearers to uphold your honour...the womanhood of India be with you as holders of your banner, sustainers of your strength. And if you die, remember that the spirit of Padmini of Chittor is enshrined with the manhood of India.[5]

REFERENCES

1. Sarojini Naidu, *The Sceptred Flute* (Kitabistan, Ahmedabad, 1969), p. 4 (All other page references in parentheses are from this edition).

2. P.E. Dastoor, *Sarojini Naidu* (Raw and Raghavan, Mysore, 1961), p. 26.
3. C.D. Narsimhaiah, *The Swan and the Eagle* (Indian Institute of Advanced Studies, Simla, 1969), p. 22.
4. P.B. Shelley, *Poetical Works,* p. 603.
5. Sarojini Naidu, *Speeches and Writings* of *Sarojini Naidu* (C.A. Natesan and Co., Madras, 1919), p. 95.

4

Identity Quest and Conventions at Cross Roads : A Study of Select Novels of Nayantara Sahgal

—Ranjit Singh

For centuries women have been exploited and victimized by male-dominated societies in India and all over the world. The continuing trend of exploitation of woman by man provokes her to revolt against the social system and aspire for its reconstitution, under a more equitable dispensation. But with the spread of education and the influence of a few institutions and organizations which have urged for women's emancipation from the age-old shackles, some signs of awakening among women have become visible. The awareness of the need for liberation from the shackles of marital bondage has been felt by many an educated woman in the India of the post-independence era.

Nayantara Sahgal, a prominent Indian-English woman novelist, in her novels presents the emergence of the new women who is no longer, "a sex object and glamour girl, fed on fake dreams of perpetual youth lulled into a passive role that requires no individuality" (Sahgal, *The Hindustan Times,* July 19, 1970), but some one who can claim to be man's equal partner. Having experienced the agony of marital discord which resulted in a divorce in her own life, Nayantara Sahgal gives a vivid and authentic account of an Indian woman's plight in the modern world and her quest for individual freedom and self-realization. This paper seeks to evaluate and examine how Sahgal through the portrayal of variegated female characters and dramatization of life-conflicting situations, marital tension and domestic traumas undertakes to point out the identity quest and the social conventions are at cross roads. For this study only four women characters namely Rashmi, Saroj, Simrit and Bhushan Singh's mother (no name is given to her in the novel) are selected from four of Sahgal's eight novels.

Different types of married women are presented in Sahgal's novels. The women portrayed in her early novels are very conventional and extremely submissive housekeepers. They are certainly tradition-bound wives who patiently put up with everything in marriage and do not think of quitting the family structure as they are hamstrung in the fabric of Indian culture. However, some of them do dare to get over their state of dreary suffering in marriage. But there are several women who undergo moments of excruciating mental torture deep within themselves. In Sahgal's fictional world marriage is often presented as an experience of conflict, frustration and a long drawn period of stress, through which characters mature and eventually find a stable identity of their own. Sahgal's women are liberated women rebelling against the inequalities and injustices interwoven in the traditional texture of marital life in India. Rashmi in *This Time of Morning*, Saroj in *Storm in Chandigarh*, Simrit in *The Day in Shadow* and Bhushan Singh's mother in *Mistaken Identity*, all certainly have a mind and will of their own, and the are brave enough to question the established norms of conventional marriage. Chaman Nahal observes that Sahgal's women are not outright rebels against marriage, but women who simply seek a better quality in marriage :

> In each case the attack is not against the institution of marriage but against the inequality and injustice that is forced upon women by men using the institution of marriage (1985, 102).

The female characters in Sahgal's *This Time of Morning* are products of a changed social condition in India and they emerge as characters endowed with greater individuality. For instance, the vivacious and outgoing Rashmi in this novel, the only daughter of Kailas and Mira, comes back to her parents, having deserted her discontented husband Dalip, an I.A.S. officer, contemplating divorce. Rakesh her childhood friend, meeting Rashmi after a long interval observes, "Now she looks displaced. It was marriage, then, that had altered her, made her a moth trapped in cement" (*This Time of Morning* 35). Rashmi feels so alienated and distraught in her married life that she simply cannot get on with her husband who differs from her so much in temperament and is almost on the verge of schizophrenia : "A part of her married a man, loved him, given herself to the task of making a home and suffered the wilderness that only two mismatched people could create." (123).

Curiously enough, Rashmi experiences all the pangs of a divided self, a vital segment of her being clamouring for separation and release from her husband, and the other part still cherishing the savoured moments of togetherness in the early years of her marriage : "I don't wish him harm but he and I — she could not even think we any longer — cannot go on together" (13). Finally, Rashmi resolves to divorce Dalip. Rashmi's decision on divorce baffles her conservative mother Mira, who is a veritable personification of the ageless spirit of female submission in the Indian context of marriage. Her daughter's bold decision is "a mortal blow to all she held scared" (146) and she wonders :

> What reason under heaven could sever the marriage bond? Women stayed married, had since time immemorial stayed married, under every conceivable circumstance, to brutal insensitive husbands, to lunatics and lepers. And Dalip, God forbid, was none of these things (146).

To Mira, Rashmi's decision is "a tasteless parody of a transplanted modernity" (146). However, it is Kailas, Rashmi's father, who understands his daughter's agony and sees in her decision "a torrential release from ancient grooves and bonds, ancient pain and suppression" (214). Rashmi takes a bold decision to work and live alone in Delhi. Eventually, an irresistible urge for communication in confidence, stemming from a certain emotional vulnerability in her impels Rashmi to move closely with Neil Berensen, a Norwegian Architect of the Peace Institute. This, finally, nudges her to share moments of closeness on bed with him. What Rashmi looks for in Neil, is a life of intense, absorbing and congenial relationship. She tells Neil : "We have to invade each other's privacy a little, force things a little or we shall, stay just where we are" (156). Commenting on the validity of Rashmi's brief love affair with Neil, Jasbir Jain lays stress, quite rightly, on her essential need for articulating her emotions in love :

> Rashmi's divorce and her relationship with Neil are not a "tasteless parody of a transplanted modernity" but an inner need for communication and involvement which remain unsatisfied. Sex is only of secondary importance (6.1 Jan. 1978 : 43).

Soon Rashmi breaks off her relationship with Neil too, as he fails to satisfy her inmost need for communication.

It is when Rashmi is about to leave for Lucknow where her father is posted as the new Chief Minister that she renews her relationship with Rakesh, her childhood friend, "who had been closer than a brother, more than a friend" (35). With a deep longing for communication within her, she asks Rakesh when the train is about to leave, "Rakesh....will you write to me? There's so much I'd like to share with you" (216). Thus she accepts Rakesh as a true companion. Sahgal's women are all on a quest for constructive and meaningful relationships with men demanding mutual understanding and involvement. Rashmi is not satisfied simply with her freedom in extra-marital relationship, but longs for communication and response, lacking in her marital relationship with Dalip and in her brief affair with Neil.

To Nayantara Sahgal failure to communicate and understand is the main cause of marital discord. Saroj in *Storm in Chandigarh* is unhappy, not being able to find a reciprocal emotional involvement with her husband Inder. Besides, the temperamental incompatibilities of the pair vitiate further their conjugal relationship. As M.L. Malhotra observes :

> Their marriage, though outwardly successful is unhappy, reeling on the rock of temperamental incompatibilities, and a radial divergence of marital ideals. Saroji is a highly sensitive, child-oriented, marital creature raised in a free atmosphere but yoked to an insensitive, self-centered, a western gloss. They belong to two different culture milieus (1971, 229).

Brought up by fairly liberal parents, Saroj has a premarital affair in her college days which she confides to her husband Inder, hoping for a clean break from the past. Unfortunately, to Inder her confession makes the beginning of a nagging suspicion. Even after four years of marriage with Saroj, and having two children, Inder continues to harbour a deep — seated doubt with regard to Saroj's loyalty, and brutally torments her with questions on her premarital relationship, while he indulges himself in an affair with their children's teacher Mara. He believes in two codes of conduct obviously, one for men and another for women.

Initially Saroj boldly puts up with Inder's idiosyncrasies for the sake of her two children and as she expects her third child, accepting to live a life entirely on his term. According to Inder, Saroj was just a wife to satisfy his physical needs and mother to take care of the children. To Inder, "A wife was one half of an enterprise, the compliant partner who presided over home and children and furthered her husband's career" (*Storm in Chandigarh*, 53). Shyam Asnani is right in stressing on the emptiness in the relationship between Saroj and Inder : "They have lived, loved, even produced and raised children and there hasn't been real understanding between them" (16.1-2 Jan.-June 1973, 54).

In course of time, Saroj realises endurance in marriage is not a virtue in itself. She makes friends with Vishal Dubey a liaison officer, who has come to settle the political problem between the Chief Ministers of Chandigarh and Haryana. It is no wonder that Saroj's parching spirit seeks love and affection elsewhere. She finds in Dubey, the understanding and mutuality in relationship which Inder has denied to her all along. As Saroj expects her third child, Dubey would take her on long walks in the jungle. Saroj who longs for "the oxygen of understanding" (220) finds it in her relationship with Dubey who instills in her the value of emancipation during the long walks together. Coming under the influence of Dubey, Saroj begins to protest against Inder's authoritarian ways and consequently, she is manhandled and abused. Meanwhile, Dubey's frequent visits to Saroj rouse the green-eyed monster in Inder. Soon the situation worsens and Saroj decides to leave Inder's home for ever asserting her individuality. Shyam Asnani comments :

> The ultimate assertion of Saroj's individuality is reminiscent of Nora's Character in Ibsen's *The Dolls House* who also revolts against her husband's inhuman behaviour and plans a flight in the similar circumstances (3.1, 1978 : 158).

Nora as a character is much more independent than Saroj who has the solid support of Dubey in executing her revolt. It is Dubey again who suggests that Saroj must go to Delhi for her confinement. With the help of Dubey who awakens a new sensibility in her, Saroj finally emerges a new woman and comes to stay in New Delhi leaving her husband behind in Chandigarh. Lakshma Sinha recognizes the dramatic significance of Saroj's departure to Delhi in these words : "Saroj leaves domesticity and timidness far behind and emerges out of her chrysalis with new found confidence. Dubey has resurrected her personality" (1987, 109).

In the earlier two novels Rashmi and Saroj actively contemplate divorce living in a state of security whereas in *The Day in Shadow* Simrit actually divorces her husband at the risk of facing misery, economic constraints, depressive bouts of loneliness and a score of other existential problems. Even as Saroj, Simrit finds herself utterly shut out of the world of her husband who never discusses business with her or in her presence. Simrit realizes that verbal communication is the missing link in her relationship with Som and tries in vain to engage him in some meaningful dialogue or other. Som pays no heed to Simrit's words, even in making ordinary decisions of everyday life : "Not even about chair covers and curtains. Even there Som had had a veto. Not even about servants" (3). Instead, Som treats her merely as a sexual object. The extreme limit of Som's chauvinism can be seen in his condemnation of his friend Lal who has murdered his wife. Significantly enough, his misogyny is directed even to his daughters. He loves his son Brij on the other hand and transfers to Brij's account, shares worth six lakhs, originally bought in the name of his wife. He deliberately keeps the shares under his control and makes his wife pay heavy taxes on the same shares even after her divorce. Moreover, the divorce in which Simrit seeks shelter, peace, freedom and independence precisely turns out to be a potential source of further trouble. The huge tax she has to pay from her meagre income, makes her feel utterly devastated and overwhelmed. She feels reduced almost to the level of a beast of burden :

> This is what an overloaded donkey feels like standing there as large as life with its back breaking and no one doing anything about it, not because they can't see it, but because it's a donkey and loads are for donkeys (56).

Eventually Simrit seeks to get the help of Raj Garg, a Christian M.L.A. to get out of the legal morass created by her divorce settlement. Raj who understands and shares her agony instills in her some positive thinking to face the world with renewed confidence in herself, thus providing her the moral support she badly needs. Raj's broad sympathies and humane attitude draw Simrit towards him in course of time and she decides to marry him.

It is significant to note that both Simrit and Saroj try their best to be good wives as long as their marriages last and never take the conventional family structure lightly. It is only circumstances beyond their control make them quit their respective households. Saroj leaves home with extreme reluctance when riots break out in Chandigarh. It is only for saving her children and the third expected child in the womb that Saroj decides to move to Delhi. Simrit too feels that "in some inescapable way a part of her would be always married to Som" (220) even after her divorce. According to Jasbir Jain :

> Simrit's divorce does not imply that marriage has failed as a social institution or that it has outlived its utility. It clearly demonstrates the need for reciprocal relationship in marriage. Nayantara's view point appears to be a desire to place marriage is the proper social and emotional perspective (1994, 42).

A similar liberated character is presented through Bhushan Singh's mother in Sahgal's latest novel *Mistaken Identity*, despite the fact that she is a product of a highly conservative age and society. Bhushan Singh recalls, for instance, how his mother had originally been confined to 'Zenana' (women's section of the house) with its high walls blocking it off from the rest of the mansion :

> Mother saw the world through the slit between her carriage curtain when she went out, more rarely through tinted glass after Father bought cars, because she preferred her carriage. And, otherwise, she saw it through barred windows (*Mistaken Identity* 26).

The senior ranee (Bhushan's mother) of the princely state of Vijaygarh in the novel, is hardly allowed any exposure to the outside world. She was married at the age of five and brought to her husband's home at thirteen and she had to wait for nine long years to be blessed with a son. Bhushan's father married thrice while his mother suffered literally in that prison house of marriage till her elopement with Yusuf.

Bhushan's mother was in no position to voice her disapproval when her husband took his second and third wives. In fact, after the third marriage of her husband, according to Bhushan "she has never been the same since. She has another ambition. She wants to turns into stone" (32). Oddly enough, society encourages such ostentatious life style of men and willingly approves of such marriages. The third marriage as Bhushan recalls : "is very public and a very popular wedding. Our public buildings were electrically illuminated by special generators and there were more singer, dancers, wrestlers, acrobats, food, drinks and poetry than the first or second time" (33). With scant regard for the feeling of Bhushan's mother, society bestows blessings on his father's marriage. Bhushan's mother believes that she alone has the right to be his wife and she is certainly not content to be the mistress of the household.

As a discarded Ranee, deprived of freedom, choice and fulfilment, Bhushan s mother comes to know Yusuf her son's prison mate very late in life when her son is about to marry Yusuf's daughter. Yusuf turns out to be an extremely kind man, sensitive to her every need and equally desirous of freedom. Deep within herself, Bhushan's mother has been all along an emancipated soul and when she comes across the right opportunity she freely expresses her thirst for freedom. Her rejecting the social convention is like coming out of a chrysalis. Ironically enough, the same society which had celebrated grandly each of the weddings of Bhushan's father taking his mother's acceptance for granted, feels quite outraged when she decides to take on another partner. Bhushan dismisses with contempt the stand taken by the society and says :

> Society has not forgiven this liaison between an illiterate ranee and her communist lover and the shameless public exhibition they make of it. But Mother and Yusuf are so love mad, they haven't noticed their notoriety, I can't say any of it surprises me as far as Mother is concerned (193-194).

In fact, Bhushan's mother "who has been sentenced to that greenish light of unfulfilled desire" (194), ill treated and despised by her husband leaves the family mansion for a fuller life with Yusuf. Bhushan recalls in vivid yet poetic terms the moment of his mother's departure :

> Early one morning she left the family mansion. I saw her hesitate for a second at the entrance and hold her breath before she walked out to star in the most sensational scandal of the generation (193).

Yusuf takes the travel hungry ranee straight to Leningrad in winter to show her the fall of snow flakes. Thus having thrown the taboos of the Zenana to the dust bins, Bhushan's mother goes happily to live with comrade Yusuf. Shyam Asnani observes :

> Unorthodox, unconventional and rebellious, she daringly breaks all traditional taboos and steps out of the palace (symbolic of traditional anchorage) forever to live openly with her son's erstwhile prison comrade the urbane Yusuf all for love (1992, 72).

In one of her interviews on being questioned about her women characters in *Mistaken Identity* the novelist observed :

> The mother of Bhushan Singh is one of the strongest in the book and partly this is the story of her liberation. She is the archetype of the woman in purdah. The woman who has been shackled all her life. She had had no say from childhood about whom she would marry, when she would marry, whether

> she wants to have children, how many and I have hinted that two were disposed of because they were girls. In all this she has been an object. She has not been a subject. And yet this woman breaks loose and becomes the most outrageously liberated creature by getting this handsome Muslim lover and they are madly in love (Varalakshmi, S., 1993, 17).

Bhushan's mother like Sahgal's early protagonists Rashmi, Saroj and Simrit, steps into the shadow of another man, Yusuf, who can understand her and communicate with her better than her husband.

Sahgal's women are thus "strivers and aspires towards freedom, towards goodness, towards a compassionate world" (Sahgal qtd. in Jan. 1994, 116). Rashmi, Saroj, Simrit and Bhushan's mother the senior Ranee stand for the emerging women of India who refuse to remain silent and submissive like conventional 'Pativratas' in marriage. It is true that all these women endeavour to escape the shackles of hapless marriages and prefer to live with their lovers who can provide them with understanding, love and warmth of companionship and help them start life afresh. Neena Arora observes :

> Sahgal's women depend on some help to escape oppression and exploitation which in their cases is usually provided by a man — a friend or a father who often helps them to come out of the miserable relationship or give them moral strength to smash the taboos and assert their identity to live a meaningful life (1991, 102).

To M.L. Malhotra :

> If Nayantara's women characters have any passion, it is the longing to be free, freedom from all restraints in word and deed, being their monomania. One and all they want to be fully alive and themselves.... No taboos or inhibitions! (1971, 224).

Thus, in Nayantara Sahgal's novels, as the women's quest for identity and social conventions are at cross-roads, they have to face many problems, conflicts, frustrations and inner stress in their married lives through which the individuals mature and eventually find a stable identity of their own.

WORKS CITED

Arora, Neena, 1991. *Nayantara Sahgal and Doris Lessing : A Feminist Study in Comparison.* New Delhi : Prestige Books.

Asnani, Shyam, M. "The Novels of Nayantara Sahgal." *Indian Literature,* 16.1-2. Jan.-June 1973 : 36-69.

——, "Portrayal of Man-Woman Relationship in the Novels of Nayantara Sahgal." *Kakatiya Journal of English Studies.* 3.1 (1978) : 151-65.

Asnani, Shyam, M. and Ramesh Chadha, 1992. "Female Quest for Identity in Nayantara Sahgal's Novels." *Quest for Identity in Indian English Writing,* Part I : Fiction. Ed. R.S. Pathak, New Delhi : Bahri Publications, 59-74.

Jain, Jasbir, "The Aesthetics of Morality : Sexual Relations in the Novels of Nayantara Sahgal." *The Journal of Indian Writing in English,* 6-1 Jan. 1978 : 41-48.

——, 1994. *Nayantara Sahgal.* Rev. ed. Jaipur : Printwell.

Malhotra, M.L., 1971. *Bridges of Literature.* Ajmer : Sunanda Publications.

Nahal, Chaman, 1985. *The New Literatures in English.* New Delhi : Allied Publishers Pvt. Ltd.

Sahgal, Nayantara, 1965. *This Time of Morning.* Delhi : Hind Pocket Books (P) Ltd.

——, 1970. *Storm in Chandigarh.* Delhi : Hind Pocket Books (P) Ltd.

——, 1971. *The Day in Shadow.* New Delhi : Penguin Books India (P) Ltd.

——, 1988 *Mistaken Identity.* London : Heinemann Ltd.

——, "Women : Persons or Possessions." *The Hindustan Times,* 19 July 1970.

Sinha, Lakshmi, 1987. "Nayantara Sahgal *Storm in Chandigarh :* A Search for Values." *Studies in Indian Fiction in English.* ed. G.S. Balarama Gupta, Gulbarga : JIWE Publications. 104-112.

Varalakshmi, S., 1993. "An Interview with Nayantara Sahgal." *Indian Women Novelists.* Set II, Vol. IV, ed. R.K. Dhawan, New Delhi : Prestige Books. 1-8.

5

Indian Writing in English : Double-Base

—B. Yadava Raju

Prof. K.R. Srinivasa Iyengar's first book on Indian Writing in English was published in 1943 by the P.E.N. All India Centre with the title Indo-Anglian literature. The book was published with a "Foreword," by the editor of the series, Smt. Sophia Wadia. In the 'Foreword' Sophia Wadia says that the country's preoccupation with politics overshadowed its literary unfoldment of the past few years in the different linguistic areas. India therefore cannot afford to be neglectful of her literary movement. In her view India's many languages are not a curse as her enemies may call them so. In fact, these many languages are channels of 'cultural enrichment.' Many educated Indians are not familiar with the literary wealth of any Indian language other than their own. Neither was any systematic attempt made to popularise the growth of the Indian literatures, nor to present gems from their masterpieces to the general public in English translation. This particular function was then being done by the Centre for India of the International P.E.N. In his Introduction to the book C.R. Reddy notes that the racial awareness need not be 'recapitulatory' of the dead past and not be 'revivalistic' in objective. It may be 'reformist,' 'critical' and 'futurist,' but the roots must be struck in 'inwardness' and the 'sap that sustains the outward growth must rise from our own depths' [p. v]. One of the aims of C.R. Reddy was to get English literature on Indian themes prescribed in schools and colleges. In order to achieve this objective he requested K.R. Srinivasa Iyengar to write a brochure on Indo-Anglian literature. According to C.R. Reddy, 'Indo-Anglian literature is not essentially different in kind from Indian literature. It is part of it...' [p. vi]. Writers like Tagore, Iqbal and Aurobindo Ghose share some of its glory from the Vaidic times. 'The soul of India transmigrates from one body to another [p. vii] but remains in essence the same. Iyengar in the chapter entitled 'The Beginnings' traces back the origins of English education in India. While referring to the Macaulay Minute of 1835 he insightfully refers to the 'filtration theory' which did not work as expected by Macaulay. Instead, it gave rise to a 'false culture,' false because it was in disharmony with normal Indian categories of experience. English education made Indian youths hanker after the thrills of urban life and finally made them incredible anachronisms in their own once happy homes. No healthy literary growth was possible on such uncongenial soil. But the later generation conversed and corresponded in English and 'Indianisms' and 'Babuisms' were the order of the day. In such circumstances, Iyengar obliquely mentions that the wit of the educated Indian seesawed between his mother tongue and English and between the Western and Oriental civilizations.[1] This resulted in a linguistic incompetence. The native Indians became neither competent in their mother tongue nor did they acquire competence in a foreign tongue. At the cost of their mother tongue, the other tongue was preferred, but the preference resulted in incompetence in both the languages. Such a situation only encouraged journalistic and political writing. But soon Indians caught up with the prevailing trend and could gradually express in English. This was supported by the meritorious work of the Anglo-Indian poets like Sir William Jones, John Leyden, Henry Derozio, Meredith Parker, David Lester Richardson, Sir Edwin Arnold and others, who derived their inspiration from 'traditional Indian themes'. Thus the early Indian writers in English drew their sustenance from English writers and

Anglo-Indian writers. It was, therefore, always bilingual connection that helped the Indian writer.

While assessing the value of Indo-Anglian poetry in his second book on the subject, entitled The Indian Contribution to English Literature [1945], Srinivasa Iyengar remarks : The best Indo-Anglian poets have given us something which neither English poetry nor any of our regional literatures can give; in other words, they have effected a true marriage of Indian process of poetic experience with English formulae of verse expression.[2] To Iyengar, to be Indian in thought and feeling and emotion and experience, yet also to court the graces and submit to the discipline of English for expression is a novel experiment in creative mutation. This is possible, obviously, only with the knowledge of both the languages and cultures. Indo-Anglian literature, then, is both an Indian literature and a variation of English literature as well. This double base, this potential double, becomes, according to Iyengar, a matter of complexity. In Iyengar's opinion the Indian is apt to think that Indo-Anglian literature is not — and could never be — as good as Bengali or Marathi or Tamil literature. He quotes Sri Aurobindo in this context : ...Some of Toru Dutt's poems, Sarojini's, Harin's have been highly placed by good English critics, and I don't think we need be more 'queasy than Englishmen themselves.... I think, as time goes on, people will become more and more polyglot and these mental barriers will begin to disappear [p. 6]. On the other hand, Iyengar also defends the Englishman who thinks that Indo-Anglian literature is not — and could never be — as good as English literature. He compares the situation to that of the birth of Sakuntala. According to the Indian legend, Sakuntala was born of the union between Menaka and Vishvamitra. But neither of them have anything to do with the daughter. But Iyengar expresses the hope that this literature would have 'some of the charm of Sakuntala' and may give 'a new Bharata for Bharat' [p. 7]. He predicts that the Indian writer in English has greater opportunity for striking out new paths and receiving quick rewards. He says that it is even possible to be agreeably and fruitfully bilingual — as many have been, and many still are [p. 8]. He emphasises the need to learn English as well as Sanskrit to achieve positions of strength and maturity in the competitive modern world. According to Iyengar, English is one of our national languages, and Indo-Anglian literature too is one of our literatures [p. 15]. Iyengar disagrees with the belief that the West impinges on India, because English education is/was a new force — part elixir, part poison — injected into Indian life; it made the building up of harmonious homes very difficult, it gave a jolt to India's traditional life; but [it] served us nobly by shocking the nation into a new awareness. It was necessary, for the first time, for the Indian to assert himself and find out who he is. This search for self-identity has not been possible without some noble and poetic expression in regional literatures as well as in English. In this connection Iyengar quotes Arthur Mayhew who writes : Under English rule in India, the impact of two civilizations may have produced unrest. But it has also sustained and stimulated life [p. 29]. The 'moment' that bred Indo-Anglian literature was an extraordinary story of endurance, assimilation and integral transformation. This was the origin of many modern Indian literatures as well as Indian writing in English. The study of English literature stimulated literary creation in Bengali, Marathi, Telugu, Tamil, Gujarati and the other languages. Some of the greatest writers of the last hundred years have been men and women educated in English. Though some of these writers may not seek creative expression in English, some of them have been unrepentant bilingualists, writing in English and their mother tongue, with equal facility, and if necessary translating their English into their mother tongue or their Bengali or Marathi into English. According to Iyengar, the filiations between the modern Indian literatures [including Indo-Anglian literature] and English literature have been close, and the links have been renewed from time to time, and the student of literary history and of comparative literature can find much to interest him in this phenomenon [p. 30].

This bilingual connection and 'double-base' have been true of the renaissance in modern Indian literature that begins with Raja Rammohan Roy who mastered many languages while still young. His interest and inquiries ranged from the rights of women and freedom of the press to English education, the revenue and judicial systems in India, religious tolerance and the plight of the Indian peasantry. He wanted India to become a new and modern country and the Indians to become a 'virile new people,' not, of course, by cutting off our moorings from the past, but by achieving a new integration of our traditional strength with the new scientific disciplines from the West. Many others followed Raja Rammohan Roy's lead in reconstructing and rebuilding the nation. Iswar Chandra Vidyasagar, Prince Dwaraknath Tagore and his son Maharshi Debenadranath Tagore, Keshub Chandra Sen, Swamy Dayananda Saraswati, the founder of the Arya Samaj are only a few instances. Kashinath Trimbak Telang and Mahadev Govind Ranade were deeply read in English and Sanskrit. Of the two, Kashinath Telang translated the Bhagavad Gita for the Sacred Books of the East Series. Later, B.R. Rajam Iyer was also a scholar steeped in English, Sanskrit and Tamil. He was also the first novelist in Tamil with his *Kamalambal*. He also published an English novel with title *Vasudeva Sastri*.

Thus, the literary scene of Indian renaissance was already electrified and charged with many scholars and social workers before Toru Dutt. Toru Dutt who began her literary career with a non-Indian and non-regional background, felt later the 'need for roots' and 'began studying Sanskrit' [p. 58]. As a result, she translated a few tales from the original Sanskrit into English verse. Iyengar remarks, She could feel her feet on hospitable soil, and satisfying the secret longings of her spirit for roots in the consciousness of the race [p. 63]. Later, Toru Dutt's cousin Romesh Chunder Dutt found time to canalize his massive scholarship and constructive patriotism into meritorious historical surveys — *A History of Civilization in Ancient India, Later Hindu Civilization, India in the*

Victorian Age, The Economic History of British India and A Brief History of Ancient and Modern Bengal. In addition to all these preoccupations, Romesh Chunder Dutt was almost possessed by the desire to turn the art of translation into fruitful purpose, for the benefit of Bengali no less than of English readers. His notable achievements include his English verse renderings of India's great epics, *the Ramayana*, and *the Mahabharata*, and selections from the Rig Veda, the Upanishads, Buddhist literature, Kalidasa's Kumarasambhava and Bharavi's Kiratarjuniya. Another notable scholar and writer was Sri Aurobindo's brother Manmohan Ghose. Though both of them were Bengalis, their influence was not limited to Bengali literature only. They influenced a score of other writers and schloars. Rabindranath's forerunners — Michale Madhusudhan Dutt, Iswar Chandra Vidyasagar, Bankim Chandra Chatterjee — had given Bengali poetry, prose and fiction a great start among the modern Indian languages. Rabindranath Tagore readily breathed this air of infinitive possibility and was drawn to Indian devotional poetry in general. A visit to England and the English Romantics exercised a potent influence on him. Shantiniketan was established where, according to Iyengar, the cultures of the East were to be brought together, and a 'living relationship was to be attempted between the West and the East : the East was to transmute the seeming West-East dichotomy into a creative unity and thus achieve a broad base for human understanding and purposive activity' [p. 101].

Next only in chronological order is Sri Aurobindo. Sri Aurobindo occupies a greater space in Iyengar's later volume than in his Indo-Anglian Literature [1943]. Iyengar says with increasing awareness that Sri Aurobindo is 'the one uncontestably outstanding figure in Indo-Anglian literature' [p. 144]. During his stay at Baroda, according to Iyengar, Sri Aurobindo 'fast achieved the feat of re-nationalizing himself' [p. 146]. Iyengar quotes Romain Rolland who saw in Sri Aurobindo 'the greatest synthesis' between Asia and

Europe and 'the last of the great Rishis' [p. 151]. His Savitri, in his own estimation, is 'an attempt to catch something of the Upanishadic and Kalidasian movement, so far as that is possible in English.' With Mulk Raj Anand, as with Bankim Chandra Chatterjee before him, political action took the form of writing novels. Iyengar says, 'He wrote of the people, for the people, and as a man of the people' [p. 333]. Anand was well aware of what was being done in regional literatures like Hindi, Punjabi, and Bengali. His nationalistic fervour and social concern grew from the circumstances and contacts with these literatures. R.K. Narayan was born in Tamil-state, but settled in Mysore where Kannada is spoken, and writes in English. He is very much part of what he describes in his fiction. He makes a special and an individual use of the English language. Raja Rao is a child of Gandhian Age and his fiction is full of modern and ancient India. Iyengar says that all his 'writing is part of Raja Rao's sadhana or spiritual experience, and so *Kanthapura*, *The Serpent and the Rope* and *The Cat and Shakespeare* should be viewed as steps — or paths — towards realization' [p. 409].

Indian Writing in English has come a long way ever since it began its journey. It is being increasingly recognised as one of the dozen or more authentic voices of India. According to Srinivasa Iyengar, Indo-Anglian literature was once 'a tool' in the hands of the leaders of the Indian renaissance 'to rouse the prostrate nation,' to 'protest against the evil of foreign domination,' has now grown 'into a creative akshay patra, amuda surabhi' [p. 703]. It is now being cultivated in our universities as an 'academic discipline', but only as an integral part of English literature studies. This, according to Iyengar, does not entail either the ignorance of English literature or of Indian literature in our own regional languages, which, according to him, would be a 'tragedy' [p. 704]. Iyengar allays all the doubts regarding the relevance of using English language for creative purposes by saying that when an Indian writer comes to use the second language like English for creative purposes, he would be actually recording a kind of half-conscious translation [from mother tongue into English] that has taken place in the mind. This is often so because most of our writers are bilingual, some equally proficient in English and the mother tongue, and some more in one than in the other. This situation, in fact, becomes the most intractable to the writer because he should take enough care not to slip into ludicrous situations. Among the post-Independence writers, Iyengar traces a general tendency to imitate the latest writing fashion in USA or elsewhere, especially among the poets. It has become customary for some of the poet-anthologists to fall foul of Sri Aurobindo and other pre-Independence poets. To these 'modernists,' the 'mystical' quality in the earlier generation of poets can be an anathema. Adil Jussawalla, R. Parthasarathy and Keki Daruwalla are among such coterie. Such pronouncements are, in the view of Iyengar, 'perverse, purblind or puerile' [p. 710]. Iyengar wonders at Ezekiel who discovers among the Sanskrit poets only 'breasts and buttocks,' and in his own collection entitled *Hymns in Darkness* there is hardly any darkness except the 'wizardry of words.' Commenting on Kamala Das's autobiography *My Story*, Iyengar says that 'her experiments in prose fiction have further stimulated interest in the poet more than in the poetry' [p. 712]. In this plethora of isms, ideas and imitations, Jayanta Mahapatra's poetry stands apart. In some of his lyrics Jayanta, according to Iyengar, seems to recapitulate 'Vedic times and themes.... The ancient spiritual quest tugs at the physicist-poet's heart-strings' [p. 713]. This becomes possible for the poet because he is always rooted in the native soil and situations. As a contrast to Jayanta Mahapatra's nativization process, A.K. Ramanujan's 'cynical desecration in a foreign culture' [p. 714] has not gone unnoticed by Iyengar's critical acumen. The theme of the poetry of the 'Parsi Quartet' that includes Gieve Patel, Adil Jussawalla and K.D. Katrak does not proceed beyond an 'uncanny sense of the anatomy of human experience...backed by a basic dedication to health and wholesomeness' [p. 714]. Adil Jussawalla has no use for the native Indian tradition which, in his opinion, is nothing but 'a vagueness of thought, an absolute faith in the mystical, and a blind reliance on the heart' [p. 718]. If these post-Independence poets are led by a kind of self-glorification,' Arvind Krishna Mehrotra is led by a kind of 'self-denigration.' According to Iyengar, both — 'self-glorification 'and 'self-denigration' are misleading. The bilingual poets like Dilip Chitre and Arun Kolatkar who write in Marathi and English, show some promising talent. Like Dilip Chitre and Arun Kolatkar, Jayasudharshana is bilingual too, and writes in both Kannada and English. Jayasudharshana, while being 'conscious of the world of modern science', retains 'his links with the roots' [p. 726]. Iyengar expresses the hope that the future Indian poetry — along with Indian poetry in English, will 'strive towards a symphony of many notes, discarding no part of human experience, rejecting no segment of our national poetic heritage since the time of the Vedic singers... [p. 730].

Commenting on the Indian drama in English, Iyengar says that though some of the recent Theatre Groups in Bombay and elsewhere have successfully produced plays in English by Indians : for example, Pratap Sharma's *A Touch of Brightness*, Asif Currimbhoy's *The Doldrummers*, Guru Charan Das's Larins Sahib, Gieve Patel's Princes and Shiv. K. Kumar's *The Last Wedding Anniversary*, by and large this genre remains confined to the top English-educated English-speaking denationalised elitocracy. As an alternative, the dramatist or playwright is compelled to skip the contemporary scene, and opt for the classical, mythological or historical themes. At any rate, Indian drama in English 'will have but a limited vogue, a minority appeal,... according to Iyengar. His observation regarding Indian drama in English is realistic, but at the same time it need not discourage the playwright if he is well-versed and well-informed about the current happenings and developments in the Indian literatures. For example, the Telugu drama, and the Marathi theatre are going strong. Some of the recent Telugu plays have held a sway over people : Rakta

Kanneru, Kukka, etc., are widely accepted and appreciated. These plays are far superior to the plays written in English by the Indian writers. This is where the Indian writer in English may have to learn from and sharpen his tools accordingly from the writer of the Indian literatures. Discussing the recent trends in Indian fiction in English Iyengar feels comfortable with some of the strides made by writers like Kamala Markandaya, Anita Desai, Arun Joshi, Shashi Deshpande and others. But relatively, the Indo-Anglian fiction remains insignificant in comparison with what is being done in U.K., U.S.A. and other commonwealth countries. Off and on writers like Salman Rushdie, Arundhati Roy, Vikram Sathe, and Jumpa Lahari have created ripples in the literary circles, but to a large extent, the fiction remains mediocre. Nevertheless, there are more Indo-Anglian fiction writers today than forty years ago. The literary awards bring the chosen writers to national attention. This is a favourable atmosphere to aspirant writers. In such a situation, according to Iyengar, Indo-Anglian literature has a unique role to play. This unique role is to expect the Indian writing in English — rather than any of the regional literatures — to project a total vision of Mother India, interpreting her aspirations and hopes and recording her arduours and frustrations and partial achievements, not only before the outside world, but also before the diverse linguistic groups within the country, and thereby promote a sense of 'national identity,' an ineffable feeling of oneness with the Mother,.... Though he has not specifically mentioned how this 'national identity' can be promoted, he leaves enough clues that this is possible only with the interaction between the Indian literatures and English. The different literatures like Tamil, Telugu, Kannada, Malayalam, Bengali and other literatures are bubbling with activity and dynamism.

It is necessary to mention that in modern times India has been producing high quality literature in nearly twenty languages. And India had strong literary traditions before the English language and literature arrived on Indian shores. Most of the works belonging to Indian English literature that have received international attention are no better than those published in Indian languages. Writers like R.K.Narayan, Mulk Raj Anand, Raja Rao, and others enjoy global reputations which are denied to some definitely superior writers writing in Indian languages. It is increasingly true that Indian English literature is less representative of Indian society than any literature in Indian languages. As such, the real India has remained as inaccessible to Western audiences as ever. One of the many possible ways out of this situation is to strengthen the translation activity. By doing so Indian English literature can really contribute something original in the sphere of Commonwealth literature. Many Indian writers in English have engaged themselves in translation activity. They include Tagore and Sri Aurobindo in the pre-Independence generation, and Arun Kolatkar, Jayanta Mahapatra, A.K. Ramanujan, Dilip Chitre and Jayasudharshana in the post-Independence generation of poets. This practice would help Indian students of Indian language literatures to reach across linguistic boundaries. This has given and will continue to give a big boost to comparative literary study in India and contribute to the emergence of a pan-Indian literary, cultural identity. This would, perhaps, be the most suitable way to pay our tribute to Prof. K.R. Srinivasa Iyengar.

REFERENCES

1. K.R. Srinivasa Iyengar [1943]. *Indo-Anglian Literature*. The P.E.N. All India Centre. Bombay : The International Book House Ltd., p. ii. All the references are to this edition and are included in the text in parentheses.
2. ——, [1985]. *Indian Writing in English*, New Delhi : Sterling Publishers Pvt. Ltd. All the further references are to this edition and are included in the text in parentheses.

6

Despair and Delight in the Novels of Mulk Raj Anand

—*B. Mishra*

Mulk Raj Anand occupies an important niche in the field of Indian writing in English. An established novelist who deals in common and day-today themes of Indian villages and towns, makes it to the sky scrappers of cities enabling us to realize the chasm between two worlds. Starting his quest as a novelist with *Untouchable* he musters enough guts to strengthen his characters to find their real fire in the furnace of fight for freedom. His simple characters smoulder within and keep the furnace burning till the fight comes to flames. A comparative look/observation of his characters between the first phase and the later phase makes our vision clear. An overall study of Anand's novels accentuates the fact that most of his works have taken birth in 'Despair' and have perfected in 'Delight.' An avid but hurried reader of novels may find Anand's works as boring and historical but a serious reader finds entering an ocean of joy with universal barrier of temporal sorrow.

The idea behind the title of this article is taken from the real chapters of life. Human life is a long and everlasting book where these two chapters are innately folded/unfolded and at times they over-ride each other. One may find it as difficult to define delight and despair as to sweet and sour. But to my view, they can be illustrated with sunshine and shower, sun and slum, happiness and sorrow *et al.* My motive behind this coinage is to discover the same in the novels of Anand. Life moves on the two wheels of despair and delight which give a slice to our existence. Anand once told P.K. Rajan philosophically :

> "Life does not admit itself to a linear approach. The approach is much more complex, incoherent, determined by instinct and emotion, impulse and idea."[1]

Since there are contradictory elements in Anand's personality, the growth of his consciousness is an existing drama for critics and scholars. His personal story can be viewed as the story of torments and ecstasies. The symbolic facts of his life are someway or the other related to his fictional impetus. Unconscious urges, repressions and fantasies colour his perception and imagination. The man who suffers is greater than the man who writes in the case of Anand. It is the personal despair and delight of Anand which is expanded in fictional terms. The fact that "Anand is an optimistic humanist who can move the most pessimistic man to action"[2] is a tribute to him.

Each novel of Anand has several layers of despair and delight. We hear in his fiction, echoes of all kinds. There are number of motivations in each of his novels. P.K. Rajan observes that the evolutionary Marxist comprehension of reality is enriched by a spiritual, metaphysical, lyrical quality in his novels. Each novel is a blend of despair and delight. K.R.S. Iyenger recognizes the genius of Anand when he remarks that Anand is a novelist who invokes "a multitude of responses."[3]

It is difficult to discuss all the novels of Anand in this article. So, we shall analyze here the first trilogy and examine specific details to show how the energies of Anand's protagonists are arrested. Because Anand claims that like Shelley he has to "stir the suppressed yearning for freedom and the forgotten inner rhythms and the natural biological urges for fulfilment."[4] Anand was keenly aware of the upward thrust of his protagonist. Independence for him is not only freedom form the alien rule but also the freedom from outworn, ethical fetters that bruised Indian spirit. Anand's pattern of despair and delight combines the most significant features of history, psychology and philosophy.

Anand's characters are born and bred in poverty. They are born to earn their own bread but the age-old tradition of keeping them under the yoke of dejection and debauchery born of exploitation deprive them of their dignity of labour. Historically they symbolize the labour class of pre-independent India but their exploitation by their masters is undoubtedly 'man's crime against man.' The characters grow in an unhealthy environment of fear and fire but that doesn't negate their potential. The prevailing conditions of the ruler and the ruled, the high and the low eat up their flesh but not bones. Their persecution without their protest is the ample proof of their simplicity and innocence. But this shows their lack of education. Despair in the characters becomes an eye opener and prove to pave the way to delight. Years of depression and dejection have strengthened their bones and revolution seems at hand. Anand keeps the hope alive and when the characters grow to a full stature, he allows them to feel their guts that the ceremony on innocence won't be drowned.

Anand's first and his slim novel *Untouchable* (1935) shows the quintessential Anand. The hero of the novel Bakha is a child of darkness. The caste system which has degenerated with the passage of time into a hydra-headed evil signifies a set of crippling injunctions. Bakha lives in a cave-like dingy, dank, one-roomed mud-house. His features are handsome but sometimes knotted and ugly. His bones are stiff and his flesh numb with the cold. On the positive side, Bakha is in stature dignified, the nature's well-built child.

Anand presents in the life of Bakha an inauspicious day punctuated by happy and sad experiences. Bakha is confronted with a reality that's stripped off all romantic illusions. When he's slapped, he faces the crisis of identity. He is presented as a victim in a recalcitrant society. His various responses to the sad and happy incidence make the perspective of hope and despair complex. The remarks of Saros Cowasjee in this connection hint at the larger implications in perspective.

"*Untouchable* opens quietly on an autumn morning and by the time the evening approaches, the author has been able to build round his hero a spiritual crisis of such breadth that it seems to embrace the whole of India."[5] When Bakha is slapped, he is full of despair. But it is not a moment of delight. Anand writes about his strength and rage in his soul. Anand writes : "The accumulated strength of his giant body glistened in him with the desire for revenge while horror, rage indignation swept over his frame."[6]

Bakha's fondness for the sugary tea gave him delight. What delighted him more than the sugary tea or the sweeter memory of his mother was his work. Work was a sort of intoxication which gave him a glowing health and plenty of easy sleep. Apart from this darkening atmosphere, the sister of Ramcharan creates for Bakha a new world full of wonder and enchantment.

Neither Gandhi nor Christianity brings for Bakha the consolation and comfort he needs. It is only the poet who can give him a new vision to liberate him from his sickening surroundings. The novel doesn't end on a note of despair paralyzing the hero into inaction. The fires of the sunset blaze on the distant horizon. Bakha looks at the magnificent orb of terrible brightness blowing on the margin of the sky. The pattern of despair and delight is given a cosmic sweep in the concluding lines of the novel. Anand writes :

> "As the brief Indian twilight came and went, sudden impulse shot through the transformation of space and time and gathered all the elements that were dispersed in the stream of his soul."[7]

Coolie comprehends deeper levels of despair and degradation with a subdued undercurrent of delight. The hero,

Munoo, a frail boy in a hostile world moves from the village to the town, from the towns to the city and then to the mountains broadening the canvas of the novel. He is eventually swept to his doom. He is more a victim than a rebel. Primitivism, capitalism, industrialism, communalism and colonialism are the various elements skillfully orchestrated into the novel. Life for Munoo is a test of his vitality and impetuosity and his fundamental right to happiness is denied to him in a hostile climate. The cotton mills in Bombay where the boy has to work exposes him to the full force of the callous capitalistic order. He drifts into a more complicated and devious world.

Munoo experiences savage struggle for survival. He has to endure the foul smell and stink, damp and sticky sweat, dust and heat and dung. In such a climate life is a despair and death a delight. The novel shows death through alienation. Despair is a pervasive feeling throughout the novel. But the element of delight is not absent. The novel is not unshaded by a touch of glamour. The glamour comes from the primitive emotions of the protagonist and the majestic sights of Nature.

Critics have viewed the Simla Chapter differently and they find it unrelated to the basic pattern. But Saros Cowasjee says forcefully that the hero must be retrieved from the horrors of Bombay. It is not without irony that the boy who comes from the hills merges into the hills after his death. The hills, streams, the waterfalls, the clouds, and crisp, cool air — all stand in sharp contrast to the heat, humidity and heartlessness of Bombay. Anand does more than pint the infernal miseries of the helpless labourers who are morbidly fatalistic. Anand makes us feel "the beauty and horror that lies beneath life's outer surface."[8]

We admire Munoo for his human and hedonistic impulses. His search for delight is menaced by the brutalizing urbanization symbolized by Bombay. He descends into the strange, airless outhouse and hears the deafening roar of the machine. There are demons outside him. Friendship and brotherhood do exist in the sickening climate of Bombay. What Bombay gives to the boy is only the congested streets and moonless sky. It is not without significance that his love for the high altitudes does not abate even in Bombay. The sudden surge of love and friendship makes the death of Munoo a memorable and moving moment.

Coolie may lack the economical and classical tightness of *untouchable* as emphasized by Marlene Fisher but it does show movement, colour and restlessness. The fact that Munoo is sustained by his memories of childhood spent in the hills, his final return to his origin is not without positive significance. His death is not without deeper metaphysical significance. The transcendental close of the novel gives a new dimension to the context of despair and delight. When Munoo is torn from his moorings, his feeling of nostalgia for his lost world is not without delight. Anand writes :

> "And through the tears, he could see the high rocks, the great granite hills, grey in the blaze of the sun and the silver line of the bees."[9]

Two Leaves and a Bud (1937) is a crucially important novel in the first trilogy, which deals with the theme of exploitation as a part of the larger colonial experience. There are oblique colonial references in the first two novels but in this novel colonialism is analyzed with greater concentration. The entire tragedy is unfolded against the dark backdrop of the tea plantation which symbolizes the might and inhumanity of the British empire. The racial problem looms larger in this novel. The Indian social life is given a new dimension. The British officials and their Indian subordinates are ranged against the defenseless coolies working in the stifling surroundings. The capitalist forces are symbolized in this novel by the British. The English men who believe in the ideology of whiteman's burden are pathologically suspicious of all Indians. Every coolie is a potential agitator for the British officials. The natural result of this distrust is the despair of the Indians working there.

Gangu, the main protagonist of *Two Leaves*, an old and infirm coolie works incessantly to keep his household oven burning. The poor working environment, with low dingy huts, without proper sanitary conditions is either a boon or bane for coolies. Notwithstanding their physical labour, some of the coolies have allowed their wives to warm the beds of their masters. This too is an endeavour to renew their identities since much depended upon the moods and temperaments of their masters. Gangu is much of an individual who's different from other coolies. His daughter Leila, too, conscious of her youth and beauty protests against Reggie Hunt's lust. Gangu tries to save his daughter from Hunt's orgies and is shot. Leila's mother dies in Gangu's arms crying for medicine. The sheer lack of a young man's courage and his faith to a system that has little concern for its followers, shatters Gangu's world. To my view, no novel of Anand is as painful as *Two Leaves* which fails to see the growth of 'a bud' born and fated to be smashed and crushed by the crooked hands of a cruel class. The novel unfolds the story of anger and awe, cries and crimes with none to sympathize except the readers.

The strain of irony is unbearable at the close of the novel when Reggie Hunt who kills Gangu and attempts to defile his daughter is discharged. Marlene Fisher gives credence to this kind of perception in her following observation :

> "Creulty and oppression do win out in *Two Leaves and a Bud* leaving Anand sick with despair and rage."[10]

But Dr. K.N. Sinha, on the contrary, feels that the novel derives its power from the 'counter pointing of good and evils' Marlene Fisher loses sight of what is good and uplifting in the novel. Gangu is much more than a scapegoat sacrificed at the altar of the narrow racial prejudices. We can notice in the doctor the qualities which sharply contrast with the lust and cruelty embodied by Reggie Hunt. If the novel is viewed as a moral allegory, it means that the novel is not without dream and delight. We ought to remember that fiction is much more than straight facts.

Reggie Hunt may symbolize untamed animality and unmitigated evil, but he's alarmed at the rising force and expectation of the labourers working in the sickening surroundings. The following lines of the book give larger implications :

> "The wild swing of their axes, the sharp sweep of their scythes, and the clean cut of their knives, filled Reggie with a belligerent passion for destruction."[11]

The sharp scythe in Leila's hand, the rustle of the breeze, the sweep of the grasses, the damp turbid smell of the sunless groves which creates an appropriate backdrop for the appearance of the python and its terrible embrace of Leila. After a god deal of writhing and wriggling, the sharp blade of Leila's instrument bruises the python. The blood on the scythes weaves together a number of emotions in the heart of the readers. The revolutionary message which is not without delight is transparent. Leila combines in her character turbulence and tenderness. Even Gangu is not too brutalized to respond to tragic situations in a deeply human manner. The novel assembles the humanistic, hellenistic and even the nihilistic impulses of the author and the protagonist of the novel.

It is thus evident that the energy of the protagonist in the first trilogy is arrested in the oppressive institutional framework. This arrest of energy in a web of prescriptions and prohibitions breeds in the hero a deep sense of despair. This cannot blind us to the sparks that occasionally flash in their soul. The social and political forces though formidable cannot black out the sun and stars for them. These heroes are aided in their search for coherence by the forces which are too big for the perpetuators of the cruel institutions to grasp. Delight which is like a faint glimmer appears with greater force in the second trilogy. This swing towards delight chiefly depends on the greater sense of the new hero's involvement and determination. The energy which is arrested in the first trilogy struggles relentlessly for its release in the second trilogy.

NOTES AND REFERENCES

1. P.K. Rajan, *Studies in M.R. Anand.*
2. S. Lakshman Shastri, Editorial, *Contemporary Indian Literature*, Nov.-Dec. 1965, p. 10.
3. K.R.S. Iyenger, Foreword to G.S. Balaramgupta's Book, Mulk Raj Anand : *A Study of his Fiction in Human Perspective*, Prakash Book Depot, 1974.
4. Mulk Raj Anand, *State Patronage of Art*, Cultural Forum, March-April, 1963, p. 6.
5. Saros Cowasjee, *So Many Freedoms*, p. 10.
6. Mulk Raj Anand, *Untouchable*, p. 55.
7. *Ibid.*
8. Ira Morris, Messages and Souvenirs, *Contemporary Indian Literature*, Nov.-Dec., 1965, p. 9.
9. Mulk Raj Anand, *Coolie*, p. 24.
10. Marlene Fisher, *The Wisdom of the Heart*, p. 52.
11. Mulk Raj Anand, *Two Leaves and Bud*, p. 146.

7

Desperation and Aspiration : Heterogenous Phases in Kamala Markandaya's *Nectar in a Sieve* and *A Handful of Rice*

—*C. Anna Latha Devi*

A host of critics have written a plethora of commentary on *Nectar in a Sieve* (1954) and *A Handful of Rice* (1966), the two novels of Kamala Markandaya which deal with the rural and urban poverty respectively. Williams states that the characters of Kamala Markandaya lie "under inescapable doom." Das is of the opinion that her novels present the Indian society realistically and Margaret Joseph analyses the tragic vision in the novels. Her novels are viewed with reference to society in general. Hence an attempt is made in this paper to analyse how two dissimilar themes desperation and aspiration form the heterogenous phases in the two novels of Kamala Markandaya.

Nectar in a Sieve, the maiden venture of Kamala Markandaya, is based on the result of industrialization of the villages which are the abode of the rural population. Her fifth novel *A Handful of Rice* reveals the novelist's deep concern for the simple villagers who migrate from their native villages to the cities in search of green pastures. In both the novels Kamala Markandaya highlights the theme of hunger realistically that they become epics of desperation. Even in the midst of ghastly and heart-rending scenes of human pangs and pains, life asserts itself. Human aspiration for a better life is discernible in the novels of Kamala Markandaya throughout.

In the novel *Nectar in a Sieve* Kamala Markandaya spotlights the despair of the farmers realistically. They are desperate because of hte rampant hunger, vagaries of natural calamities, ruthless machines and heartless men. When an Indian village is on the threshold of industrialization, the peasant community suffer both physically and mentally. Nathan and Rukmani are representatives of millions of tenant farmers in India and their life is an example of the havoc caused by industrialization. The whole novel thus reveals the story of an Indian village shaken to its roots by the onslaught of modernization.

Nathan being an industrious tenant farmer leads a life of contentment in his soil. His wedding with Rukmani brings showers of joy and happiness. Rukmani, the daughter of a headman who is out of power and pelf is married to below her status. But she is hopeful of a better prospect in her husband's place. Her youthful heart sinks at the sight of his unfinished mud house. She bears the first shock of her life passively because of the assertive words of Nathan, "in a few years we can move — may be even buy a house such as your father's" (*Nectar,* 10).

The farmer couple Nathan and Rukmani till the land, water the plants and manure the crops in a joint venture hoping for a rich harvest. As a tenant farmer Nathan has to work for long hours every day, even then his meagre income is uncertain. Whether drought or floods Nathan becomes a tragic victim of the vagaries of nature. If the crops are good his family feasts if not fasts. It is quite obvious that Indian agriculture is a gamble of the monsoons which are unpredictable. The farmers have to live from harvest to harvest, toiling, praying and waiting in suspense. Rukmani pathetically ponders, "to those who live by the land there must always come times of hardships.... Sometimes we eat and sometimes we starve" (*Nectar,* 136). Still she is hopeful because she believes that her little rice "will last until times are better" (*Nectar,* 47). Later when Nathan has a nightmare about the loss of paddy, she comforts him, "never fear, all will be well" (*Nectar,* 84). When the White Doctor Kenny shows his deep concern for them at the time of their crisis, Rukmani asserts, "do not concern yourself. We are in God's hands" (*Nectar,* 133).

The concept of happiness of the rural people is very simple. They lead their poor life on the elemental verge with their dire needs of food, clothing and shelter. Rukmani describes her blissful state :

> While the sun shines on you and the fields are green and beautiful to the eye, and your husband sees beauty in you which no one has seen before, and have a good store of grain laid away for hard times, a roof over you and a sweet stirring in your body, what more can a woman ask for? My heart sang and my feet were light as I went about my work, getting up at sunrise and going to sleep content. Peace and quite were ours (*Nectar,* 12-13).

But the sweet harmony of the peasant's life is disrupted mercilessly by the intrusion of industrialization and the consequent urbanization. The tannery's imperceptible and lasting consequences filter down to all the layers of the village, geographical, economic, social and moral. The calm, serene and peaceful atmosphere of the village is destroyed. The water of the river contains the stinking waste material of the tannery and the productivity of the land is decreased.

Nathan, as a typical tenant farmer is wedded to the land and he knows no other profession except that behind the plough. He expects that with a series of favourable seasons, he will be affluent enough to buy for himself the land he tills on lease. Often the monsoon plays ducks and drakes but Nathan is not upset by the changing seasons. "While there was land there was hope" for Nathan (*Nectar,* 136). Those who live at the mercy of the land always experience tragedy in their lives. "The fruit of the peasant's labour goes either to the landlord or is destroyed by the ravages of nature" (Jain, 79-80). But he waits patiently aspiring for golden times.

Despite poverty and hunger, the tannery contributes to the disintegration of Nathan's family. Rukmani sorrowfully recollects, "my sons had left because it frowned on them; one of them had been destroyed by its ruthlessness" (*Nectar,* 136). When her sons desert the soil and leave for distant lands seeking better prospects, as a sorrowful mother, she bids them farewell with a heavy heart and a deep sigh. But Nathan exports his wife not to think of trials but of joys.

Exodus to alien lands and urban areas is the consequences of industrialization of the villages. Though Nathan has extreme emotional involvement with the soil in which he has sweated for about three decades, he is forced to evict his familiar abode because his land is sold to the tannery owners for a high price. This news leaves the old man in downcast spirit. He suffers endlessly. He cannot contemplate a life away from his beloved land. This has effaced all his hopes.

Even when he is desperate, Nathan takes a quick decision to go to urban lands in search of pastures new. He is hoping to find better opportunities there. Soon he finds that they are misfits in the city. Their meagre belongings are stolen and they are reduced to near beggary. Their search for their son is futile. Hence Nathan feels disillusioned and he says, "It is better that we should go now, while it is still light" (*Nectar,* 164).

The city has nothing to offer to the farmer couple. Rukmani's spirit is not curtailed by any tragic situation. She faces the worst of blows boldly and offers her service as a writer of letters. She hopefully remarks, "I am sure if I write letters as well as read them, I shall earn even more" (*Nectar,* 168). Her aspiration in the midst of desperation is to save money so that they could go back to the village and settle down there in peace. Though her venture is not successful, it speaks volumes of Rukmani's far-sightedness.

The final blow that Rukmani receives from the cruel hand of fate is by means of Nathan's death. To her misfortunes never come single; they come in battalion. Even at the last moment of his life Nathan consoles his wife with the words "do not grieve" (*Nectar,* 187). Rukmani swallows her grief. Her frustration is transmitted by her renewed hope in the village life and she decides to return to her native village. Her will is strong and assertive. The novel ends with a note of aspiration, when Selvam reassuringly tells his withered mother, "Don't worry, we shall manage" (*Nectar,* 189).

Rukmani's dropping spirit elevates not only at the heartening words of her son but also at the familiar sight of the rural abode which she has cherished for so many years. She happily ponders, "I looked about me at the land and it was life to my starving spirit. I felt the earth beneath my feet and wept for happiness" (*Nectar,* 188). What she has aspired, she has achieved. In her village she hopes to start a brand new life. Firkal aptly remarks :

> Kamala Markandaya's *Nectar in a Sieve* demonstrates the importance of faith in life as a great sustaining power. It is her firm faith that helps Rukmani to draw nectar in a sieve (87).

In *A Handful of Rice* the scene shifts from the paddy fields of an Indian village to the sprawling city. From idyllic tranquility, the rustic characters of Kamala Markandaya begin their sojourn to the disquieting pressure of city life. Through the story of Ravi, the novelist highlights the problems of the city in relation to the struggle for survival. She emphasizes the theme of urban poverty and the related desperation. Though urban or rural, the problem faced by the poor is common. The novel is a realistic exploration of the problems in the city.

Cities too exert pressure on the lives of the inhabitants and they struggle hard against the various forces. The cities have become unsafe to live and survival has become very difficult. In a city the human values are almost dead and people often prey on each other. Struggle for survival is so stark that there is little ray for fine human sentiments.

Markandaya's theme of urban poverty is explicit from the opening scene of the novel *A Handful of Rice.* Ravishankar, the central character forces his entry into a tailor's house crying desperately for food, "I am hungry, I want a meal" (*Handful,* 6). Ravi is an example to show how man can stoop and become gradually changed in his struggle for a handful of rice.

Economic conditions compel Ravi to turn his back to his peasant past and he flees from his native village to seek his fortune in the city. As Srivastava points out, "Ravi is an impractical youth, wriggling out his rural shell, but dreaming of dizzy heights and then afflicted by the denial" (103). Contrary to the expectation of Ravi, the city offers no scope for him. It is full of social evils. It is the seat of black marketeers, hoarders, bootleggers and cheats. "Grab or go under" (*Handful,* 117) are the watchwords of city dwellers. Ravi compares the city to a jungle. He describes, "in this jungle one has to fight fiercely, with whatever weapons one had" (*Handful,* 198). Cities have "traps specially set to seduce your men away from right to wrong" (*Handful,* 202). He strives hard in the city because unscrupulous individuals exploit the ignorance of people like Ravi and feather their own nests. P.S. Chauhan comments, "the city becomes the symbol of...violence and inhumanity" (145).

Initially in his desperate search for food, Ravi breaks into a tailor's house abandoning his "decency" (*Handful,* 12). Later he aspires to marry the daughter of the tailor and improve the conditions of his life. As against his aspiration when the tailor dies he has to step into his shoes and shoulder the joint family and he contemplates "perhaps tomorrow it will be easier" (*Handful,* 144).

Ravi is obsessed with the thought of acquiring wealth. When he goes into the luxurious houses of memsahibs he is distracted to find the silk hangings, tall windows, gleaming doors and shining furniture. He would touch the satin-wood surfaces, sinking an inquiry toe into the inch-thick carpets. To live like this "without worry, without wanting every need and craving satisfied" (*Handful,* 83), is his life-long dream. Perhaps it is this which makes him to take life as a challenge. He often shouts, "I want more. I want more. I want a bed... Day beds, night beds, double beds, divans" (*Handful,* 75) because he has every right to demand. He is optimistic when he says that he can rank with the rich people "if we stop thinking like stupid water-buffaloes" (*Handful,* 76). The luxurious life of the rich makes him aspire for better prospects.

It is difficult to understand the dimensions of Ravi's desires and aspirations. He is very sensitive to the class structure and wants to reach the status of the rich by fair or foul means. "The class structure of the rich and the poor has taken firm root and disparities widen with the poor being deprived of basic essentials of food and proper medical care and housing..." (Jha, 31). He is desperate when he finds the corrupt ways in which money has been acquired. He is disillusioned when he is underpaid for his back breaking labour of stitching clothes or in smuggling foreign goods when they had been boycotted during the freedom struggle. He is frustrated to see the wide gulf between the rich and the poor, which has taken firm foot in the society. He is sorry to note the pathetic conditions of the poor like himself who are deprived of even the bare essentials of life.

Ravi undersells his labour to Eve, the fashionable shop which buys the clothes he stitches and sells it at a very high rate. Ravi sees with astonishment :

> ...one of their coats. It did not look the same hex;
> it had become vastly richer, more sumptuous, since
> leaving his hands — he had to look twice to make
> sure it was the same. But there was no doubt about

> it.... Pleasure filled him...until his eyes travelled down the straw hand-span waist where the price taf was Rs. 125/-.... Ravi was stunned (*Handful*, 69).

Due to poverty, the old people and the children are liable to be infected with diseases. This is becasue they have little immunity to fight against diseases. Their constitution is weak due to malnutrition. Ravi's son is attacked by meningitis. With his meagre income he is unable to give him medical treatment at the right time. When his wife asks him to call a doctor, he in an agony of helplessness cries out :

> A doctor, what! are we memsahibs or something to send for a doctor for every ache and pain? Will you pay his bill? (*Handful,* 228)

Though the death of his son shatters Ravi he does not lose hope. He takes life as a challenge.

In a fire of desperation smoulderig in his heart he joins a mob shouting "rice, rice today" (*Handful,* 233). The crowd loots the rice godown. He struggles and gets very close to the rice bags, but fails to get even a handful of rice. Yet he is hopeful that the clouds of poverty may pass and a bright day will dawn supplying all his needs.

At another time Ravi indulges in looting and destruction of the rich people's sites. He takes a brick to hurl the rich man's locality but he restrains himself. Good sense prevails upon him and he keeps away from evil doing. He is a refined man who hopes for a better life. So he says, "But tomorrow, yes, tomorrow" (*Handful,* 237).

The ultimate triumph of conscience makes Ravi leave his evil doing is an assertion of the novelist's belief in the essential goodness of man. Ravi turns his back to the dark sub-human underworld and looks up to the human world of emotion and conscience. The triumph of conscience no doubt exhibits the novelist's assertive vision of life.

Kamala Markandaya depicts the two phases of life desperation and aspiration. In spite of social evils which are present in the world she has an assertive vision of life. Nathan, Rukmani and Ravi believe that there is an affirmation of life in the midst of colossal human suffering. The characters of Kamala Markandaya show great powers of heart and soul even in moments of crisis and calamities.

The novels of Kamala Markandaya do not end in a note of despair. A ray of light shines through human suffering. The negative aspects of life lead to a positive vision. All the characters in the novels experience troubles and turmoils in life. But they rise above their desperation triumphantly because of their aspiration. Though both the novels are tragic stories dealing with the theme of starvation and suffering, they end on a progressive note of quiet strength and resolution revealing the heterogeneous phases in Kamala Markandaya's novels. What emerges at the end of her novels is the aspiration of the characters to regenerate and reconstruct a new world order where all the polarities are reconciled and the sharp edges of life are blunted.

WORKS CITED

Primary Sources

Markandaya, Kamala. *Nectar in a Sieve.* New York : John Day, 1954.

——. *A Handful of Rice.* New Delhi : Hind Pocket Books, 1966.

Secondary Sources

Chauhan, P.S. "Kamala Markandaya : Sense and Sensibility." *Literary Criterion* 12, 2-3 (1976) : 134-47.

Firkal. "Imagination and the other Modern Feminist Poetics and Indo-Anglian Fiction," *Gender and Literature.* Ed. Iqbal Kaur. Delhi : B.R. Publishers, 1992.

Jain, N.K. "Kamala Markandaya : *Nectar in a Sieve*," *Major Indian Novels : An Evaluation.* Ed. N.S. Pradhan. New Delhi : Arnold Heinemann, 1985, 74-87.

Jha, Rekha, "Political Encounter," *The Novels of Kamala Markandaya and Ruth Prawer Jhavwala* : A Study in East West Encounter. New Delhi : Prestige, 1990, 16-47.

Srivastava, Ramesh K. "Markandaya's *Nectar in a Sieve* as a Tragedy," *Six Indian Novelists in English.* Amritsar : Guru Nanak Dev University, 1987, 134-44.

8

A Horse and Two Goats : A Critical Evaluation

—*Fed Mathew*

R.K. Narayan's last but one collection of short stories *A Horse and Two Goats*, seems to provide a fertile ground for criticism. Many scholars of eminence, like William Walsh, P.S. Sundaram and M.K. Naik have made efforts and thrown much light upon the abstruse nature of Narayan's writings. His deceptive simplicity, the Indian narrative technique and ironic vision place some obstacles in the critical path to commit a penetrating observation over Narayan's short stories. Critics, therefore, praise his sense of humour, the endless capacity to entertain the audience, but evade the serious attempt to find out the genius behind the universal appeal of his fiction. The present paper is a brief attempt at unravelling the profundity of R.K. Narayan, the supreme story teller.

Most of Narayan's contemporaries, like Mulk Raj Anand, Manohar Malgonkar, Kamala Das and Khushwant Singh, in spite of their great diversity do partake a sense of purpose in their short stories. R.K. Narayan's short stories, however, do not seem to share this common feature, explicitly. They seem to be well-made stories, with some plain strokes of realism, to entertain the audience eternally. But being a genius his insistent pursuit of the same old track makes it obvious that his deceptive naivety is rather deliberate. The universal appeal of his stories, which reveal his recurrent deceptive simplicity compels us to go a bit deep into the essence of his writings which I presume to be derived from the age old notions of Indian philosophy.

Although the initial review of *A Horse and Two Goats* which appeared in the London Magazine, commented upon the title story as "strangely disappointing,"[1] the later critics gave it due praise. P.S. Sundaram opines that "this was the best story in the collection, or if that seems unfair, shares with 'Uncle' that honour."[2] William Walsh, a decade later, goes a step further by adding that the stories maintain "the delicate fabric of human relationships which are strained or tangled by knots of incomprehension...."[3] But hardly a year had passed before M.K. Naik raised his dessenting voice : "Narayan's technique of the short story clearly shows him subscribing to the idea of the 'well-made short story.' Almost all his short stories are compact and neatly structured. The only exceptions are some of the later stories like *Uncle*, *Annamalai* and *A Horse and Two Goats*, which tend to be rather "discursive," as C.V. Venugopal has rightly pointed out."[4] This claim seems to be doubtful as the piece belongs to his mature days and seems to uphold his vision of literature as a comprehensive and artistic medium of expression.

The original edition of the book included only four stories, namely, *A Horse and Two Goats*, *Uncle*, *Annamalai*, *A Breath of Lucifer*. The later editions included a former story *Seventh House*. These five stories seems to be quite compact as they deal with the same theme of incomprehension, treated from various angles. The little story treats it with two strangers, an illiterate rustic and a modern pragmatic foreigner from New York. The second does it with an adopted son and his uncle, whereas the third and the fourth have masters and servants, and the fifth culminates in the vacillations of the hero to comprehend and commit himself. Through these stories, one might argue, Narayan transforms the theme of incomprehension to that of illusion or Maya in Indian philosophy.

1. Analysis

(a) Narayan's short stories are generally well made. They have a proper introduction, a body and a conclusion. Although Narayan follows the Indian narrative technique, in which incidents generate a chain of incidents, gradually winding to climax, with all the necessary realistic touches. The title story has a beautiful introduction in which the theme is properly introduced with a prophetic simile. Munni goes to the shop to purchase the provision on credit. He waits long enough to begin his pleasing talk with the shopkeeper. As the conversation proceeds, he indulges in the scandal of the postman and his wife to elicit a pleasing response from the shopkeeper. He goes to the extend of spinning fanciful tales of his forthcoming birthday and his fortunate daughter. But the whole attempt fails. The Shopkeeper does not concede to a fresh loan.

The introduction is followed by the main body of the story. Narayan quietly allows the evasive narration to glide into a detailed description of both Munni and the red faced American tourist. He handles so dexterously the medium of conversation that the natures, dispositions and behaviour patterns of both the characters are made very clear. At the outset of the conversation itself both the characters are introduced properly. Although the visiting card added a further threat to the already scared Munni, with impending arrest, the soothing cigarette brought in a sense of cognizance between Munni and the puzzled foreigner. The topic gradually turns to the horse which fascinates both. Munni is ecstatic about religious beliefs and spiritual attributes while the foreigner is fascinated by its artistic, cultural and finally pragmatic aspects. Munni gradually transcends himself by soaring into a spiritual realm through the recollections of his bright childhood, traditional religious rites and beliefs, and finally passed on to eschatology. The tourist descends from polished, formal speech to business talk, concerning his financial status and problems of transportation and it eventually touches the rock bottom of pure business. The spiritual elevation of the uncouth villager and the pragmatic descent of the foreigner are built upon their encounter with the horse.

The very title itself is ambiguous. The two constituents of the title richly suggest the two cultures, the east and the west, the rustic and the modern. Being a symbol, it can also allude to idealism and practical wisdom. In spite of all these deliberate allusions, the dominant stress in placed on the element of truth. Each one infers his own subjective truth from the circumstance. The friendly visiting card of the foreigner is an arrest warrant to Munni. When the native simpleton speaks about the beheading of the thief the foreigner recognizes it as about the chopping of wood. Munni's whole religious sermon is mere business talk for the other. Finally, Munni's goats are the foreigner's horse. The simple message is that truth is conditional, it is subjective. The realities of Munni and that of the other are different. One's truth is illusion to the other. The reaction of Munni's wife at the end is the final stroke emphasizing the theme of illusion. M.K. Naik's observation that Narayan has an ironic vision of life definitely holds good. The theme of truth and realization, is repeated in the mind of the reader. The confusion in the minds of the characters is transmitted into the hearts of the readers for a final reconsideration.

(b) In the second story *Uncle*, the adopted son has some misgivings about his uncle; from the beginning to the end his doubts are maintained without much of a change. If the characters of the title story are two entirely strange persons, here we have a more intimately related pair, and so the strain is more extensive. As in the case of the other stories, *Uncle* also has an introduction : the incident between the narrator and his friend Suresh. Suresh questions him about his father and finally baffles him with his verdict that his uncle had impersonated. The silence of his beloved aunt over the incident intensifies the mystery.

It is in the body, the content that, the note of incomprehension is expressed from various angles. The note of misunderstanding between the uncle and his adopted son becomes quite complex with the emergence of Jayaraj, the photographer, with his subdued talk and dim portrait. Although his uncle had taken proper care in all his activities he has never cleared the original doubts of the boy. The recurrent suppression of his natural curiosity intensifies his ardent desire. In addition to it, his encounter with Jayaraj and suggestive conversation with his uncle and them with the bald man, along with his offer of the faded portrait in a completely changed atmosphere, compels the boy to run away from his shop. The fall of evening is given extraordinary importance and the effect of this change is in the mind of the boy. The very visage of Jayaraj has drastically changed to that of the devil, and his awe-inspiring store room has become a store of impending doom.

> The Muslim tailor, though contributed substantial evidence towards the positive side of his uncle, provides ample proof towards his connection with Rangoon. Till the end of the story, suspense and confusion are retained. The theme of incomprehension takes the form of variations in subjective comprehension : for Jayaraj and his friend his uncle is an impostor; for the tailor he is a saviour; and for the boy he is a loving uncle. The sudden change of the evening instills terror in the mind of the boy who, though he always wanted to stay with Jayaraj, now quickly decides to fight with him. The portrait incident makes the confusion complete. The disposition of the boy, skillfully illustrates the subjective nature of truth. In the first story, truth has finally dawned on the readers mind while the second one keeps the reader at bay. The misunderstanding of the adopted soon about his uncle, aunt and his parentage, does not end in himself; they are transmitted into the readers mind for a final clarification of one's own identity. The identity of

the self in a world of illusion is beyond comprehension.

(c) The third story *Annamalai* deals with the same theme of incomprehension on a different plane, namely, the master-servant relationship. As in the case of other stories, this also has a prophetic similie as introduction. The very letter, itself initiates the interplay of confusion. The narrator is unable to identify the writer. Annamalai, even at the end of the story, looms large as a mystery beyond rationalization. His identity, his village, his notions and even his name are all enmeshed in vague observations. We are at a loss to identify him properly even after pages of detailed description.

Annamalai's past blurs in a misty ambiguity as it has two versions. One is recounted by Annamalai to his present master, which is a monotonous tale about master and inadequate wages. The other version which he proudly presents before the lady-neighbour has all the ingredients meant to be impressive such as fortunate days happy family, daughter and granddaughter. The same is the case with his present. This work in the garden is a case in point. He divides the plants into two divisions as flower plants and weeds. He has, in fact, no idea of gardening. He destroys certain plants with his superstitious premonitions. Although his knowledge of gardening is much of a boast, he least bothers to obey the orders of his master. He works as the pleases. He proons the garden when his friend's cow is in need of it. His master's notion of gardening is entirely different but he accepts 'Malai' as he is. His conduct with neighbours and others is also dubious. He seems to sell the flowers, but when the master is present he cringes to please him. When all is said and done, the question whether he is a saviour or destroyer of plants remains unanswered.

When we proceed to details, the polarization and clash of contradictory versions become quite visible. The two instances of the village have great relevance from this view point. Annamalai's ethics dictates him to withhold the lamb of the pledged sheep. But the master and the readers find it crude, indecent and illegal. The tailor's contract settled by the village elders and the subsequent expense of travel to renew it are a sheer waste to our eyes while for Annamalai, they are just and accurate.

The conclusion is also equally puzzling. Annamalai went out without receiving his gift. It was rather his right to get such a gift. But, strangely, he does not wait to receive it. As his self-esteem was greatly questioned, he might have deemed it unfair according to his ethos to accept such a gift. Thus, the whole story is an interplay of subjective visions clashing with one another and subsiding in the general haze of reality. The subjectivity of reality is the recurring motif of the story. The apparently rational convictions of an individual loses their authoritative absoluteness when viewed from the opposite angle. The terra firma of one's indubitable judgements changes into a taunting slippery ground.

(d) The fourth story *A Breath of Lucifer*, also shares the same background as the third one — the relationship between master and servant. The physically crippled state of the master enriches the meaning of the whole incident. The smudge on the glass and his hallucination set forth in the prologue, are richly suggestive. Master's misgiving about the physical features of the self-proclaimed male nurse, Sam gradually takes root in Sam's reminiscences in which he was Lucifer, enticing Marie. This introductory terror reaches the climax at the turn of the central incident.

The birthday of Sam and the day fixed for removing the bandage of his eyes, strangely co-inside and Sam duly celebrates the day. The self-proclaimed saviour of patients, the angel just short of a lamp announces fire, Lucifer's fire, and seems to become Lucifer himself. Sam's musings fire on fire, tiger, mines, Marie, colonel and so on are either real or imaginary. The narrator is unable to verify them. They are both real and imaginary for him. As Annamalai who is the saviour of plants becomes their destroyer Sam the angel who is the saviour of patients becomes Sam the Lucifer. The limitations of objectivity in contrast with the predominance of subjectivity in every sphere of perception is the repeated message.

As in the case of *Annamalai*, the virtual remnant of the whole incident is a piece of an epistle. The letter comes at the outset of *Annamalai*, while Sam's postcard marks the end of it. The physical features of Sam, his works, his past, his future, everything is enmeshed in a big question mark. The experiences of the narrator, though seemingly factual, lose their physical entity and transcend to the superhuman realm where reality and illusion converge.

(e) *The Seventh House* goes a step ahead in dealing with the common theme. The mind of the hero is divided, reminding us of Hamlet's procastination. He is unable to arrive at a clear-cut decision. The story opens with a typical conversation in which the acute vigilance and care of the narrator is contrasted with the extreme levity of the doctor. His convictions are being questioned and gradually he is shown as susceptible to superstitions. The flash back of his marriage is very significant as it was settled through a compromiser. The hero later, goes in search of the astrologer, leaving the doctor and scientific temper.

The climax of the story is reached by narrating the present disposition of the hero. His scientific temper enabled him to marry his lady love. But her incessant decline in health coupled with the inefficiency of the doctor compelled him to consult astrological counsel. The first remedy of the Fortune teller is unheeded but the second seems to him to be viable.

The clash of subjective visions, as if connected in a chain, occurs one by one. The gravity of the husband in contrast with the levity of the doctor is the staring point and it proceeds to the artificial compromise where tradition and modernity clash. His confrontation with the fortune-teller and the two prescriptions, his frantic and misguided search and the final anti-climax at the right turn of things brought about by the well intentioned driver are the subsequent instances.

The intensity of these confrontations is further developed as one moves to the conclusion in which the chain of clash and confrontation is extended to the heart of the hero. When he finally falls short of aspiration, the readers are at a loss to ascertain it as falling short of aspiration or the rehabilitation of his scientific temper. The ambiguity at the conclusion seems to suggest the harsh truth that one has to trudge through this loose, sally of illusions to reach the final realization.

2. Evaluation

When we evaluate these five stories, it becomes obvious that these well made stories share many a common feature. They have similarity both in structure and content. Although they seem to be desultory in nature they have a well-knit arrangement, in which interplay of different strands, loosely interwoven, is only one of the deliberate strokes of the supreme story-teller. The instances are scattered in the plot, but each one intensifies the central idea of the story. Besides these, thematic unity is also very conspicuous. The plots and the so-called sub-plots spin around the central theme, evincing a similar strand either by similarity or by contrast.

As we have already seen, the prophetic similes which function as the introduction set the mind of the reader for the full unravelling of the theme through the central instances. Each of the five stories is share this aspect. The futile interview with the shopman for a fresh loan of provisions does it in the title story. The interaction between the narrator and his classmate Suresh engenders the element of doubt and Suresh finally passes the verdict that his uncle has impersonated. The very first letter of *Annamalai* introduces the element of confusion and the narrator is unable to identify the identity of the writer. The self-introduction of Sam spiced with the details of his physical features, along with this childhood role as Lucifer, initiates the element of terror, which reaches its zenith at his total abandonment of the narrator. The opening conversation of the *Seventh House* evinces the extreme callousness of the doctor and his predictable consequent failure, both of which foreshadow the final predicament of the hero.

The interplay of internal strands, though different in each story intensifies the central theme by providing an ever-increasing profundity through allusions. In the title story, very many topics appear almost casually in the conversation of both the characters. The talk of the foreigner, for example, moves to his past life in New York city and to his past-time of chopping woods. The power failures, along with the consequent agony of life is a very meaningful stroke to reveal the dark side of the modern life. The chopping of woods and the ignition of the hearth with the whole of Sunday times go a step further to enable the reader to visualize the seedy side of western culture. The digressions of Munni also serve the same function, by providing glimpses of relief through religion, in the life of a rustic Indian.

In *Annamalai* the twist of internal strands is more skilful. The moral outlook of each character is beautifully disclosed; the notions of gardening of the master and the gardener are entirely different. Annamalai works as he pleased. His approach to the lady neighbour and his relatives in the village is still more confusing. The lamb of the pledged sheep and his contract with the tailor add a new dimension to the whole story. This subjective vision of morality is amply illustrated by Annamalai's final rejection of the promised bonus at his retirement. The moral outlook of both, the master and the reader, is put into question by these alternate strokes.

The self-proclaimed male nurse Sam, his interaction with the colonel, his experience in operation theatres, his drinking habit and his final absconding provide an added plane for the story the *Breath of Lucifer*. The reconciliation scene of the *Seventh House*, in which the totally puzzled child, the confused audience and, finally, the artificial reconciliation bring about an added dimension.

The plots and the sub-plots spin around the same theme and thus accelerate the total effect of the story. The second story *Uncle* as a case in point, in which the sub-plot, Jayaraj and his studio are developed in such a way that it shares the dominant qualities of the main incident. Mr. Jayaraj is presented as the well-wisher who gradually evolves to be the embodiment of devil and finally passes out without giving any exact clues. He is almost the replica of the uncle who is both a loving protector on the one hand and an impersonator on the other. Even the photo has its corresponding one, the dim portrait with all the dark ambivalence.

Another sub-plot which has so much similarity is found in the *Breath of Lucifer*. The reminiscences of Sam reveal his resemblance to Lucifer and his first successful attempt as Lucifer in a play. As the story proceeds, it is revealed that Sam had seduced Mary and still continues to do so. In the main event the narrator seems to be enticed by Lucifer. In addition to that the appearance and disappearance of Sam can be compared with the birthday party, the fire, and the subsequent night escapade, where clarity seems to evade eternally.

When we proceed from one story to another, the story-teller enhances the total effect of the story. The thematic intensity gradually grows to supreme heights, as we proceed from the two strangers of the title story to the ultimate vacillation of the hero in the last story. The loving husband is unable to reconcile himself with the superstition. Although the third and the fourth have the same character pattern, the fourth is more intense as the master is completely handicapped. His illusion is beyond any limit as he is physically crippled, to ascertain anything. In the *Seventh House* the hero's mind is sharply divided, he is the embodiment of uncertainty.

Thus these stories are well-made to the core, as they sustain coherence both in structure and theme. The only question which comes from these observations is if they are well-structured ones, what is the ultimate message of these stories. R.K. Narayan deals with the same theme, stories after stories. Why is he so much obsessed with this single theme of incomprehension? In other words, the subjectivity of truth, the notion of illusion has something more than the status of a theme in the vision of the author.

To comprehend the relevance of 'incomprehension' in Narayan's literary world, a close analysis of the common theme may be helpful. The theme of incomprehension, in reality, is a constant search of the characters to understand and realize the reality. The intensity of this quest for reality accelerates from story to story. The characters in the first story, as they are deprived of a common medium of conversation, fail to grasp even the topic of conversation, whereas in the fifth story, the hero is sharply divided in the mind, his scientific temper and religious beliefs play dominant roles and his consequent vacillations between reason and emotion is the culmination of this quest.

The scene in the title story from this perspective is equally revealing. The learned and the rustic, the west and the east grope in darkness to ascertain the reality. The lack of a common medium of interaction enables the free play of subjective interpretations, unravelling the complexity of each person. The semblance of realization reached at the end also falls short of reality. Reality, till the end, evades one's grasp.

The theme develops from reality to identity in the second story *Uncle*. The identify of the uncle and also of the narrator loom large throughout the story. The loving uncle of the adopted boy evolves to be an impersonated doctor and the boy is elevated to be the fortunate son of a doctor. The search to ascertain identity goes on, and ends in vain. When we come to *Annamalai* the epitome of confusion, the quest penetrates space and time with which one often ensures the veracity of things. Annamalai's past and present are equally puzzling. His old village and the present place of residence are also beyond proper comprehension. The general bewilderment further puzzles the reader by adding an edge of ethical parameter. Annamalai's illusions and the so-called perceptions of the narrator scarcely converge to identify one from the other.

It is in the fourth and fifth stories that Narayan stretches the theme to supernatural and sub-conscious realms. The narrator in the *Breath of Lucifer* is physically crippled and had already considered the smudge in the eyes as the smudge in the glass. He is compelled to assure the identity of his own saviour Sam, who proclaims to be an experienced male nurse. His attempt at verifying Sam passes to a supernatural realm as Sam turns out to be the Lucifer, the embodiment of evil. The evolution of the saviour Sam to Lucier and the final disappearance from the question whether the evil and the supernatural can exert power over the mortals. To be more precise, the illusion of reality passes on to illusions of the supernatural.

The final story gives the theme its maximum effect by transferring the whole quest into the mind of the hero and giving it a psychological bend. His education and scientific temper stand on one side whereas his religious leaning coupled with his emotions pull him to the opposite. His reason fails to sustain its initial exuberance, as he encounters the onslaught of sheer existence. He is on the verge of giving way to superstition and decides to appease the Mars. His anxious efforts to become unfaithful to his wife finally give way to another impulse, rather than to reason, to return home. The vacillations of the hero and his final inability to know the reality almost amount to existential anguish. Thus Narayan gradually develops comical theme of incomprehension into the serious quest of reality.

3. Message

As a result of our ardent search, we have come to the conclusion that the stories in this collection share a number of similarities. They are well-made stories, they have thematic and structural unity. They deal with the theme of incomprehension which gradually penetrates deeper layers of reality, identity and illusion. Now the only question that remains is the message of the stories. Do they have any message at all?

Critics are generally reticent over the explicit and implicit connotations of Narayan's deceptively simple style. But the recurrence of the theme, with a meticulously planned structure, compels us to go deep into it.

It is beyond doubt that, the theme of incomprehension, which is almost an obsession in Narayan's short stories, is the message. Incomprehension in Indian philosophy is illusion or Maya. Dr. Chandradhar Sharma's definition of Maya may make the observation clear. "Maya or Avidya" according to Shankara, "is not pure illusion. It is not only absence of knowledge. It is also positive wrong knowledge."[5] The title story is a typical case in point. The story deals with the absence of knowledge in the characters and finally comes to positive wrong knowledge. Both Munni and the foreigner are confirmed in their misconception and the truth simply evades their grasp to the end. The narrator in *Annamalai* is deprived of any accurate knowledge of both the past and the present of his gardener. When it comes to Sam, the absence of knowledge both of Sam's physical features and the narrator's surroundings confronts the narrator and the reader alike. The ambivalence elevated to superhuman levels always adds to the positive assertion of wrong knowledge.

Maya according to Shankara operates in three ways, as positive wrong knowledge, as doubt and as absence of knowledge.[6] As in the case of the other two, the trait of doubt also looms large in these stories. *Uncle* and *Seventh House*, stress it at the expense of the other two. The adopted son initiates his search in doubt, his unabated doubt does not find its satiation even from his beloved aunt. The intervening characters like the tailor and Jairaj only intensity the darkness. The final search of the hero also ends in nothing solid. He has the identity crisis. In *Seventh House* the notion of doubt is very elaborately treated. The hero is an embodiment of doubt and the consequent procrastination. The doctor's inability to diagnose the disease of his beloved keeps him a constant devotee of doubts and misgivings. His frantic search for a remedy, his vacillations between superstition and scientific treatment and his final submission to impulse are all the effects of his inherent doubt. Doubt and misgivings when grown beyond a level culminate in nervous breakdown. The hero just manages to eschew this ultimate predicament.

In addition to this, Michael Gorra's observation of Narayan's novels that his treatment of history and the existing physical world are greatly influenced by a great ideal of non-attachment and indifference, the effect of Maya, strengthen our stand.

> "For Narayan deals with history only by denying its importance, in much the same way as the orthodox Hindu denies the existence of the physical world. Both are forms of Maya, or both depend on a concern with material reality, and Narayan's omission of visual detail is finally inextricable from Malgudi's abstraction from history."[7]

Narayan's Indian Psyche and ethos naturally colour his vision of life and they penetrate consciously or unconsciously into the fabric of story-telling. As he himself sketches the world of the story-teller, different components such as stories, philosophy and moral codes are inter-related and so his stories do have this extra edge. "Literature" he holds, "is not a branch of study to be placed in a separate compartment for the edification only of scholars, but a comprehensive and artistic medium of expression to benefit the literate and the illiterate alike."[8] It is, therefore, obvious that his artistic medium is comprehensive and it does possess the message. The elusive glide of the content coupled with obvious and deliberate yarns of triviality, a common trait of his short stories, creates a naivety in his writing and thus enshrines the hard kernel which is often bypassed. His own lapses, both linguistic and semantic, has also a major share for this omission.

From these observations, namely, the stories of this collection are well-made ones, they have thematic and structural unity, they deal with the theme of incomprehension which is systematically developed into the Indian concept of Maya, we conclude that these stories, though not flawless have their own validity.

NOTES

1. *London Magazine*, September, 1970, p. 95.
2. P.S. Sundaram, *R.K. Narayan*, (New Delhi : Arnold Heinmann India 1930), p. 123.
3. William Walsh, *R.K. Narayan : A Critical Appreciation* (New Delhi : Allied Pub., 1982), p. 106.
4. M.K. Naik, *The Ironic Vision : A Study of the Fiction of R.K. Narayan* (New Delhi : Sterling Pub., 1983), p. 99.

   Cfr. C.V. Venugopal, *The Indian Short Story in English : A Survey* (Bareilly, 1975), p. 87.
5. Chandradhar Sharma, *A Critical Survey of Indian Philosophy* (Delhi : Motilal Banarsidas, 1960), p. 252.
6. Confr. *Ibid.*, p. 276.
7. A.L. McLeod (ed.), *R.K. Narayan : Critical Perspectives* : Michael Gorra : History, Maya, Dharma : The Novels of R.K. Narayan (New Delhi : Sterling Pub.), 1994, p. 52.
8. R.K. Narayan, *Gods, Demons and Others* (Mysore : Indian Thought, 1967), p. 4.

9

Journey Beyond the Senses : An Analysis of Anita Desai's *Journey to Ithaca*

—O.P. Budholia

Anita Desai as a novelist occupies a distinct and distinctive place in the realm of contemporary Indian English fiction. She is a trend-setting novelist for laying bare the inner recesses and the existential trauma of human beings. She makes known to us the unconscious motifs of human psyche, the problem of human relationships, the protagonist's quest for identity almost in all her novels from *Cry, the Peacock* to *Fasting, Feasting*, but her *Journey to Ithaca* (1995) makes some definitive movements in her structural and visionary perpectives. The entire structural scheme, being divided into four well balanced chapters, is patterned skillfully on a new device of *Prologue* and *Epilogue*. The seeds for higher human values have already been sown by her in *Clear Light of Day* and in *Baumgartner Bombay*; but they sprout to full swing in *Journey to Ithaca*.

The inclusion of *Prologue* helps her disclose the inner human motives for higher values of life. In *Prologue*, the early life of Matteo, the hero of the novel, is made very clear to the readers. To a philosophic child like Matteo, the school was like a "theorem set with in a larger theorem."[1] So, this mathematical precision created in him a failure as a student at his early age. The readers through *Prologue* are informed that the school life "baffled him life the geometry and algebra" (18). Whenever, he was inquired of his activities in the school, his answers to questions appeared sullen and monosyllabic. In *Epilogue*, the readers are passed on knowledge of the journey of Matteo the India, his marriage with Sophie and the role of his parents in nurturing their children — Giacoma and Isabel after his departure from Italy to India. The anxiety of Matteo's parents brings forth two main aspects of Matteo's life : his withdrawal from the school and the appointment of Fabian as a teacher for his further studies. Fabian acquaints him with Hermann Hesse's *Journey to the East* which enkindles in him a curiosity towards the philosophy of *Vedanta*. Another remarkable incident lies in his marriage with Sophie who "was a journalist" (30). After this marriage, both Sophie and Matteo left for India.

Chapter first of this novel reveals Sophie and Matteo's departure from Italy to India, their apparent contradictions for the East-West encounters, their experiences of *Kumbh Mela* at Allahabad, their arrival at an ashram in Bihar and again their aversion towards the activities of the ashram. Both Sophie and Matteo had "a design, a pattern, to their wanderings" (35). An analogical matrix in the psychic depth of Matteo becomes perceptible when he begins to learn Sanskrit here. Sophie, on the other hand, feels suffocated and always complains to Matteo against the unsavoury atmosphere of the ashram.

Chapter second brings into being yet another challenge to Matteo. Till now, Sophie is pregnant and she wished to leave this place for another one on a mountain of the Himalayan regions for her safer delivery. On the advice of the doctor, both Sophie and Matteo come to an ashram at Himalayan region. This ashram is run by a beautiful young woman who is known as the Mother. But Sophie suspects the spiritual authority of the Mother : "It sounds as if she gets up on a stage and hypnotises you all like a magician" (102). Sophie with her womanly emotions becomes jealous of the Mother and regards her "a monster spider who had spun this web to catch these silly flies (127). The jealousy of a woman makes her enquire all about the past of the Mother. Her inquisitiveness leads her to discover her arrival in India as a dancer, "looking for a rich somebody to pick her up" (131). Like Sita in *Where Shall We Go This Summer*, Sophie becomes rebellious against the forced decision of her husband. With her future anxieties of a mother, she leaves the company of her husband and comes back to Italy to her parents. In Italy, she tries to fill the absence of Matteo in the company of another gentleman, Paolo whom she meets in a party. He also finds this mature woman quite fascinating. But Sophie still experiences the over powering effect of the Matteo-consciousness on her : "Her life with Matteo had spoilt her life with a man like Paolo; it was no longer possible" (155). Anita Desai thus upholds sanctity of the relations between husband and wife. Chapter third gives a new turn to the story, as it reveals Sophie's ceaseless efforts for discovering the past of Laila. She inquires of her from the doctor and finds the secrets how she became the mother from Laila, the dancer. A daughter of Alma and Hameed, Laila rebels against the traditional code of Muslim religion and leaves her home in search of her spiritual existence. Like Maggie Tulliver in *The Mill on the Floss*, she is a rebel against her social norms and craves for her self-identity.

At the Al Azhar University, her yearning for freedom is perceptible when she addresses her fellow students "better to go to prison than live as slaves" (172). Laila as a revolutionary student becomes a source of affliction to Alma and Hameed. Even at her seventeen, she determines to break off the traditional custom which snares her like the coil of a serpent. Her stay at Paris upsets her aunt Francoise and uncle Bertrand by the rebellious thoughts. When her uncle asks her to eat the meat, she refuses it and confesses : "I am a vegetarian. No one will make me eat the flesh of slaughtered animals" (185). In Paris, instead of purchasing Islamic books, she purchases the books of the Oriental philosophy. Above all, as luck would have it, she meets a troupe of Krishna lila and joins this troupe for learning the Oriental art of dance. Now, she learns the classical art of dance from Krishnaji, but the art of dance does not bind her for a long time and she gives it up for realizing the higher vision of God. Chapter fourth describes 'Sophie's arrival in Bombay to Krishnaji's house in order to know the past life of Laila.' Sophie recognizes Krishnaji, because she has seen him as a young dancer in Paris, Venice and Laussane. As he listens to the name of Laila, he revives his past life and confesses his relations with her as a "father" and as a "teacher." The diary episode in this chapter becomes the real source of Laila's Journey to the East and her meeting with Swami Pramanandji.

There are three characters who strive in search of the higher vision of human life : Laila, Sophie and Matteo. Apparently, Matteo has shown some seeds of *Adhyatma* in his early life. He questions his teacher Fabian as a boy about an esoteric experience. He thinks over the relationships between the body and the spirit thus : "It seemed that in time, all substance from one image could flow in to the other and only one would remain : Leo He must grow, I must disappear" (24). The growth of "He" becomes suggestive of his divine attributes and the disappearance of "I" symbolizes the extinction of his egoism. Matteo as a seeker after truth thinks of unveiling the mystery of life and death. Both husband and wife thus arrive at Bombay in an ashram. But Sophie lacks the faith of Matteo and as a young wife, she always remains in search of her existence as a woman with her husband. The novelist propounds the domestic and social vision through Sophie and Matteo — the psychological realism of a young couple. After the pregnancy of Sophie, their arrival in an ashram in Himalayan region brings some new reflections into being. This ashram thus represents the true interests of the devotee irrespective of his caste and creed. Working on the universal norms of life, Desai follows the secular image of India by making Laila confess about the presence of God in the heart of man. Laila as mother also refuses to accept any kind of formalism for the realization of ultimate truth. The Mother as a Muslim girl does not hold back to be initiated by a Hindu saint. She remarks about the futility of all religions thus :

> This is no church, my friends, this in no temple or mosque or Vihara. We have no religion. Religion? Like the black crows up in the tree caw-caw-caw, scolding, scolding! But, do they crow at us now? No, they are silent! We have silenced them.... Religion makes one ashamed, makes one guilty, makes one fearful. The Master has told you not to feel guilty not to feel ashamed, not to be afraid (p. 98).

The image of "the black crow" in the above passage brings forth the hollowness and emptiness of all religions. The sound of the crow — "caw, caw, caw" is linked with the meaningless sound of different religions which have nothing to do with the absolute reality. When there comes a protest against Laila's Muslim identity in the ashram, the Master shifts this ashram to another place in the Himalayan region. He gives an example of Kabir who was himself a Muslim, but led his entire life "in the holy city of Benares and he wrote songs of Rama" (134). Matteo as such comes to the right place, now, for his regeneration as a *sadhaka*.

The Mother thus exemplifies an ideal life of high attributes while teaching her disciples : "You must know I mean honey made from spiritual nectar, to nourish your souls. All organizations are useless, Matteo, useless and dry and empty, if they do not contain the nectar of the spirit. I want it to be rich, rich, rich with this nectar" (118).

The "nectar" here symbolizes the essence of life. Matteo works on the advice of the Mother as *sadhaka* with all patience. The western ideology for work is analysed ("work is work and should bear fruits," 125) with reference to Indian hypothesis of "niskama karma." Here is Matteo who confesses the higher and nobler vision of "niskama karma" in the teachings of the Mother before his wife, Sophie : "She teaches us to work without desiring the fruit from that work. Isn't that a higher way of life" (125). In this ashram, love is regarded as the nucleus for God realization. Matteo too acknowledges his sacred love towards the Mother :

> Matteo : Sophie, my love for her isn't the love one feels for a beautiful or glamourous or intriguing woman, a legend, as you say. You must see that! There is a difference between sacred and proface love, Listen, in her presence I feel I am more alive than I am in the presence of any other living creature.... When I leave her, I feel I am falling, down, down in to darkness. No, not darkness but greyness, flatness, emptiness (141).

The constant jealousy of a woman in Sophie makes her depart from India to Italy, but the Matteo-consciousness so overpowers her as she arrives in India again. She discovers now the past life of Laila as student, as a rebel in the Al Azhar University, as a dancer and as seeker of a spiritual Guru in Swami Premanand ji. Evidently, the deeper plan of the novelist is to envisage the varied groups of human relationships for a common pursuit of *Adhyatma*. As a novelist, Desai does not spare even a character like Laila for the instinctual and impulsive flights of human mind. Here is an example for two apparent contradictions in Laila's mind : psychic aberrations and a self-confidence to overcome them :

> Faces leered at me, smiling : /Are we not fine enough for you? From somewhere strength came to me/And I repelled them,/Knowing it better to die/Fighting Evil/Than to live without His Grace (p. 301).

Sophie is thus satisfied with her inquiry about the Mother and comes back to the ashram. She is stunned to see the ashram deserted by the spiritual journey of the Mother. Sophie perceives the higher position of Matteo as a seeker after truth in the guidance of the mother : "The urgency to see Matteo, to tell and reveal, had so overtaken her, she had not thought that for Matteo too, the wheel had turned" (303). The "Wheel" image gives the metamorphosis of Matteo as a regenerated man. Sophie thinks and burns with the fire of spiritual thoughts. She finally determines to follow the ideas of Matteo as a seeker. When she says to Diya "I'll have to," and adds "what else" (305). She now intends for completing an inner journey of consciousness like Matteo for esoteric experiences. Thus, Desai through her visionary perspectives achieves a great success in this novel by outlining the higher values of human love, humanism, realism, mysticism and a unified code for the universal vision of brotherhood.

As a novelist Desai succeeds in revealing the subtle and intense expositions of human psyche first in *Clear Light of Day*, in *In Custody* and then in *Baumgartner's Bombay*. *Baumgartner's Bombay* brings in to being the emotional states of a European Jew who explores the basic question of identity as an Indian citizen. This novel prepares the foreground for *Journey to Ithaca* by revealing a super-sensitive mental state of the protagonist. The central issue in *Journey to Ithaca* is not the search for identity of existence, but a "Search for truth, ultimate reality, beauty, joy, ecstasy or whatever form truth has" (4).

The three characters, Laila Sophie and Matteo come to India as the seekers after truth. As a young wife with the western-oriented approach to life, Sophie desires to fulfil the dream of her womanhood but this is not possible in an unruly and stuffy arranged life of the ashram. She feels neglected among the other pilgrims in the ashram : "She scrambled to her feet and returned to eat some bread from the night before and drink a tumbler of tea given her, and even smoked a cigarette furtively behind a hut.... Feeling both guilty and grateful to be excluded" (53-54).

The smoking of cigarette "furtively" becomes symbolic of two things : first she breaks the code of the ashram; and secondly, she relieves herself momentarily from her tense nervous system due to an inferiority complex as an ashramite.

Again, the smoking of Sophie brings froth the apparent contradictions of her mind : the guilt and gratefulness. She feels guilty, for she smokes furtively as an ashramite and feels grateful as she does not like to develop any association and reconciliation with any of the pilgrims in the ashram. As an expatriate, she experiences the dilemma of her identity. The sense of belongingness so vexes and overpowers her that she questions her husband : "Couldn't we stay in our own country? To die there?" (57). Disenchanted as a ashramite, even the very mention of the word "ashram" baffles her so much so that she longs for her home. Weeping like a child she cries, "I want to go home" (89).

Matteo is yet another important character who aspires to accomplish his higher existence of life. As a devotee, he finds solace when he is blessed by the presence of divine Mother. During his illness in an ashram of Bihar, the doctor attending to him suggests that "Matteo doesn't need a doctor, he needs a *guru*" (147). Matteo and Sophie have a basic difference in their respective approach to life : Matteo represents all that comes from the heart, while Sophie represents all that comes from the mind. Imbued with saintly attributes, Matteo acknowledges the grace and blessings of the Mother thus : "Her presence heightens and illuminates the experience of living as no one else's does.... When she appears, everything comes to life, it flowers, it brightens" (110). Thus, the Mother as container and repository of all powers and energy creates a spiritual awareness in Matteo.

The third character who becomes rebellious like other heroines of Anita Desai for her spiritual quest is Laila. Spending her childhood in Alexandria, she is educated in Paris and Venice and finally comes to India for her spiritual emancipation. Laila as a Muslim girl revolts against her parental religion, and endures the panics of life in her search for godhead, first in Paris and then in India. As a dancer, she fails, but as a seeker after truth, she succeeds in fulfilling the final goal of her life. There are two women who revolt in this novel against their surroundings : Sophie and Laila. Sophie longs for worldly freedom while Laila aspires for spiritual freedom. As a rebellious daughter of Alma and Hameed, she exhibits "an amber of curiosity". Since her early childhood, her curious nature makes her to give up "all orthodox religions" (110).

As the novelist analyses the psychic depth of the characters, her language tends to be situational and contextual. For example, the conversation between Sophie and Matteo becomes a good piece of symbolic and psychological language. Matteo as a seeker after truth finds two kinds of paths while reading the story of *Katha upanishad* : the path of Joy and path of pleasure. The linguistic meaning of these two words for Sophie is more or less the same. She seems awe-stricken when Matteo distinguishes the linguistic properties of these two words :

> Sophie's lips felt dry, and she spoke through those dry lips hoarsely, "I can't understand what you mean. The path of pleasure, the path of joy. To me, they are the same, they are not the separate. But I see that you are saying I am the fool, the one who takes the path of pleasure and that you are the wise one (295).

Sophie expresses her contempt towards other people in the ashram through non-verbal language. She does not like to give up her European identity among the ashramites in India. So, she does not try to understand the mystical yet the false language of the people at the ashram. She excludes herself from the environment of the ashram due to the "lack of the language" (34). She rather tries to understand the language of birds and animals through their gestures, and motions, but ignores willingly to understand the language of people at the ashram. Here is an example by which Sophie comprehends the language of the animals through sound :

> The pai dogs that barked in the village and in other villages, plaintively or aggressively, pleasingly or

> even conversationally as though addressing each other over great distance in the dark, were more comprehensible to her : she listened to their dialogues with greater understanding and sympathy. Once, she was certain she heard a pack of jackals howling, as eerily as wolves and this roused the dogs to frenzy : she felt their fear in her own veins (53).

The phrases "jackals howling" as "eerily as wolves" and the "dogs to frenzy" are indicative of Sophie's turmoil in her mind. The fear of her conscious mind creates the fear in her unconscious mind. The animal image haunts her like a psychosis patient. She thus becomes nightmarish and sees her new-born babe as a snake.

Sometimes, Anita Desai like a linguist distinguished between native and non-native variety of English. Sophie as an ashramite does not understand the regional pronunciation of English. Even Matteo hears a woman, speaking the typical regional variety of English :

> She was speaking very slowly and clearly, enunciating each word very precisely. Almost as if it were lesson in elocution, but it took Matteo sometime to make out that she spoke in English, for her voice and accent sounded so Indian in its pronunciation of "ds" and "ts" rolled "rs" and *heavy emphasis on the first syllable* (74).

The different images used in this novel make the language of the writer symbolic and suggestive. The images like "the gravelled path," "dust-filmed glass," "a velvet tassel," "a cream-flecked smile" prepare the foreground for narrative pattern. Again, Sophie used the image of "a monster spider" for the Mother and for her spinning web to catch "these silly flies." The images like "breast like a sword" and "an invisible crevice" are functional, for they reveal the hidden and interior regions which are beyond the purview of any written language.

Anita Desai in *Journey to Ithaca* has thus united varied groups of people from different parts of the world in order to present cosmic vision of human life. The novel transcends the barriers of caste and creed. The incomplete journey of Hugo in *Baumgartner's Bombay* for his spiritual quest comes to its completion in Journey to Ithaca. The chief protagonist of this novel, Laila, defies her social code and comes above the narrow round of caste, creed and a particular religion for attaining the higher vision of human life. The novelist thus professes the universal validity that all religions of the world come to a single stream, representing the religion of humanity. In this novel, Desai also raises a question of the universal confirming : how to bring *bhava parivartan* (spiritual change) in man. The novel thus ends with a hope of mankind's regeneration through self-analysing process.

REFERENCES

Anita Desai, *Journey to Ithaca*. (London : A Minerva Paperback. 1996), p. 17. All subsequent references are to this edition and page number follows each citation.

10

Crisis in Human Values : In the *Alphabet of Lust* by Kamala Das*

—*Vinod Kumar Maheshwari*

Kamala Das has emerged as one of the most influential writers in Indo-Anglian literature in the post-independent India. She is a winner of the PEN International Award for poetry and the Kerala Sahitya Akademi Award for fiction; and she has written prolifically in Malayalam and to a substantial degree in English too. She writes with understanding and insight on different aspects of social life in India. Even as hers is a feminine viewpoint by virtue of her being a woman writer, she is not a biased commentator as the members of the Women's LIB are generally found to be in blaming the men-folk for misplaced and miserable existence in the modern world.

In the *Alphabet of Lust*, Kamala Das has reflected upon the life-style of an educated upper middle-class woman in a forthright manner without being prejudiced in any way by the burden of traditional Indian values on women. In this novel, she has analysed with verve and understanding the existential parameters of an upper class Indian woman in the socio-political profile of the contemporary India. Her implied argument is that Indian woman is no longer a mysterious jigsaw puzzle; she willy-nilly has got to face the modern

* Paper presented at National Conference organised by Chhathisgarh English Teachers Association at Raipur in October, 2000.

situations, and in facing them, she is left with narrow options; either to betray herself and go up the social ladder; or be prepared for an uneventful life of silent misery of a typical Indian housewife. This is how the novel presents the crisis in human values.

The story of *Alphabet of Lust* is basically concerned with the miserable plight of Indian women who are caught in deplorable situations to which they as individual would never have opted voluntarily in a better social atmosphere. As human beings, they have their own urges of life; but finding themselves in unresponsive and inhospitable social conditions, for their meaningful growth, they are lured into situations from which there is no easy way of escape. Manasi, the heroine of this novel, is such a person. She is a poetess in terms of her creative urge; but her being married to government official, stationed in Bombay, with a routinised limited outlook is a grave hindrance to her, to speak psychologically.

As the story starts, Manasi is found in absorbing conversation with one of her admirers from earlier days when she was unmarried. Vijay was meeting her after twenty years. Then, they were staying at Calcutta. Vijay had an elder brother 'with whom she had a short love affair which lasted until he died in an air-crash.' Here, the novelist observingly comments : "If he had lived she would have been the sister-in-law of the young and corrupt politician (that is, Vijay) who was seated beside her now, smoking a Benson and Hedges cigarette. She would not have been the wife of a struggling Government official named Mitra who looked old enough to be her father. But then she would not have been a poetess, for her poetry had burst out of the mire of her utter hopelessness like a red lotus[1] (9). It means that Manasi with all mental disaffection was a talented woman. She told Vijay that she was then forty years and that her eldest daughter studying in Lucknow was nineteen. Vijay also came to know that Manasi had to send her daughter to Lucknow just to keep her free from the ill-tempered atmosphere at home.

To Manasi, her girlhood admirer Vijay was a changed man. 'As an adolescent on a visit to her ancestral home in Bengal, he had been a pale-skinned boy with skinny knees. Now he was a hefty man, bronzed in the face with the sun, and with straight black hair combed neatly back, revealing the smoothness of his brow. He gave her a slow smile. If she had not heard all the scandals regarding his promiscuous love life she would have been charmed by that smile. But now she only felt a revulsion' (7). However, as the novel proceeds, one finds that Manasi's revulsion towards Vijay is greatly softened; and a stage comes when Vijay was given the post of Minister for Iron and Steel; consequently, he sent an emissary (one, Krishnan) to Manasi to come to Delhi and meet him. She accepted the invitation from the Iron and Steel Minister, Vijay[2] to meet him at Delhi. In fact, her mind had become astir after she was informed by her husband that Vijay had become the Minister for Iron and Steel. 'Your childhood friend is now a minister,' cried out the man in joy. But she glanced once at the news-item and remained silent. 'Now we have also become influential people,' said the husband, grinning. She flared up at his words. 'Do you think I am the kind of person who will go to Delhi and beg for favours?' she asked him (17).

Kamala Das has described the disturbed condition of Manasi, showing how restless she was. Restless, she walked up and down and then settled herself near the window of her own bedroom, to soothen her bruised nerves; but it had an adverse effect on her. 'From it, only the depressing view of another dingy building was visible. A room as small as her and similarly impoverished was laid bare before her eyes. The voile curtains at the window had been pulled back. A man lay curled up on a cheap cot which held no sheet but only a worn out mattress. Another of those Government servants, she told herself, staring at the unnatural condition of his face, the faded hair thinning at the crown. Another man who thinks even during the act of love making about his next increment.

How like old garments these men looked faded with the dhobi's innumerable. She felt pity for herself' (17).

In comparison to these washed out men of government, Manasi felt that she was still attractive, active and alive. The younger set of people considered her a revolutionary poetess. 'But her husband, the mild Mr. Mitra, had faded with the years, signing on millions of files until he had become to her only a shabby appendage which she had to tote with her while she went to public functions to preside' (17). This is how the still beautiful young poetess Mrs. Manasi Mitra toyed up with a number of possibilities in future when she would be a prominent political figure — that is, a woman of great importance and public influence; and in that eventuality, if she happened to marry again, her present husband, Mr. Mitra might fare no better than a part of her cosmetics in the changed conditions. Interpretatively, it can be stated that Manasi's psychological journey is from her traumatic shock at the time of marriage with Mr. Mitra after the death of her lover in an air-crash to the post-marital disillusionment with her family life, and now, as she looks forward for a new turn in her life, following her meeting with the Iron and Steel Minister, Vijay and his invitation to meet with him, she visualises the possibility of her break with her husband and her disaffection-filled married life.

As she ponders about her past, present and future, she is a little bit agitated to realise that she has a lovely daughter, Superna to be married to a good-natured husband. In her disturbed reveries, Manasi failed to realise that in her future, she might get more and more disillusioned as a woman of ideals and bubbling emotions. While preparing her mind seized with diverse conflicts in regard to her integrity as woman, she decided to meet Vijay; and as events rolled out, she would be meeting with new situations in which withal her fame, and power, money and status, she would lose the finer graces of womanhood. Here, one is reminded of James Joyce's poser : 'What is the fun of attaining heaven, when the soul is lost?'

For Manasi, the glory and achievement came with this type of saddened realisation.

Even as the future would bring unexpected surprises for her, her mind was already dizzy with unborn anxiety. When Francis Bacon speculated that the road to power is treacherously slippery, he touched upon the levers of an abiding truth. With women in the twentieth century, the validity of the Baconian observation is insistently alive. To D.H. Lawrence, success is a bitch-goddess; and in Manasi's case, it turns out to be so. Her boyhood friend, Vijay holds out unending possibilities for Manasi if she cared to associate with him after her breaking marital ties with Mr. Mitra. Vijay's short visit to Manasi, it appears, was engineered by Milton's Satan who had pushed his plan successfully. 'After the visitor had left, Manasi walked over to her dressing mirror. She shut the door and took off all her clothes. Was she beautiful enough to satisfy Vijay's hunger for her body? Had not her breasts sagged a little, just a little? Hadn't her thighs become flabby? Was she not a tarnished trophy, too shabby to be offered to the youthful politician who was a notorious philanderer? He had mated with the best looking girls of several countries. He had had mistresses galore. He was trained in the art of unemotional love-making by that notorious lecher, Sadasiva Rao who was supposed to conduct erotic orgies in his drawing room, in which all his friends and their girls participated' (29).

'Why did Vijay need her at all? She was not the kind of woman who liked sexual acrobatics. She felt shy to undress in front of her own husband. And to think that for some diamonds she was to shed her shyness, her long-cherished chastity.... She found herself looking pale in the mirror. The mirror which had held her reflection for the past twenty years suddenly made her very uneasy. Was it accusing her of greed? Of vanity? She turned her face away' (29).

The novelist knows it searchingly that Manasi was in a state of inner turmoil. The defence woven around her ideal of a *Pativrata* were vanishing one by one because Vijay's offer to her was too unresistingly tempestuous to be easily overcome and ignored, which is specifically true in case of an Indian woman who is sensitive and well-formed, given to scrappy brushings periodically with her marital partner. With initial reluctance, her husband allowed Manasi to leave for Delhi to Vijay Raje, the Minister for Iron and Steel. Soon after meeting Manasi, this accomplished politician and philandering crook saw to it that the talented poetess, Manasi, is converted to his viewpoint so that in future as the situation arises he would be able to use the talents of Manasi to his advantage. At cajolery, Vijay was expert : 'Why should you know any of these things, Manasi? he asked. You are above fashion, above convention, above every accepted rule. You are genius. All you need to know is to write poetry, and that you do supremely well.'

'I do not want to be only a poetess,' she said. 'I want to be woman who can be admired and loved.'

'How like a child you speak, exclaimed Vijay. Today I am going to introduce you to the Prime Minister, who wished to meet you. We are dining with the Minister for Information and Broadcasting who has also invited the Prime Minister' (31). Manasi felt a little shaky and hesitant to meet these high dignitaries as Vijay's friend because she had no proper clothes to wear for such occasions; but he tried to placate her by saying : 'Any man would think it an honour to be introduced to you. You have not heard what the intelligentsia say about your writings, my dearest one' (31).

The upshot of this cajolery and placating was that at Simla, Manasi realised that she was no longer a *Pativrata* woman. It was a turning point of grave solemnity for the rest of her life. No doubt she would reach to the pinnacle of glory; but her womanly spirit would lead her to realise the enormity of cost at which the glory was attained. After the die was cast, she would have on occasions a feeling of self-estrangement and ruefulness for crossing the *Lakshman Rekha* at the bidding of externally motivated forces epitomised in persons like Vijay Raje and his associates.

It is true that Manasi would finally become the Prime Minister after a sudden paralytic stroke to the aging Prime Minister under whom she had worked politically; and otherwise in terms of her womanly talents. If one takes stock of Manasi's chequered life span from her lover's death in an air-crash leaving her pregnant, to pave the way for the birth of her daughter, Superna; and then her marrying a government official, Amol mitra followed by her escapade with Vijay Raje, one just has to take a pause and think about the attendant difficulties and temptations to a woman who is beautiful and talented — as it was so with the poetess Manasi.

From the tenor of the story in the novel, *Alphabet of Lust*, it is evidenced that there is hardly any place for a section of young, talented women to live their life with dignity, poise and understanding in our social set up — unless they are prepared to rent their body, off and on, to those who are politically influential and monetarily strong! Woman's poise and serenity is now measured in terms of her capacity to serve the powerful patrons from the sphere of politics or public offices with bouts of carnal pleasure. The true spirit of morality stares helplessly at the profile of things prevailing in the country. One can take a cue from what the novelist expresses in her novel. It is Vijay telling Manasi : 'The Prime Minister has fallen for you, and wants you to join his cabinet as the Minister of Information and Broadcasting.'

'What a pack of idiots rule this country,' cried Manasi, laughing heartily. 'Be serious,' Manasi, said Vijay. 'They are trying to shunt the present man to some State as a Governor. He is seventy-one. Very rigid in his views. He cannot see eye to eye with the younger generation. You will be ideal for the post, but....'

Manasi straightened up all of a sudden. 'But?' she asked him. 'Why do you say 'but?' '

'The Prime Minister is a womaniser,' said Vijay. 'He will not leave you alone. Your name will soon be mud in the country.'

'But that is the sort of mud that is being worshipped in this country,' she said.

Vijay, I am willing to do whatever the Prime Minister wants me to do. It is not as if I am a chaste woman now. A *pativrata* you saw to it that I became a mere tart. I rented out my body for a pair of diamond earrings. And hereafter for power I shall rent it out to the most influential tenant, I can hope to get.

Manasi began to laugh loudly. At the sight of her reddened face Vijay was frightened.

Was she getting hysterical? He tried to fondle her face but she brushed his hands away. 'From today I am no longer your woman, she said. I am the Prime Minister's private property. If one is willing to drown oneself, one might enter the depths of the sea rather than die in the shallow waters, near the shore' (40-41).

It is a fine pen-portrayal of a woman, disillusioned with the world from top to its lower social levels. The novelist has also elucidated that the chastity-bereft Manasi had no illusions about the conventional values. To Vijay who pressed her to marry him replied negatively on the ground that she was still a married woman and that her husband was Amol Mitra. On her blank assertion of being Mrs. Mitra, he tauntingly commented : 'Last night did you remember Amol Mitra while you climbed my thighs like a leopardess? Manasi, if I am to be blamed, you are to be blamed too. We were victims of pure animal lust' (41).

To this extent, Vijay's assertion may be justified. However, an element of deception creeps in when he observes : 'But in my behaviour and attitude there was a redeeming factor. I loved you. I love you, Manasi, you bitch' (41).

There is a ring of condemnation of Manasi as he tried to show himself as a true lover. 'She laughed again, ignoring his rude remark. You are not worthy of me, Vijay Raje, she said. If this is to be a hunt for the right man, let me hunt in my own way. I was satisfied to be Amol's wife. I was happy to be feeding him and looking after his home. But you trapped me with offers of gems which I had never even touched. You brought out the worst in me. I shall never be again what I was, never be able to write honestly about the goodness of men. I am finished as a writer....'

Manasi went to the bed and lay down. She felt depressed. Her world was collapsing before her eyes. Her integrity which she had valued had died with this trip. If she could love Vijay, she would have been able to forgive herself but lusting for his young body was not love. I want to die, she cried, oh, Vijay, I want to die. I cannot go back and face my husband (41-42). In order to free her mind of depressive thoughts, Vijay suggested her to take rest for an hour or so; and on his own part, he started self-talking on the latest trends in politics. Feeling repentant, Manasi tried to make her thoughts vocal : "I want to return to my quiet home in Bombay and be again what I was. But that is now impossible, isn't it? I have become soiled. Peace is a dead dove rotting in my alcove. It shall never be resurrected from the dead. After all it is no phoenix. Oh Amol, what a lot I lost in this gamble : I shall never be able to look at you in the face. I am debased. I am hopelessly soiled" (43). Here, a reference may be made to an excerpt from Kamala Das's poem, *The Stone Age* :

> ....Ask me why like
> A great tree, felled, he slumps against my breasts.
> And sleeps, ask me why life is short and love is
> Shorter still, ask me what is this and what its price....

The meaning is very much palpable. If, according to Disraeli, 'every man has a price,' it is equally relevant to say that in modern world every shade of bliss is priced. This is how the poetess Manasi got stigmatised.

Manasi was in deep remorse; her heart-rending suffering is a painful reminder for all of us to note that there is something radically wrong with our life-pattern. There is a corruption galore in our body-politic. If in this novel, Manasi belongs to an upper middle class society, it does not mean that the condition of women in other classes is cheerful. The sinister scenario of money and political or bureaucratic power nexus is very much pervasive in India. It is, therefore, not far to say that the story of Manasi is enacted times without number almost in every populated habitant. The daily newspapers' reports vouch for it; but the strongest irony of the contemporary history is that even as we pay obeisance to the Father of the Nation and the glorious, republican constitution, we hardly care to wrestle with the basic problem in which innocent women become the victims of lust, living out the remaining span of their life in shadowy existence with hopeless misery.

We worship several gods and goddesses but we placidly ignore Tulsidas's observation that Ram resides in every heart and that to be human is to follow as far as practicable in the footsteps of Maryada Purushottam Ram. That we have hardly taken any serious step to crystrallise the truth of God within us. The Father of the Nation, Mahatma Gandhi used to remind us that the manual work-ethic is the core of any human progress; but after independence, we have started worshipping money, status and power more and more with the result that the crisis in human values has become too deep-seated to be eradicated by mere wishful thinking or through the periodical sermons of the leaders. We talk of 'internet progress' but we hardly care to educate public to learn the art of delicacy in male-female relationship by restraining the violent facets of carnality. Then, allied with work-ethic, the social landscape can be peopled with men and women of sanity. So long as this facet of life is ignored, the money and political power combine would strangle to pieces the ideals of love, understanding and graceful living. Here lies the crux of the crisis in human values. Once man-woman relationship is perverted from within and distorted from outside, there is no end to human perversion. This is how the novel, *Alphabet of Lust,* tackles the problem of crumbling human values.

WORKS CITED

1. Kamala Das, *Alphabet of Lust* (New Delhi : Orient Paper Books, 1976). All parenthetical page references are to this edition.
2. *The Times of India*, 10 December 1992.

NOTES AND REFERENCES

1. Sadashiv Rao, a powerful political leader from Bombay. Highly unscrupulous, he had no respect for moral code.
2. Vijay Raje is the younger brother of Manasi's lover who died in an air-crash before she got married to Amol Mitra.

11

A Comparative Study of Mulk Raj Anand's *Untouchable* & Sharan Kumar Limbale's "Akkarmashi"

—Shiv Kumar Yadav

"Truth is always stranger than fiction" is an age-old dictum. The relation between truth and fiction is somewhat like history and myth respectively as John Beattie explains, "History and myth...are not the same, although there may be an element of history in myth, as there certainly is of myth in history."[1] Fiction like myth is weaved in and around fact, history and truth but also being governed by man (author) and milieu (environment). Mulk Raj Anand also opines in the similar vein : "The novelist presumes to be God Almighty and indulges in the sport of creating a world of his own in his novel."[2] In order to have complete control over his puppets (characters), Anand declined the advice of Gandhi to write a straightforward pamphlet about Harijans.[3] The fictional form provides an ample opportunity to an author to be a deliberate victim of selective amnesia to justify his ways to his characters and viewpoints. On the other hand, an autobiographer who narrates his life's events and experiences, certainly within his own term and frame of references including his prejudice and bias, gives a transparent opportunity to a reader to get his story verified in the light of other sources of fact and truth *i.e.*, history.

This paper seeks to compare Mulk Raj Anand's *Untouchable*, a fiction and Sharan Kumar Limbale's

"Akkarmashi" a fact (an autobiography), which narrate the plight and sufferings of a large segment of the Hindu society which acquired different names in different periods of the Indian history — Antyaj or Chandals (exterior castes), Achoot (untouchables), Harijan (children of God), Scheduled Caste (a constitutional name), and now Dalit (depressed, a self-assumed socio-historical name). Anand's novels like *The Untouchable*, *The Coolie* and *The Big Heart* have been written with a motive to prop the economical and social questions of the Indian society. His "Compassion for the Waifs, the disinherited, the lowly, the lost — in a word Daridranarayan the Lord & incarnate Poverty)"[4] is unquestionable. But his depiction of an untouchable in his *Untouchable* and the three solutions offered by him regarding the removal of untouchability, it seems to me, is just like touching the tip of an iceberg of the complex 'chronic and perhaps racial disease of Hindu collective consciousness, if it is compared with Limbale's "Akkarmashi."

The "Akkarmashi," originally written in Marathi and later on translated into Hindi by Dr. Surya Narayan Ransubhe in 1991 depicts the agony and sufferings of Sharan Kumar Limbale in particular and of the Hindu untouchables in general. Limbale's description is so truthful and revealing that it belittles E.M. Forster's tall claim regarding Anand's *Untouchable*. Forster claims, *Untouchable* could only have been written by an Indian and by an Indian who observed from outside. No European, however, sympathetic could have created the character of Bakha, because he would not have known enough about his troubles. And no untouchable could have written the book, because he would have been involved in indignation and self-pity.[5] If Forster claims that 'however, sympathetic' a European cannot create the character of Bakha, it can also be claimed in the line of his own logic that however compassionate, a Hindu caste cannot depict the plight and suffering of Sharan Kumar, an 'Akkarmashi, a word of Marathi means, in the worlds of Dr. Ransubhe, "Akkarmashi ka arth hai Jarajputra, Avaidh Santan, Samaj dwara amanya sambandho se janmi santati, istri ki majboori ko dekhkar, use rakhail bananewale sampann aur amanviya purush sambandho se janami santati, aisi santati ko marathi mein Akkarmashi kahte hain."[6] [Meaning of akkarmashi is love-child, Illicit-child, offspring born out of socially unacceptable relationship, offspring born out of a relationship in which a woman has been made a mistress by a well-do-do and inhuman person, by exploiting her helplessness. This sort of offspring is known as 'akkarmashi' in Marathi.] This paper also attempts to underline the viewpoint that a 'participant observer' (sufferer), despite the possibility of being victim of indignation and self pity can reveal the truth and gauze the density of agony more pungently in comparison to 'non-participant observer' (sympathiser).

Anand's *Untouchable* was germinated in early Twenties and published in 1935. And till today it has been published in thirty plus languages of the world, which certainly underlines its well deserved and unreserved acceptance everywhere. He wrote this novel, after being inspired by "a poignant story about a sweeper boy, Uka, by Mahatma Gandhi in *Young India* written with the utmost simplicity".[7] Later on, he got his manuscripts heard by Gandhiji and after that pruned it to its extant size and contents. The influence of Gandhi on Anand is an open secret, but in *The Untouchable* he is so enchanted with Gandhism that he visualises the problem of untouchability thoroughly through the lens of Gandhi having few disagreements.

The Untouchable appeared nearly more than 50 years before 'the Akkarmashi' but failed to capture the complete scene of sufferings of untouchables prevalent at that time. If we take the glimpses of painful experiences of Bakha, following significant incidents come to the fore : Morning abuse of his father (suar ka aulad, haramjada — son of a pig, illegally-begotten); the slap on the face as he accidentally touched a caste Hindu, disapproving eyes of shopkeepers who sold jalebis to him, behaviour of 'charity bread' giver woman; recollection of the story about the doctors' refusal to give medicine to his father when Bakha was ill, the temple incident of Sohini and aftermath; Bakha's hesitation to take sweets from Ramcharan, abuse of the housewife because he carried her injured child home to her and so 'polluted' the little one by his touch; quarrel between colonel Hutchinson and his wife when Bakha was brought to Colonel's residence. If we analyse these incidents of Bakha's life, it is very much clear that Anand's depiction revolves around the problem of untouchability practised by the Hindu Castes and their hypocrisy as well as untouchability among untouchables. The oblique reference of love-child of Gulabo — "Ramcharan, true son of his mother, Gulabo, if he want's his father's son, but of the richman, his mother's lover"[8] by Anand shows his concern regarding the Hindu castes hypocrisy.

In the "Akkarmashi," Sharan's story runs like this : Sharan, not only an untouchable but an akkarmashi also, belongs to Hannur village somewhere on the boundary of Maharashtra and Karnataka. His story begins from his maternal grandmother, Santamai, of Mahar caste, a deserted woman, having only one daughter — the mother of Sharan Kumar, who lives with a Muslim, Mahmud Dastgir, referred as Dada by Sharan, within the framework of modern institution of 'live-in-relationship.' Dada himself a 'deserted' husband without any issue, lives with Santamai, as a committed partner, Masa Mai only daughter of Santa Mai from her first husband and mother of Sharan Kumar, marries Vithal Kamble of Baslegaon and gives birth of three sons. The eldest son dies very early. Hanmanta Limbale, as Patel of Baslegaon, under whose suzerainty Vithal Kamble works as an annual contract labour and receives Rs. 800, exploits the helplessness (due to acute poverty) of Vithal Kamble by making his wife his (Limbale's) mistress. In turn, he supports them in the rainy season. But it does not work for longer time and eventually Kamble deserts Masamai and deprives her of two sons. Masamai does not marry again.

Hanmanta Limbale likes her decision and makes a separate arrangement of her at Akkalkot, where Sharan appears on this earth as an 'Akkarmashi.' Later on, disenchantment grows in Limbale, and he starts levelling accusations of being faithless against Masamai so the paternity claim of Sharan Kumar can be disowned. Being mentally agonised of his accusations and tortured of atrocities, she returns to her mother Santamai along with Sharan. Here Sharan grows under the unconditional love of Santamai and her live-in-partner Dada, Mahamud Dastgir, and also collects his experiences as an untouchable as well as an 'Akkarmashi.' Masamai, here, again becomes mistress of another 'touchable' Yashwant Sidramappa Patel, a prominent person of Hannur village, where they live, and gives birth of eight more "akkarmashi" — six females and two males. Sharan obtains his Bachelor Degree in 1978 and gets appointment for the post of Telephone Operator. Sharan writes in the preface of "The Akkarmashi" — his autobiography "Mere Saale Subhash Ki Atmakatha bhi isi prakar ki hai. Uski Maa Achoot, Pita Berar Samaj Ka. Pita Amir, Mahanagarpalika Ka Sadasya; Aur Maa? Mahanagarpalika Ki Chaturth Shreni Ki Majdoor Aurat.[9] [Biography of my brother-in-law is the same. His mother, an untouchable, father from Berar society. The father — rich a member of Metropolitan Council, and the Mother? fourth grade woman labour of Metropolitan Council.] This is not the story of Sharan, it is only his genealogy and chronology. As a matter of fact his story of sufferings and miseries is the story of an untouchable of the post-independent, democratic republic, secular and socialistic India. Despite several constitutional and legal measures initiated by the State still we have a number of 'Sharan' and 'Subhash.'

The story of Bakha in the *Untouchable*, it seems to me, is just a struggle for emancipation from the sufferings of untouchability while the "Akkarmashi" apart from being a struggle for emancipation from the human bondage, it is also a craving quest for identity. Mathematically, we can say that if the "Akkarmashi" is almost universal set of miseries, the

Untouchable just its subset. In the description of every incident, Sharan shows the injuries and scars caused by glaring discriminations and atrocities perpetuated by the caste Hindus. Space limitation does not permit to narrate all the painful experiences of Sharan's life her, but few incidents need to be described. In the very beginning, we find how the students of untouchable community enjoy the left-over, remnants and droppings of the 'touchable' at the end of the picnic. When Sharan describes this incident of the picnic, his mother, Masamai, complains "Ghar ke logo ke liye usme se thoda le aata to kya bigarta? Bacha hua anna amrit hota hai.[10] [It wouldn't have caused you any harm if you would have brought some of that (droppings) for we people. The droppings are like nectar.] Another event also clearly shows the acute poverty prevalent among untouchables. Sharan narrates : "Fasal ke dino mein janwar jyada kha lete. Jwar ke bhutte khane ke bad unke gobar mein phule huae dane dikhte, Dano mein bhare huae aise gobar ko Santamai alag se rakhati. Ghar lautate samay raaste mein nadi ke pani mein us gobar ko Santamai dhoti. Gobar nikal jata, dane alag ho jate. Maa un dano ko sukhati. Sukhane ke bad woh kam ho jate. Mujhe lagta, unhe sukhana hi nahi chahiye, Sukhane ka bad to we kam ho jate. Dane sukhane ke bad hum ghar lautate. Un dano ko woh chakki mein khud peesti, gati hui."[11] [In the harvesting season, cattle would eat more than they could digest. The undigested grains were visible in the dung. Santamai would keep such dung separately, while returning home, Satamai would clear the dung in the river water. Thus gains and dung would get separated. Maa would dry the grains. The amount of grains would get lessened after being dried. It seems to me, that must not be dried as it would get lessened. We would return home after having dried the grains. She would grind the grains herself while singing in the grinding stones.] Here we find even animals are more fortunate than the untouchables who get more fodder than they needed. Sharan narrates further that Santamai would never give the bread of those grains to him and his brothers and sisters. She alone would consume those pieces of bread. They would eat "Chani"-dried pieces of carrion when they would have scarcity of food. Stones would serve the pupose of bath-soap and alkaline soil as detergent. Sharan would use the soap-lather floating in the river, but only on the condition that he would help the person from whose clothes soap-lather floats.

Sharan's story impels one to analyse the reasons responsible for the sub-animal status of untouchables in our society. Sharan, even, can't claim his lineage among untouchables as his biological father is a Patel, a Savarna. Savarna calls him an untouchable and the untouchable calls him an "akkarmashi." We come across a situation when the two Patels — the father of Sharan and the father of other brothers and sisters Limbale and Sidramappa visit Masamai together. She is unwilling, but Sidramappa wants that she should share bed with Limbale for the night. Is Masamai more than an animal?

The revelation of facts regarding the conditions of untouchables in the "Akkarmashi" questions the efficacy of the three solutions to the problem of untouchability offered by Anand — change of faith, Gandhi's approach and Machine. As a matter of fact, Anand himself rejects the first option as it is evident when Bakha recalls his father's reaction regarding the change of faith..."that he had refused to leave the Hindu fold, saying that the religion which was good enough for his forefathers was good enough for him."[12] Further, again, "To Bakha....the few words which she (wife of the Colonel) had uttered carried a dread a hundred times more terrible than the fear inspired by the whole tirade of abuse by the touched man."[13] Regarding the other two solutions, "Bakha is duly impressed, feels more hopeful of the future than at any time since the day dawned, and returns to his house to tell his father about the Mahatma and about the machine that will clear dung without anyone having to handle it."[14] Very promptly, E.M. Forster appears in support of Anand to justify his solutions, when he says, "It is the necessary climax, and it has mounted up with triple effect. Bakha returns to his father and his wretched bed, thinking now of the Mahatma, now of the Machine. His Indian day is over and the next day will be like it, but on the surface of the earth if not in the depths of the sky, a change is at hand."[15] "The Akkarmashi" appears in the Nineties, and cries loudly where is the change.

Gandhi fails to understand the problem despite this, Bipin Chandra writes, "experience in South Africa was unique in one respect. By virtue of being a British-educated barrister, he demanded may things as a matter of right, such as first class tickets and rooms in hotels, which other Indian before him had never probably even had the courage to ask for Perhaps, they believed that they were discriminated against because they were not 'civilized' that is 'westernized.' Gandhiji's experiences, the first of a westernized Indian in South Africa, demonstrated clearly to him and to them that the real cause lay elsewhere, in the assumption of racial superiority by the white rulers."[16] The same 'experienced' Gandhi tries to see the problem of casteism and untouchability as an unrelated issue, and according to him, certainly not rooted in the Varnashram as it is not found in Hindu's original scriptures. He assumes untouchability just a deviance so its eradication is sufficient enough to ensure all sort of justice to the untouchable. Probably, he couldn't see that the caste names of untouchables are the words of abuse for the 'touchables.' Arundhati Roy underlines this agony of untouchables in her masterpiece, "They were also demanding that untouchables no longer be addressed by their caste names. The demanded not to be addressed as Achoo Parayan or Kelan Paravan, or Kuttan Pulayan, but just as Achoo, or Kelan, or Kuttan."[17] If 'untouchability' has its physical dimension only, then how does 'Gulabo' and 'Masamai' become the mothers of the touchables. And being a confirmed believer of his own assumption, his "Harijan campaign included a programme of internal reform by Harijan, promotion of education, cleanliness and hygiene, giving up the eating of carrion and beef, giving up liquor and the abolition of untouchability among themselves."[18] Even Anand differs from Gandhi although very mildly. When Bakha hears Gandhi saying, "In order to emancipate themselves they have to purify themselves. They have to rid themselves of evil habits, like drinking liquor and eating carrion"[19] he felt, "That is not fair."[20] Gandhi does not see that, "In fact, Sanskritisation depends upon resource availability, mobilisation and accessibility at the level of the lower castes"[21] and "the sankritising castes may even face a threat or challenge from the dominant castes."[22]

The Third solution — Machine — certainly brings a change in the physical dimension of untouchability but what about its psychological dimension. A comrade in *The God of Small Things*, speaks, "But frankly speaking, comrade, Change is one thing, Acceptance is another."[23] Sharan Kumar goes to another village for hair-cutting where his identity as an untouchable is not known to the barber.

Bakha is a fictional character while Sharan, a living individual. Sharan Limbale could have written his own story in fictional form and then might have ensured enough scope and freedom to make his story an epic of sufferings of untouchables of India as a whole. But Sharan just narrates his story and never tries to visit the past saving few anecdotes of Santamai and others, nor visualise the future. And that's why like Bakha who "is only partly the prototypical 'untouchable,' for he is also himself, a unique individual, even in some measure in exceptional untouchable."[24] Sharan is also 'an' untouchable not 'the' untouchable but his story comes very close to the sufferings of untouchables as a whole cutting across the regions of India. Sexual exploitation of the untouchable woman by the touchable man has been prevalent in every part of India. "Sexual exploitation of tenant of womenfolk was rampant to such an extent particularly in Masaurha Zamindari, that the foremost peasant leader of Bihar in the Zamindari period, Swami Sahajanand Saraswati notes in his autobiography "Mere Jeevan Sangarsh (My Life

Struggle), that tenants outside Masaurha were unwilling to get their daughters married there."[25]

Comparing the intensity and density of sufferings of untouchables described in the *Untouchable* and the "Akkarmashi," the later seems to be the story of the Twenties or even more earlier while the former is of the Sixties and Seventies. The *Untouchable* has earned a worldwide publicity and evoked sympathy for untouchables, but I wonder, no one questioned that it was very less than the reality. Bakha once suffers from "spiritual nausea," when he learns that he is "the cause of the mem-sahib's anger,[26] but I perceive, this, as the "spiritual nausea" of Anand's learned humanism. Similarity does exist between 'Bakha' and 'Sharan' and that is of — helplessness, self pity and indignation, throughout the narratives of Anand and Limbale.

The *Untouchable* ends with some solutions, as Anand perceives the whole things only externally and mechanically as an observer, but the "Akkarmashi" ends with the baptism of Sharan's son. Sharan gives a name 'Anarya' as he perceives the whole things 'culturally and psychologically' as a 'sufferer' hence wishes to return to his 'historical' or 'mythical' root as even after many millenniums, his integration couldn't get completed into the Aryans' fold despite Gandhiji's long fasting before the Poona pact.

REFERENCES

1. John Beattie's *Other Culture*, Routledge & Kegan Paul, 1964, p. 24.
2. Mulk Raj Anand's, *Untouchable*, Arnold Associates, 1981 p. 181
3. *Ibid.*
4. K.R. Srinivas Iyengar's *Indian Writing in English*, Sterling Publishers, New Delhi, p. 332
5. E.M. Forster's Preface to the *Untouchable* by Mulk Raj Anand, p. 9
6. Sharam Kumar Limbale's "Akkarmashi" [Translated edition (Hindi), Granth Akademi, New Delhi, 199], p. 5
7. Mulk Raj Anand's *Untouchable*, Arnold Associates, 1981, p. 179.

8. *Ibid.*, p. 99
9. Sharan Kumar Limbale's "Akkarmashi" [Translated edition (Hindi), Granth Akademi, New Delhi, 1991], p. 9.
10. *Ibid.*, p. 14.
11. *Ibid.*, p. 23.
12. Mulk Raj Anand's *Untouchable*, Arnold Associates, 1981, p. 138.
13. *Ibid.*, p. 149.
14. *Ibid.*, p. 173.
15. *Ibid.*, p. 10
16. Bipin Chandra's *India's Struggle for Independence*, Penguin India, 1992, p. 172.
17. Aundhati Roy's *The God of Small Things*, India Ink, 1998, p. 69.
18. Bipin Chandra's *India's Struggle for Independence*, Penguin India, 1992, p. 294.
19. Mulk Raj Anand's *Untouchable*, Arnold Associates, 1981, p. 165.
20. *Ibid.*
21. K.L. Sharma's *Indian Society*, NCERT, 1987, p. 145.
22. *Ibid.*
23. Aundhati Roy's *The God of Small Things*, India Ink, 1998, p. 279.
24. K.R.S. Iyengar's *Indian Writing in English*, Sterling Publishers, p. 338.
25. A.N. Das's *The Republic of Bihar*, Penguin India, 1992, p. 122.
26. Mulk Raj Anand's *Untouchable*, Arnold Associates, 1981, p. 149.

12

The Social Values in the Novels of Kamala Markandaya

—Chhote Lal Khatri

Kamala Markandaya is unquestionably one of the most outstanding women novelists on the canvas of Indo-Anglian fiction. An interesting aspect of the modern Indian Renaissance has been the creative release of the feminine sensibility. Her novels in comparison with those of contemporary women writers, seem to be more fully reflective of the awakened feminine sensibility in modern India as she attempts to project the image of the changing traditional society. The variety and the complexity of the achieved content of her novels represent a major trend in the history of Indo-English novel. In her novels, Markandaya not only displays a flow for virtuosity which orders and patterns her feelings and ideas resulting in a truly enjoyable work of art, but also rejects the image of national consciousness on many levels of aesthetic awareness. The variety and the quality of the 'felt life' in her fiction renders it label proof in that it indicates the direction to a plausible resolution of, rather than other definite solutions to human problems.[1]

Markandaya's novels implied largely social and economic background, physical features, dress and behaviour in person. Markandaya has seen India at close quarters and has acquired an intimate view of its ideas, ideals and various modes of life. She is as well acquainted with western ideals and mode of life. The major themes of the novels are the social, cultural and economic clash of these two modes. During the bitterness, which had prevailed in the thirties and forties at the height of the freedom struggle, the writer's attitudes were mostly biased against the Britishers. Bitter memories associated with the British rule which overshadowed the pleasant experiences with individual Englishmen, disappeared in the fifties. The hold of traditions was gradually relaxing while a new culture was born of the clash between the East and the West and it was merging imperceptibly but decisively. The large audience of the educated class was questioning the age. The old social dogmas and society were being re-interpreted with their new found knowledge. The Indian novelist today works mainly against this background. Indian society has always been a group society in which the "atomization of the West is still foreign." The drama in these novels unfolds in the broad social content in which one life reflects another. One sees this in the tension between the new urbanized class and their village kinsmen; between minority groups and those who still seek to hold monolithic barriers; between the masses and those in public office; between the young and their middle aged parents and guardians.

Kamala Markandaya's acquaintance with Indian life is as authentic as her understanding of the Englishmen and their character. She spent a few years studying the life of South Indian peasants before marrying on Englishman and settling down in London. Culture being ingrained in the personality of the nation, it is visible not only in domestic habits or sartorial concerns but also in beliefs and convictions. Markandaya's major theme has been the cultural clash of the two modes of life, she has seen so closely.

Markandaya has constantly been preoccupied by the East-West conflict of modes and convictions of which she herself is a living example. This clash between the Eastern and Western "values leads to an inevitable quest for identity; which she has ably dwelt upon in most of her novels in different contexts and with varying flavour. But she lacks the epic dimension of Raja Rao and the sharp sociological concerns of Mulk Raj Anand who have also dealt with the theme of East-West encounter in some of their novels."[2]

In *Nectar in a Sieve*, her first novel this dichotomy of values is captured in a most compelling way. It is the lot of Nathan and Rukmani to till the land belonging to another paying an exorbitant rent for it and getting hardly a square meal a day as reward even after the best harvest. But Rukmani is content to live in the soulful quietude of her little village till this garden of Eden is ravaged by a serpent in the form of tannery. "Like Maxuders the town people came with cart loads of bricks, stones and cement to build this hideous superstructure while their supervisor directed the operation with loud voice and many gestures but doing not a stroke of work himself"[3] [24]. The proprietor "the red-faced white man does not live in the village and only came and went" [26] thus laying the foundations of an industrial society based on the principles of exploitation of labour and asenteeism. The tannery began to rear its ugly head devouring green open spaces polluting the clean wholesome atmosphere and tempting simple gullible peasants into greed, ambition and immorality. Some like Kunthi are jubilant at the change and consider "the tannery...a boon to us" [27]. She asks Rukmani, "Are you not glad that our village is no longer a clump of huts but small town? Soon there will be shop and tea stall even a bioscope" [29]. Rukmani's spirit however revolts against this deflowering of pristine innocence. Her intuitive preception warns her against the impending disasters and she knows that the tannery does not auger well for the village. She cried, "They many live in our midst but I can never accept them for they lay their hands upon us and we are turned from tilling to barters and hard our silver since we cannot spend it and see our children go without the goods their children gorge and it is only in the hope that one day things will be as they were that we have done these things. But like a mythical demon the whole village is devoured by the tannery that turns into a spiritual waste land. It is all noise and crowds every where and rude young hooligans idling in the street in the dirty bazar and uncouth behaviour and no man thinks of another but schemes only for his money" [37].

The ravage caused by draught or by excessive and unreasonable rain leads the former to the brink of starvation so that he must sell his possessions like vessels and clothes to pay the rent. In security and privation, however harrowing by themselves are not the greatest calamities suffered by the landless farmer. When the land he tills is taken away from him so that he is forced to leave the village it is the ultimate in social inequality and economic disparity that has arisen out of the western system of intermediary landholders. Rukmani and Nathan are forced to break stones in the quarry outsides the city on the advice of Puli. They know nothing of this job and can only make a pittance.

Nectar in a Sieve, a touching tragic tale though compared to Pearl S. Buck's *The Good Earth* and Alan Paton's *Cry, the Beloved Country*, has according to K.R. Srinivas Iyengar, "a nearer and apter analogy" with K.V. Venkatramani's *Murugan, the Tiller*. Finally, they are evicted from the land. Wang Lang, of *The Good Earth* and Murugan of *Murugan, the Tiller* are as devoted and attached to their land as Nathan is in *Nectar in a Sieve*. Olan in assistance to her husband Wang Lang and Sita in *Murugan the Tiller* though a widow are seen to face the same circumstances as our Rukmani of *Nectar in a Sieve*.

India's grinding poverty affects the Western people most of all though it is the West that is in many ways responsible for it. Even Kenny tells Rukmani that he would return to his country when tired of India's follies and stupidities, 'Your eternal shameful poverty.' One of these stupidities is the social structure in India.

Iyengar remarks, "if *Nectar in a Sieve* recalls Venkatramani's *Murugan, the Tiller*, Markandaya's *Some Inner*

Fury recalls his *Kandan the Patriot*. Where Venkatramani is poetical and masculine, Markandaya is suggestive and feminine. If her writing is less rich in imagery, it has more ease and partakes more of life's fitful fever."[4] But, of course there is a world of difference between Rukmani and Mira, the heroine of *Some Inner Fury*. Mira is a creature of imagination and memory, and her naturalness, and sophistication are in uneasy partnership. Flushed with a new sense of independence, and provoked by constant humiliation and repression, rises against both foreign domination and parental tutelage. She falls in love with the Governor's Military aide Richard Marlowe. Despite her mother's admonition that "it is not right for a young woman to go among young men. Mira over looks and ignores all social taboos inhibitions. She goes with her lover on a long pre-marital honeymoon. Only political and national barren under the relationship to divide them into"[5] [51]. your people and my people. Almost as in a typical Hardy novel, intensifies clash and malignant forces are let loose. Mira quietly retires with her ghostly memories and from time to time the slow pain comes "seeping up, filling up my throat with grief, flowing from throat to temple" [52].

Roshan Merchant is another such emancipated young lady, Oxford-educated and divorced. She too is torn between the cultural and social demands of East-West orthodoxy. "Born in one world, educated in another. She moved in both worlds with ease and non-chalance [68]. She went to dances and parties and both Englishmen and Indians were eager to partner her. Mira and Roshan are members of a newly emergent society in which young-men in Western clothes and English accents...flaunted their unorthodox and a few girls with shingled hair and advanced views aired them" [91]. When Kitsamy returns from Oxford, "still in the hold of Western culture" [93], its brazen ways, its painted women and its easy morality. He is engaged to a girl of his mother's choice. With a heavy heart he tries to forget the English girl he loved. Premala is let loose till he capitulates willingly. Premala's mother explains that the novelist, "readily understood the need for this strange new pattern of courtship, deplorable no doubt, but what the times demanded" [97]. The marriage is solemnized with the customary, ostentation. Premala appeals to Mira's mother for such a marriage, partly because she is traditioal in many ways. Unlike the emancipated Mira, she prefers to sit at Kit's feet and feels a little uncomfortable in the house that Kit has done up in the western style. His parent's home was equipped to cope with both the Europeans and the Indians, with "two dining rooms, two kitchens even tow sets of servants" [81]. She misses her home and Dodamma, who had shorn head and wore no blouse under her sari but contributed to the housekeeping by supervising the servants. When Kit's foster-brother Govind comes suddenly on an evening, Premala is joyous and welcomes him in the traditional way of home coming with a tray laden with small cup of curd, fruit nuts and sliced copra. Only the betel leaves were missing. Even the westernized Kit had missed. "Our food...I've only just realised how much" [92].

A Silence of Desire explores the theme of the clash between traditionalism and modernism, between faith and reason represented by Sarojini and Dandekar who form a married couple in the novel. "Her religious tutelage had been rather more earnest than his own and often had answers to the conundrums which his less amiable, non-Hindu friends set him not of course that she would supply them, until he had indicated that perhaps, she might"[6] [120]. He was more disturbed by the fact that Sarojini is bound up in socio-cultural beliefs that imply reposing faith in a Swamy for her cure. That Rajam herself was cured by the Swamy, comes as a shock to him. Sarojini tells him : "I do not expect you to understand. You with your western notions, your superior talk of ignorance and superstition when all it means is that you don't know what lies beyond reason and you prefer not to find out" [35]. The influence of western culture is keenly seen in the office. There is Joseph who believed in "first love and was even said to practise it" [23].

If beggars, prostitutes and peasants symbolise the economic backwardness of the nation, the Swamis are the spokesmen of traditional values. In *Possession*[7] the Swamy and Caroline represent tow divergent approaches to life, the spiritual (*i.e.*, oriental) the material (western) but the Swamy is shown also as capable of understanding the historical forces and his voice is the voice of wisdom and Uma Parmeshwaran says : "This Swamy is a 'charlatan' whereas that of *A Silence of Desire* is a genuine nuptic. Anasuya the narrator of the novel is a writer and friend of caroline and Valmiki. Valmiki a goat-herd who paints amateurishly but attracts her attention"[8] [95]. After taking the blessings from the Swamy, Valmiki leaves for England, but there he seems to find no source of inspiration, Valmiki grows up in Caroline's house tended by the Indian Tamil cook and the English housekeeper Mrs. Peabody. In Mrs. Peabody's opinion "the Indian cook didn't know where to start never having the habit of work"[9] [97]. When the Indian cook refuses the invitation of Mrs. Peabody she takes it as an insult. Anasuya explains his role he "padded...unobtrusively...all without a record glance at me, in the tradition that his caste of mine both acquiesced in" [97]. Gradually Valmiki becomes westernised; he kisses Anasuya on the cheeks when earlier he had compared her to his sister brought her "Parijata" flowers. Now his inspiration of painting is not spiritualism but the western aesthetic beauty. The Swamy's visit to England, at the invitation of his English disciples, revitalize the cords of culture.

Caroline too cannot pull herself away completely from her social superiority and continues making fun of the Indian sense of punctuality "the oriental's wish to finger every pie" to never go whole-hog-sings its bristles but never do it in. *A Handful of Rice* portrays the socio-cultural economic class very vividly. Once again Markandaya gives a picture of the Indian village where people "lived between bouts of gentle and acute poverty the kind in which the weakest went to the walls the old ones and the babies dying of tuberculosis dysentery the falling fever, recurrent fever and any other names for what was basically simply nothing but starvation"[10][220]. In the city, life for the poor is no different but no one complains not even Nalini. She says people of their kind can never be rich the memsahib who had a lot of clothes stitched in India because "things were so cheap here...knows she would never be able to afford so many clothes once she leaves India" [209]. She had no sympathy for the workman who made this possible. She has no sympathy for Ravi for the delay in delivering the clothes due to Appu's death. Ravi is shocked at her callousness : "Did this women realise how they lived? In her community did they simply carry straight after a death as if nothing happened"?[39]. Marriages in India are not found on love. Jayamma was much younger than Appu she did not love him but she nursed him devotedly as a wife should out of a strong sense of duty [169].

In *The Coffer Dams*, the conflict is in real encounter between Indian and English engineers. The small British colony includes Helen, who is Clinton's wife and Millie Rawlings, the Chief Engineer's wife. There were few occasions when they met socially and when the neutral Englishmen like Helen and Leferve did, the others raged agaisnt them. The Rawlings were appalled to see Leferve bring Gopal Rao as a companion to their dinner. Look what the lad's brought in, "cried Millie Rawlings though her husband asked her not to make a scene, and very cleverly refused to shake hands with Gopal Rao"[148]. Helen is different. She is drawn towards Bashiam when she assures him "Look at me I've never been a memsahib. You are not some kind of freak to me. We're alike. We're freaks only to the caste we come from, not to each other"[180]. Regarding the dead bodies Clinton says "their bodies can be incorporated into the structure" [182]. But the tribal do not consent saying "until the bodies of our dead are returned to us so that the rites may be correctly performed and their soul depart in peace. Krishnan joins their demands and Helen is also with them. When Bashiam barely escapes death, Helen is shocked and charges her husband for it."

In *The Nowhere Man* the cultural ties of the east cannot be sundered easily by the expatriate Srinivas and his wife. Vasantha is stunned to know about the marriage of her son to an English girl, that she stands outside too shocked to move. The English lady unused to open emotions reflects. "The way these Indians went to pieces. Different from one's own kind who would close the door and pull down the blind decently, not stand above letting the whole world see"[11] [52]. Vasantha's son is embarrassed by his mother who sticks to Indiness to such an extent that she sticks out. "Like a sore thumb when a son is born to him he specifically asks his mother not to come, not even if she is ready to sleep on the ground in the kitchen. He says so because they don't do things like that in this country." *Two Virgins* has the theme of adolescence and growing up, of love and conflict between parents and children, of contrasts between village and city.[12] The emphasis is laid on the change in the rural life brought about by the modern hedonistic civilisation in the country after independence. The changes are perceived through the eyes of Saroja, the village girl and the her sister, Lalitha of the city. Markandaya has drawn the consequences of the western influence that has ruined Indian traditional society and the social evils of this tradition that impeded its progress, but Nissim Ezekiel says that an "Indian writer living permanently abroad cannot always be trusted to write knowingly about." The two virgins lived with Appa, Amma and Aunt Alemalu. She had no husband and therefore no status when Appa says joint family is an anachronism aunt says "just tell me to go I will, I know have out lived my usefulness....I am only a widow, less than the dust so do not torment yourself about my fate"[18]. In the monkey incident Chingleput tells Saroja "it ought to have left to die as its mother intended when she abandoned it because the tribe would never accept a cripple"[205]. The Golden Honeycomb is once more the problems of socio-cultural adjustments of the East and West. Humanity is all but gets split up by externals into different water-tight compartments and that can be diffused only with love and understanding. The Brahmin Minister did not enter the birth chamber at the birth of the prince because it was unclean and did so only after purification. The Dewan's wife Vatsala did not allow the Resident to defile her household. When he did so, he had to walk in his stockinged feet. After he had drunk from a silver goblet Vatsala had it melted down to purify it. The Dowager Maharani's widowhood is given a detailed description to familiarize an audience ignorant of it. Bawajiraj II's flirtations with Mohini, her being pregnant with his child are viewed with a moral disgust by the British. Bawajiraj's wife Shanta Devi lives a life apart from her husband reconciled to the belief that "she must submit to men in general and her husband in particular". The wife did not take her husband's name as Vatsala did not and even Rukmani in Nectar in a Sieve did not.

Markandaya seems to be troubled by the division in humanity. Her stories acquire a lasting value which flowers from their tragic vision. She seems committed to the belief that wrongs must be righted. In so far as there is latent optimism, the solutions are possible. Her novels amply exhibit her commitment to the social values of one's roots. One exists as long as one's roots are intact. Nathan dies when he is evicted from his land but Rukmani struggles successfully because her roots are in her children.

Premala in *Some Inner Fury* dies when her roots are scorched, when she is taken away from her traditional way of life and asked to be a society lady. Similarly, Sarojini in *A Silence of Desire* survives the Western onslaught because she is rooted in the primitive pantheism. On the whole Kamala Markandaya appears to be a rational feminist with her roots in the cultural ethos of India.

REFERENCES

1. Madhusudan Prasad, *Perspectives on Kamala Markandaya*, Ghaziabad.

2. Rekha Jha, *The Novels of Kamala Markandaya and Ruth Jhabvala : A Study in East-West Encounter*, Prestige Books, New Delhi.
3. Kamala Markandaya, *Nectar in a Sieve*, Sagar Publication, New Delhi.
4. K.R. Srinivas Iyengar, *Indian Writing in English,* Sterling, New Delhi, 1989, p. 439.
5. Kamala Markandaya, *Some Inner Fury*, London, 1957.
6. Kamala Markandaya, *A Silence of Desire*, London, 1961.
7. Uma Permeshwaran, *A Study of Representative Indo-English Novelists* (*Native, aliens expatriates*), New Delhi, 1976.
8. Kamala Markandaya, *Possession*, Jaico, New Delhi.
9. Kamala Markandaya, *A Handful of Rice*, Delhi, 1966.
10. Kamala Markandaya, *The Coffer Dams,* Delhi, 1969.
11. Kamala Markandaya, *The Nowhere Man*, London, 1973.
12. Kamala Markandaya, *Two Virgins*, Vikas Publication, New Delhi.

13

Images in Sarojini Naidu's Poetry

—Ashok Kumar Bachchan

Sarojini Naidu is a poet of keen sensibility and rich imagination and her poetry offers a delightful feast of similes and metaphors. Her images are usually impressive and impressionistic; they are also varied and sublime. She draws her lovely images mostly from the world of nature and the fairy kingdoms; but her images drawn from the native sources, from the myth, legend and folk life are no less captivating. The images are delicate, sensuous and romantic. Her imagery is highly influenced by P.B. Shelley, John Keats, early Yeats and Rabindranath Tagore.

Sarojini Naidu is greatly influenced by Omar Khayyam and other Persian poets because she spent her early formative years in a stimulating Muslim city like Hyderabad. She shows her keen interest in taking some lively images from Muslim life and culture and the Islamic world. Most of her poems have been composed in her youthful period. Thus they are always aglow with her vigorous imagination and youthful fancy. Her poetry is naturally marked by a freshness of imagination which transforms common objects of nature and human life into something miraculously fresh and uncommon. She expresses her feelings through sensuous imagery which is usually highly imaginative and suggestive. Not only are her sense perceptions quick and alert, she also has a rare gift of communicating these perceptions by vivid, picturesque and sensuous imagery. V.S. Narvane comments on the Indian character of her imagery :

> However, the strongest feature of Sarojini's poetry is her vivid imagery, her most memorable lines are those in which she has presented beautiful and graphic pictures by fusing together several visual impressions. It should be stressed, once again, that these images can be appreciated only by those who have retained their sensitivity to the subtle stimuli which come from the Indian environment, and who still have a feeling for aspects of Indian life now rarely experienced in our modern cities.[1]

Coromandel Fishers is a realistic lyric which depicts the happy, busy life of the fishers who go out with the morning light. The feeling of love and brotherhood and the fishermen's attachment with the sea is supported and reinforced by the imagery of protected childhood. The symbolism of morning light lends authenticity to the sense. Here one finds simile, metaphor and image — all in one. The wind howling all night is the child crying all night and the child lying quiet asleep in the arms of his mother is the wind silent at dawn.

The sensuous, romantic imagery in the following lines is quite appealing :

> Sweet is the shade of the coconut glade, and
> the scent of the mango grove,
> And sweet are the sands at the full o' the
> moon with the sound of the voices we love.
> But sweeter, O brothers, the kiss of the spray and
> the dance of the wild foam's glee;
> Row, brothers, row to the blue of the verge,
> Where the low sky mates with the sea.[2] (pp. 6-7)

The impact of Wordsworth can be felt distinctly on the imagery. The image of 'the dance of the wild foam's glee' is reminiscent of Wordsworth's golden daffodils. 'The waves behind them danced, but they/outdid the sparkling waves in glee....[3] There is another startling image in 'blue of the verge, where the low sky mates with the sea.' Sea is a dream to the fishermen, a dream they must pursue afresh everyday.

Palanquin Bearers is a simple folk song, portraying the picture of a vanished aspect of rural life. In the shelleyon style the poet has compared the noble lady inside the palanquin to a number of objects :

> Lightly, O lightly, we bear her along,
> She sways like a flower in the wind of our song;
> She skims like a bird on the foam of a stream,
> She floats like a laugh from the lips of a dream.
> Gaily, O gaily, we glide and we sing,
> We bear her along like a pearl on a string. (p. 3)

The lady 'sways like a flower,' 'skims like a bird,' 'floats like a laugh' and the palanquin bearers bear her along 'like a pearl on a string.' Again, the bride :

> 'hangs like a star in the dew of our song;
> She springs like a beam on the brow of the tide,
> She falls like a tear from the eyes of a bride.' (p. 3)

Here we find both concrete and abstract images. There are vivid and concrete images executed with gnomic terseness like skimming on the foam of a stream, a beam springing on the brow of the tide and tears falling from the eyes of a bride. There are also some vague images in the manner of the pre-Raphaelites, like laughter from the lips of a dream, swinging like a flower in the wind of a song. 'Swinging,' 'hanging,' 'springing' and 'falling' are good kinetic images in themselves. The image 'She falls like a tear from the eyes of a bride' is highly imaginative and suggestive. Cousins does not find any thought in the poem but is impressed by its imagery and romantic setting. He comments that the poem 'is without slightest suspicion of literature, yet its charm is instantaneous and complete.'[4] The images indicate a lightness of touch, a buoyancy, and create a dream-like atmosphere.

In *Indian Love Song* Sarojini Naidu introduces impressionistic images. The lover's eagerness for complete identification with each other has been beautifully expressed through a series of romantic images. The sensuous and the subtle seem to be mingling in the image :

> 'Like a serpent to the calling voice of flutes,
> Glides my heart into thy fingers, O my love!' (p. 16)

The second stanza offers a bunch of a similes. The lover expresses his complete absorption in love :

> Like the perfume in the petals of a rose,
> Hides that heart within my bosom, O my love!
> Like a garland, like a jewel, like a dove
> That hangs its nest in the asoka-tree. (p. 16)

The beloved's heart is hidden in the lover's bosom 'like perfume in the petals of a rose', 'like a garland, like a jewel, like a dove' (p. 16). The concluding lines have a lovely impressionistic image :

> Lie still, O love, until the morning sows
> Her tents of gold on fields of ivory. (p. 16)

In praise of Gulmohur Blossoms' besides visual images like 'the glimmering red of a bridal robe' and 'rich red of a wild bird's wing' there is a suggestive image in 'the mystic blaze of the gem that burns/on the brow of a serpent king' (p. 94) which gains richness from Oriental sources.

The second stanza offers a lovely image which is concrete as well as typically Indian in character :

> Or the blood that poured from a thousand breasts
> To succour a Rajput queen? (p. 94)

But the most suggestive image appears in the concluding lines where the rich hue of the gulmohur blossoms is compared with the light that leaps from the funeral pyre of a true, devoted wife.

In *Golden Cassia* the string of metaphors picturise the flowers in their exotic splendour.

The poet finds that they are more than mere woodland flowers scattered on the way. They have been compared with various objects. They are like 'some new-fallen star,' 'or golden lamps for a fairy shrine' (p. 96). In this poem Sarojini Naidu conceives of spring as a woman wearing anklet in her feet. The image of bright anklet-bells from a maiden's feet is startling. The mixed feeling of joy and pain of the Indian bride is imaged suggestively in 'or the gleaming tears that some fair bride shed/Remembering her lost maidenhead' (p. 96).

In *Vasant Panchami* the poet employs natural imagery to intensify the effect and enhance the thematic appeal. The poem has a native flavour and is written in the vein of Hindi poetry. The young widow's grief stricken heart is 'like sorrow-trodden grass' (p. 91) Her dark and dry life is like a 'fallen flower' and faded leaf (p. 91).

In *The Water Hyacinth* epithets are piled up to describe the alluring beauty of the flower. The poem maintains a sort of aesthetic balance between soft surfaces of nature and the harsh realities of life. The destructive principle of nature inherent in the flower is compared to cruel fate which wrecks human life. The image of 'winged insidious fate' is startling. A powerful sense of morality which pervades everything on earth is aptly symbolized by the dense spread of the flower on the surface of water. The struggle for existence is dramatically symbolized.

June Sunset reflects the poet's fascination for nature. Sarojini Naidu traces out the sunset scene at different levels. The second stanza offers a lovely kinetic image of a gentian pushing through a wet earth and then a metaphor also in the foot of the shower passing through the fields. The effect is gained by the use of concrete imagery :

A brown quail cries from the tamarisk bushes,
A bulbul calls from the cassia-plume,
And thro' the wet earth the gentian pushes
Her spikes of silvery bloom.

> Where'er the foot of the bright shower passes
> Fragrant and fresh delights unfold. (p. 192)

The poem *Autumn Song* begins with a suggestive image of sunset hanging on a cloud like a joy on the heart of sorrow:

> 'Like a joy on the heart of a sorrow,
> The sunset hangs on a cloud.' (p. 23)

The poem ends with a simile. The poet, in her sad and melancholy mood finds her dream shattering like fluttering pale autumn leaves :

> My heart is weary and sad and alone,
> For its dreams like the fluttering leaves have gone. (p. 23)

In *Night Fall in the City of Hyderabad* the image employed are precise and evocative. The splendour and beauty of the royal city is captured by the natural imagery :

> See how the speckled sky burns like a pigeon's throat,
> Jewelled with embers of opal and peridote.
> See the white river that flashes and scintillates,
> curved like a tusk from the mouth of the city-gates. (p. 55)

The image of the star-studded sky burning like a pigeon's throat is picturesque and romantic. The sky at night fall in the city burns like a pigeon's throat; perhaps like the thought of a bride whose throat quivers with glittering ornaments. Another evocative image appears in the concluding lines where night is imaged as the majestic arrival of a queen :

> Over the city bridge Night comes majestical,
> Borne like a queen to a sumptuous festival. (p. 56)

Leili is a nature poem with a Muslim theme but Hindu ethos. Leili is a Persian word for night. The first stanza suggests the approach of night through concrete events and images namely, 'The serpents are asleep among the poppies' (p. 31) poppies, which have associations with sleep and dreams; the fireflies, who would be visible only during night, lighting the panther's way; (p. 31) the introduction for the panther's way the epithet 'soundless', and the interjection 'o soft!' (p. 31) by the lotus buds stirring upon the stream like dreaming maidens. The natural imagery employed here beautifully sets the scene of night's quietude. In the second stanza the image of moon shining as a castemark on the brow of Heaven is a great achievement in itself. Cousins responds rapturously to this caste-mark image and observes :

> The figuring of the moon as a castemark on the forehead of heaven is itself a unique achievement of the imagination in poetry in the English language. It lifts India to the literary heavens : it threatens the throne of Diana (the goddess of moon in the Roman mythology) of the classics; it releases Luna (another name for the goddess Moon) from the work of asylum keeper (Luna is associated with lunacy madness), and gives her instead the office of remembrancer to Earth that the Divine is imprinted on the open face of nature.[5]

In *Life* Sarojini Naidu employs vivid, concrete images to set the children's innocent world of colour and fantasy. In childhood, life is full of rosy dream; it is like 'a lovely stalactite of dreams' (p. 35). The image of life as a lovely stalactite is highly suggestive of children's world of careless joy. There is a kinetic image also. The morning is suggested beautifully by the image of the sea billows leaping in the 'flames of amber and of amethyst' (p. 35). It is morning time, hence, one can easily imagine a play of colours on the leaping waves. Both the images build up the children's world of joy and dreams.

Past and Future has a different echo of Tennyson on its imagery. The poem offers a memorable image. The past has been visualized as a mountain cell where old hermit-memories dwell in consecrated claim :

> The new hath come and now the old retries.
> And so the past becomes a mountain-cell,

Where lone, apart, old hermit-memories dwell
In consecrated calm, forgotten yet.
Of the keen heart that hastens to forget
Old longings in fulfilling new desires. (p. 34)

These lines are reminiscent of Tennyson's lines in *Morte D' Arthur* :

The old order changeth, yielding place to new
And God fulfills Himself in many ways,
Lest one good custom should corrupt the world.[6]

Future is unknown and uncertain, hence it is aptly imaged as a timid person :

And now the Soul stands in a vague, intense
Expectancy and anguish of suspense,
On the dim chamber-threshold...lo ! he sees
Like a strange, fated bride as yet unknown,
His timid future shrinking there alone,
Beneath her marriage-veil of mysteries (p. 34).

The poem, *The Snake Charmer* is nothing but a catalogue of images put together. Sarojini Naidu captures the folk spirit by employing images drawn from the world of nature. The charmer wooes his pet as his bride or fiance with love and concern. The snake emerges from its hide-outs in nature like a bride. The imagery is powerful, for it combines the natural, humane and personal worlds without any sense of interference. The poem attains tremendous appeal due to its lovely images and romantic setting. The images like the 'moonlight-tangled meshes of perfume' (p. 8) and 'clustering *keoras* guard the squirrel's slumber' (p. 8) are typically romantic. The concluding stanza has a very suggestive image, the snake is subtle bride and 'silver-breasted moonbeam of desire' (p. 8). The image sets up a folk scene where the Charmer treats his pet with love and reverence.

It is hard to forget the delight of the intensely sensuous imagery of *Indian Dancers*. The poet recreates the scene with the visuals and rhythmic movements of Indian dancers while dancing. The sensory and kinetic images evoke the cosmological principle underlying the pattern of Indian dance.

The poem *Invincible* deals with concrete images. The image of life being crushed like broken grain between the grinding stones of pain is quite tough and realistic. Sarojini Naidu challenges fate :

> O fate, betwixt the grinding-stones of Pain,
> Tho' you have crushed my life like broken grain.
> (p. 174)

The second stanza presents a beautiful image of soul reblossoming like a grove :

> Tho' in the flame of Sorrow you have thrust
> My flowering soul and trod it into dust,
> Behold, it doth reblossom like a grove
> To shelter under quickening boughs of Love. (p. 174)

In Salutation to the Eternal Peace contains some highly evocative and picturesque image. The image of 'life's ripening harvest-fields' which falls within Time's bending sickle's compass is highly suggestive :

> Men say the world is full of fear and hate,
> And all life's ripening harvest-fields await
> The restless sickle of relentless fate. (p. 137)

There are some lovely picturesque images which are highly suggestive also :

> 'When from the climbing terraces of corn
> I watch the golden orioles of Thy morn' (p. 137)

And 'who know the silver wings that gleam and glide,/The homing pigeons of Thine eventide?' (p. 137). There is yet another equally evocative image, 'who dream in twilight granaries thou dost bless/with delicate sheaves of mellow silences?' (p. 137).

Alabaster is a fine metaphor for the poet's heart itself. Her heart is always full of dreams and songs, and it is treasured countless sweet and bitter memories of her life.

Sarojini Naidu's love poems are full of romantic imagery. *The Dance of Love* speaks of the ecstasy and pain in the heart of the lovers. The sweet music and the subtle stepping of dance wake in their heart both the ecstasy and pain of love. The passionate world of lovers with their strange aches and ecstasies has been appropriately supported by the sensuous imagery :

> The music sighs and slumbers,
> It stirs and sleeps again...
> Hush, it wakes and weeps and murmurs
> Like a woman's heart in pain;
> Now it laughs and calls and coaxes,
> Like a lover in the night.
> Now it pants with sudden longing
> Now it sobs with spent delight. (p. 73)

Humayun to Zubeida offers a number of images. Zubeida, the beloved haunts her lover's 'waking like a dream' (p. 22), his slumber 'like a moon,' (p. 22) and pervading him 'like a musky scent' (p. 22) and possessing him 'like a tune' (p. 22). Humayun, the lover, wishes to be possessed by his beloved. He expresses his feelings of love through a string of similes which throw up lovely images.

A Rajput Love Song is full of metaphors and lovely images. The lover has been separated by the dawn to meet again at night but the lover is not at all ready to be separated from her beloved only for a few hours. The beloved, Parvati, is not worried at all, for her love is always with her in the form of the 'basil-wreath' in her tresses, the jewelled golden bangle on her mind, the scent of the Keora in her clothes, the 'vermilion tassel' in her girdles, 'the scented fan' on her pillow and the 'sandal lute or silver lamp' (p. 80) in her shrine. She expresses her passionate longings of love through a chain of images, all drawn from a woman's delicate world. Amar Singh, the lover, replies in the same tone and style, only the images here are drawn from a warrior's world. He also feels the constant presence of his beloved in 'the hooded hawk' (p. 81) on his hand, the 'heronfeather' (p. 81) on his turban, the sword at his side, a shield against his enemies and amulet against life's perils.

Ecstasy is a fine love lyric which deals with the feeling of joy and pain. Here a simile illumines and turns into a vivid image. A beautiful flower 'smitten with rain' (p. 25) could be an apt image for a maiden's soul smitten by love.

In *The Temple* sequence of love poems, one notices both sensuous and sublime images. *Ecstasy* opens with a metaphor which turns into a glowing image. The lines recall a typical Indian valleys with rods of flowers is a fine kinetic image. Flower could be an apt metaphor for a lover. The maiden has got him and crushed the burning petals of his lips between hers. The sensuous image of the maiden crushing the burning petals of a 'miraculous flower' (p. 212) which stands for a lover, reminds one of Keats's equally sensuous lines :

> 'O for a beaker full of the warm south,
> full of the true blushful Hippocrane.
> With beaded bubbles winking at the brim,
> And purple stained mouth.'[7]

The second stanza visualizes spring unbinding the 'tresses of rich perfume/To lure the purple honey-bees to their enchanted death' (p. 212). Again a kinetic and sensuous image reminds us of Keats's lines :

> Thee sitting careless on a granary floor,
> Thy hair soft-lifted by the winnowing wind.[8]

In *Desire of Love* the maiden is willing to undergo any amount of suffering and sacrifice to instill into her beloved and 'immortal breath' (p. 216) and to fashion into a God. The metaphor of refashioning into God may appear vague to the Western readers unacquainted with Indian thought but it is quite appropriate in the Indian context and goes well with the Indian philosophical outlook.

In *The Offering* the maiden worships her love not only with her beauty and youth, but with her heart's deathless passion, love itself. There are lovely images : beauty is 'like a rare blossom to Love's glowing shrine' (p. 211), youth is like a pearl flung into 'Love's lustrous wine' (p. 211) and glory and fame are like camphor and curd to pour upon 'Love's bright and sacrificial flame' (p. 211). The image of camphor and curd may appear quaint and meaningless to the Western readers unfamiliar with the Indian mode of worship but it corresponds well with the Indian way of thinking.

Dr. James H. Cousins observes :

> 'To the untravelled western readers, 'Camphor' as a figure of speech will carry queer shades of meaning built up out of clothing and moths; and 'curds' will be flavorous only of dining rooms or convalescence. But one who has shared the offering substance of life to some power of the inner worlds, or who has passed his hands through the smoke from camphor, that burns to nothing in token of the participant's desire to be lost in the fame of the Divine, will find through such figures an entrance to the strongest place in the life of India, the place of religious devotion and the perpetual presence."[9]

There are some striking images in Sarojini Naidu's patriotic poems also. *The Gift of India* is a kind of homage to the heroic sons of India who sacrificed their lives in the First world war, fighting from the side of the Allies. They died unknown and unlamented on the foreign soil. There is a bunch of similes which throw up scintillating images : The dead bodies of the great sons of India were 'gathered like pearls' (p. 146) and consigned to 'alien graves' (p. 146). They live in oblivion like the shells scattered on Egyptian sands and again 'they are strewn like blossoms mown down by chance' (p. 146). The images instensify the thematic appeal of the poem.

In *To India*, the poet reminds the Mother India of her past glory and wishes her to emerge out from her gloom of slavery as a triumphant power. She employs here a sublime image of a bride begetting new glories from the ageless womb of time for the desired poetic effect :

Rise, Mother, rise, regenerate from thy gloom,
And, like a bride high-mated with the spheres,
Beget new glories from thine ageless womb! (p. 58)

Renunciation shows the poet's intense urge to serve her country. She appeals to her people to spread the fragrance of their great deeds not only in their country but in the whole of the world. The imagery is vivid, concrete and powerful. The image of carrier birds bearing message has roots in the native consciousness. Its use in English language is like a fresh breeze to the western readers.

An image in Sarojini Naidu's poetry stands for a whole range of experience and vision. *Champak Blossoms* of Sarojini Naidu, for example, has amber petals, ivory petals, petals of carven jade and they lure forests, fields and valleys with their sweetness. They are 'radiant blossom' that fling their champak blossoms involves the whole chain of experience, Sarojini Naidu's images are soft and delicate with feminine emphasis on colour and beauty.

Lotika Basu is severely critical of the adjectival and metaphorical excess in Sarojini Naidu's poetry. She comments:

> One gets rather tired of the brilliant metaphors and similes. Thy introduce an element of artificiality in her poems. It makes them as exotic that wither and die when compared to the natural simplicity and bare beauty of the work of the greatest artists. A few of her poems seems to be written only for the sake of her metaphors and similes.[10]

But Lotika Basu is rather indifferent to the great potentiality of Sarojini Naidu's handling of metaphors and similes as pictorial flocks of imagistic perception. Sarojini Naidu has discovered a novel way of organizing poetic emotion which led to *chhayabad* in modern Indian poetry. The critic fails to see the historical compulsions behind the Indian writer's work.

Sarojini Naidu's image confirms the fact that she is a poet of high poetic sensibility and imagination. Her poetry may not reflect seriously on life's intricacies but she definitely makes the scenes look real in colours and tunes, and they bespeak for her extraordinary range of imagery. A post-modernist may regard her imagery merely fanciful when he forgets that she is a free singer.

REFERENCES

1. V.S. Narvane, *Sarojini Naidu* (Orient Longmans, New Delhi, 1980), p. 139.
2. Sarojini Naidu, *The Sceptred Flute* : Songs of India (Kitabistan, Allahabad, 1969), pp. 6-7.

   (All other page references in parentheses are from this edition).
3. Mark Van Doren (ed.) *Wordsworth Selected Poetry* (1950). Modern Library College Edition (New York), Paperback, p. 494.
4. James H. Cousins, *The Renaissance in India* (Ganesh and Co., Madras, 1918), pp. 259-60.
5. Cousins, *op. cit.,* p. 265.
6. Douglas Bush (ed.), *The Selected Poetry of Tennyson,* (The Modern Library, New York, 1951), p. 320.
7. H.W. Garrod (ed.), *The Poetical Works of John Keats,* (Oxford University Press, London, 1956), p. 207.
8. *Ibid.,* p. 219.
9. Cousins, *op. cit.,* p. 256.
10. Lotika Basu, *Indian Writers of English Verse* (Calcutta University Press, Calcutta, 1933), p. 93.

14

Myth and Reality of Values in Kamala Das's Poetry

—*J.K. Nair*

Art and literature are born out of polarities in personal impulses and social values. Social values, ironically, has a mask of human progress, but they do not always offer a strategy for creative development to the individual members, but rather would insist on the perpetuation of society's rigid notions on enlightenment and progress. We are travelling in time on the wheels of a civilization that has always endeavoured to impose a sort of discriminative value systems on its peoples. If so, values have two different faces; one, the vital ingredients for an ideal human society, and the other a sort of deceitful, discriminative and double-edged set of laws tacitly operating within a given social set up. When the individual comes head-on with the latter, there arise conflicts within and without. Art and literature are products of such conflicts within the creative minds. "Creation presumes uninterrupted tension between form and matter, between evolution and the mind and between history and values" (Camus 238). In the modern Indo-English feminist literature, particularly fiction and poetry, more fiercely than in any other literature of the world, is manifested this tension 'between history and values.'

The most characteristic feature of modern feminist literature is the pervading sense of alienation, an estrangement from the mainstream of history and civilization. This sense of alienation is certainly not a product of feminist imagination, but rather the result of a historical, civilizational and literary abandonment of women and their activities. The women protagonists of the modern feminist novels and poetry are mouthpieces of Indian woman who often mock at the dichotomized and biased human culture.

The gender inequities are no associated with any particular civilization. This evil has travelled down from the primordial period to our times. Since human civilization itself has evolved incessantly ignoring the vital half of its race, *i.e.*, women, the concerns voiced in the modern feminist writings are as relevant and momentous as the question of man's existence itself. This fact has prompted Helen Cixous to say : "If women were to set themselves to transform History, it can safely be said that every aspect of History would be completely altered" (487). The marginalization of this 'better half' by generations together is in fact head-on with the Nature's blue print of evolution; Nature trusts femininity and bestows on it the maximum responsibility of advancing evolution towards progressive directions. Moreover, human society is founded on the gregarious instinct of man as a creature; and each component of the human social set up is theoretically cemented together by the ingredient of love, and love is predominantly a female instinct. This precious and unique phenomenon of femininity in Nature manifests itself in the form of unrestrained maternal charities, catered to all and sundry equanimously. Nevertheless, since the dawn of civilization, the male principle has been overacting itself as a phenomenal exploiter and sabotager of the female principle at all practical counters. Elaine Showalter aptly recalls a passage from Gerda Lerner on women's experience "in its own terms." Says Lerner :

> Women have been left out of history not because of the evil conspiracies of men in general or male historians in particular, but because we have considered history only in male centred terms. We

> have missed women and their activities, because we have asked questions of history, which are inappropriate to women.... (470).

Though in the West feminism grew as an ideology alongside the concept of Renaissance humanism, it emerged as a literary theory at a later stage. In fact the very bricks for the foundation of modern feminist literature were laid by the writings of Simon de Beauvoir in France and Virginia Woolf in England. In the hands of these amazing women personalities, the feminist cause that was hitherto only a movement has been elevated to aesthetic heights.

These revolutionary upheavals on the other part of the world notwithstanding, the Indian women still had little opportunity to board the train of the modern feminist thinkers, mainly due to the sophisticated nature of Indian social set up. In a rigid social structure like India's, revolting against any accepted values would mean risking an existential conflict with the society as a whole. Thus, with the awareness of the comparatively freer existence of women on the other side of the globe, Indian women felt themselves to be like caged animals. And the partly emancipated women of the West functioned as teasers for these 'caged animals.' To break the stronger social bars around themselves than those around their Western counterparts, women needed extra energy and intrepidity in the Indian context.

It is only in the middle of the twentieth century, more precisely after the advent of Independence in 1947 in India, there emerged a prominent cultural awakening demanding the recognition of the feminist niceties and prerogatives, both in the social and naturalistic parameters. As a result of the spread of learning and awareness in the post-Independence era, particularly after the sixties, Indian feminist writings in English abundantly revealed a hitherto unknown Indian feminine psyche. Veena Noble Dass evaluates this awakening among Indian women writers in the following words :

> Very often these works do not offer a tangible solution for the feminist. But the experiences rendered through the feminine consciousness invariably point to an inner exhilaration suggesting the beginning of fresh awakening, a much sought-after precept of the feminists. Indian English Fiction, Poetry, and Drama are replete with the male-female confrontation, problems of adolescence, and coming of age, with special reference to women, explicit and latent pleadings for equality, liberty and self-preservation, even risking the normal safeguarding of hallowed tradition (11-12).

In so far as the novel is concerned there are many names to reckon with in this context. But the advancement has not been so rapid in other genres of Indian writings in English including poetry. Kamala Das is a loner in poetry. She plays a very significant role in making the feminist concerns and points of view violently clarified and made transparent through her poetry. In this context, no feminist revolutionaries, more particularly in the Indo-Anglian poetry, is as important as Kamala Das. In the words of Sunanda P. Chavan : "Kamala Das embodies the most significant stage of development of Indian feminine poetic sensibility not yet reached by her contemporaries" (60). In fact no Indian woman poet, other than Das, has ever dared to stretch her "two-dimensional/Nudity on sheets of weeklies, monthlies/Quarterlies, a sad sacrifice" (Loud Posters, OP, 47).

As a poet, Kamala Das successfully poetizes the modern Indian feminist violence and rebellion in accordance with the celebrities of the twentieth century Western women's liberation movement, like Simon De Beauvoir and Virginia Woolf. In the context of modern India, hers is a unique poetic innovation and experiment of superimposing the violent and revolutionary ideas of the Western women's liberation movement upon the Indian women's world of rigid and unbending traditions. Her entire poetic property has since been an evidence of her unique personal temper and temperament, and stands to prove that given the opportunity of freedom and transparency in thought and action, Indian woman too can break the 'Bell Jar' (to borrow the expression of Sylvia Plath), and come out of the seemingly unassertive and submissive calm and quietude of her world, and go hand in hand with her Western counterparts in aspiring and exacting for a dignified status for women rather than putting up with the humiliations of sexual expatiations and subservience that they are subjected to in the Indian social milieu.

In the characteristically unrelenting Indian socio-cultural milieu, where any surface commotion does not percolate very easily, particularly when it is against traditions and conventions, Kamala Das makes a poetic revolt by way of introspectively pondering upon the unfortunate state of existence in which Indian women conduct themselves. Like a seasoned artist, she penetrates her imaginative insight to sympathetically understand the possible average grievances of the Indian woman as extremely exploited agent in the social, ethical, moral, and existential circumstances.

No traditional Indian woman-poet, Kamala Das felt, has ever endeavoured to question the legitimacy of their own fosterage as social beings. They wrote a kind of poetry that has customarily tried to lure their own class to the feet of man-made gods or man-gods. In Das's own words :

> The prescribed themes for women's writings were God and domestic bliss. Nothing else. This body, this physicality was to be ignored. We had Avvayyar, Mirabai, but they wrote of God, they sang of God. That was allowed. But what happens to you, what happens to a woman, when a man becomes her god, her living god? Has she no right to write about that god? (My Instinct...156).

In fact the whole poetic rebellion in Kamala Das is just a way of recording her protest against a culture that has rendered both man and woman into mutual non-entities in being life-partners. The man-made institutions constantly and continuously rendered woman into an utter dependent agent on man as a result of the male-oriented social systems. Women gradually got conditioned to the strategically proposed systems and traditions. Kamala Das's poetry, with its absolute transparencies of what it means by being a woman, particularly as a life partner, creates in man a sort of stirring sensibility. In her poem *The Old Playhouse* she expresses this *angst* very powerfully. Says she :

...You called me wife,
I was taught to break saccharine into your tea and
To offer at the right moment the vitamins. Cowering
Beneath your monstrous ego I ate the magic loaf and
Became a dwarf.... (OP, 1).

The expression 'You called me wife' hints at the very mechanical nature of the interpersonal relations between the woman persona and her man. It is only under a social compulsion that the relationship stands, and nothing transpires between the two hearts. Also 'Cowering/Beneath' man's 'monstrous ego' woman has been eating the 'magic loaf' right from the dawn of civilization and has remained a 'dwarf' historically. It is the collective psyche of women speaking out from a sudden awakening. If so, Kamala Das's real rebellion is against a social conspiracy in which humanity has been divided into many a social strata thus fulfilling history's ultimate and insidious 'divide and rule' purpose.

No other voice in Indian literature could ever revolt with such tribal fury and violence as has been sounded in Das's poems against traditions and conventions. She has daringly defied the phallus with such expressions as :

Woman, is this happiness, this lying buried
Beneath a man? It's time again to come alive,
The world extends a lot beyond his six foot frame.
(Conflagration, D, 20)

She is here vibrantly declaring her inner most feeling that the six foot male-frame is not only insufficient for her aspirations, but also incapable of subjugating her identity which, she feels, is as profound and mysterious as Nature itself. In a sense she wants to suggest that man can neither control, nor fulfil her personal needs of identity as a woman and as a creative principle. In the naturalistic context male principle is a mediate phenomenon, and the female principle is the immediate base. It is her umbilical association and relation with the created beings that makes woman comparatively superior to man.

The modern poetic counterparts of Das have established their own places in the Indo-Anglian poetic milieu, but the exclusiveness of Das's poetic arguments lies in the fact that none of her contemporary poets, male or female, has shown the courage to directly assault the traditions, and question the legitimacy of culture and its antecedents. Ironically, they more or less display a tacit acceptance of these human institutions (not humane attributes), and their poetry emerges out of their concern over the symptoms of decadence of culture. Kamala Das, on the other hand, confronts like a rebel with the glorified nastiness of the so-called human culture and civilization. In her poem *Ode To Lynx* she says :

> "Civilization irks me with its cunning ways
> I connect only with candour."
>
> (CP, 88)

To her the entire gamut of the history of human civilization and progress looks like a grotesque edifice of Gothic horrors. This denunciation, this defiance of human advance and progress, finds expression in her poem *Daughter of the Century* wherein she says :

> We ate our forefathers
> To gather the vigour for living.
> Our grandchildren shall perhaps eat us
> When their turn arrives.
>
> (OSK, 130)

The 'eat' metaphor used to express the manner in which we ate the tradition, and in turn hope our children to do the same is inflatedly cannibalistic. Nothing short of cannibalism can serve the purpose of expressing the fury and agony of Kamala Das. In the above cannibal metaphor, Kamala Das implies that one generation flourishes after having massacred and smashed the earlier one. If so, from generation to generation, what perspires is not progress. On the other hand, it is all a vain show of failure in standing up to the credentials of the hopes and desires. In effect she wants to confirm poetically that generations after generations, it is always that failure to be that stares into the eyes of the individuals. The entire gamut of the edifice of culture all through the ages shows the same symptoms of failure and distress. Therefore, there is nothing to be really proud of the human traditions that invariably hurdle the women folk to a marginalized status of being non-entities. Here, what Satchidanandan observes is worth quoting. Says he :

> She refuses to glorify the historical past; her nostalgias are confined to certain moments of love and tenderness in her personal past, hence her natural opposition to all forms of revivalism. She rejects the patriarchal value system that is based on egoism, greed for power, expansionism, hero-cult, violence, war, mindless exploitation of man and nature, the misuse of intelligence and the supremacy of reason and theory over sensitiveness and experience (16-17).

The barbarous face of the so-called civilization is even more fiercely revealed it the following lines of the poem *Daughter of the Century*, which clarifies her stand :

> We mated like gods but begot only our killers
> Each mother suckles her own enemy.

As a matter of fact, the whole and sole pride of woman, naturally speaking, is in her achievement in the name of her children. But in the above lines, instead of being proud of her progeny, she curses them just to show as to how grossly her importance was eroded by the powers that should have come to her proud satisfaction. The abnormal manner of diverting and directing her anger towards the issues speaks for the painful manner in which she suffered the companionship of her perennially failing partner in love.

At more places than one, Das hints that the evolution of human society is strictly in contrast to the self-reflecting, self-fulfilling idealized greatness of human birth. Asks she :

> Who can say for certain that we are superior
> To the maggots that eat us in the end?
>
> (*Daughter of the Century*)

The macabre self-image of the individual here conflicts with the reality of the disciplined society. All kinds of animosity seep through the interstices of modern life, a sort of maggot culture feeds upon it, transforming the pragmatism of hatred into an essential commodity of everyday existence.

The human evolution as a species is meant to be greater than any of its kind on earth. But the manner in which the history of civilization evolved state of inequalities at almost all practical counters of society makes human life shallow, a farce that has no serious purpose. Kamala Das categorically asserts that it is the institutions and systems that divert the human life to a path bristling with thorns. Such systems are not in conformity with the Nature's purpose of evolution and progress. Says she :

> The ultimate discovery will be
> that we rare immortal;
> the only things mortal being
> systems and arrangements,
> even our pains continuing
> in the devourers who constitute the world.
>
> (Composition, D, 29)

Generations may come and generations may go. The 'systems and arrangements,' being purely temporary, may outdate the earlier ones in chronological order. But at the same time the very 'pains' of being human in the 'systems and arrangements' that perennially inflict a gross failure on the very spirit of being human would ultimately become the cementing forces of the intactness of humanism, as the ultimate desired goal of being-in-the world. Very simply, all her desire is for the human society to be more and more human in being immortal. What differentiates Kamala Das from other Indian poets of her times in this existential concern, this expression of anger against the set discriminative values of the present-day society. While it is true that her whole poetic property is against the backdrop of feminist concerns, she rather takes a broader view of human life and its tribulations, and argues out her cause with relevant questions that cover the whole humanity. Whatever she utters poetically is immediately connectable to its human significance. Das's poetic personae represent the quintessential woman in her manifold aspects, rebelling against what is, with an underlying reminder of what should be true of humanity. In her poetry there is an unceasing content of restlessness, which in effect turns out to be a inconsolable 'cry' of the occasion. When such a 'cry' gets attended by a sense of self-pity, her poetry becomes a vibrant symbolic gesture of showing a rebellious will to fight out for her cause. And she fights for a world that is free from discriminative value systems, hypocrisies and prejudiced laws.

WORKS CITED

Primary Sources

Das, Kamala, *Collected Poems*, (CP)
Decendants (D)
My Instinct, My Guru (My Instinct...)
Only the Soul Knows How to Sing (OSK)
The Old Playhouse and Other Poems (OP)

Secondary Sources

Camus, Albert, *The Rebel*, Hamish Hamilton, London, Fourth Impression, October 1959, tr. Anthony Bower.

Chavan, Sunanda P., "The Moderns II : Kamala Das," *The Fair Voice : A Study of Indian Women Poets in English*, New Delhi : Sterling Publishers Pvt. Ltd., 1984.

Cixous, Helen, Castration or Decapitation, tr. Annette Kuhn, Feminism : *Contemporary Literary Criticism; Literary and Cultural Studes*, second edition, Robert Con Davis and Ronalt Schleifer (ed.), Longman, New York, 1989.

Dass, Veena Noble, Feminism and Literature, *Feminism and Literature*,Veena Noble Dass (ed.), Prestige Books, New Delhi, 1995.

Satchidanandan, K., Transcending the Body, *Only the Soul Knows How to Sing, Selections from Kamala Das*, D.C. Books, Kottayam, Kerala, 1996.

Showalter, Elaine, Feminist Criticism, *Feminism-Contemporary Literary Criticism, Literary and Cultural Studies*, second edition, Robert Con Davis and Ronalt Schleifer (ed.), Longman, New York, 1989.

15

Tiger Must Be Tiger : An Evaluation of Brahminical Values in R.K. Narayan's *A Tiger for Malgudi*

—*P. Rajendra Karmarkar*

The idea of tiger, an image of strong man designed for regulating the behaviour of the country, is scintillating and significant especially when sense of responsibility rated at 2 percent and India gauged as one of the topmost corrupt countries, and country's population (2.25 to 2.75 per cent per year) races menacingly to overtake China's record, and 'the largest democracy' gets the strictures from the International Human Rights Watch for its human rights violations and democracy turns out to be skin-deep owing to the prevalence of the Casteism.

Tiger must be tiger with all its might and dignity. It should not turn into a symbolic fox noted for cunning and treachery by changing natural eating habit from carnivorous to herbivorous, as it is innately a flesh-eater like human being and noted for its magnificence, majesty, and ferocity. Vegetarianism was self-imposed especially by the ancient Brahmins and was given much propagation after Buddhism advocated the principle of non-violence (*Ahimsa*) which led to the origin of vegetarianism. Brahmins prescribed vegetarianism as a counter strategy against the growing popularity of Buddhism.

India's constitution maker, Dr. B.R. Ambedkar says, 'Democracy in India is only a top dressing in an Indian soil, which is essentially undemocratic.' Ambedkar indicates that India, a divided house, lacks equality, fraternity and freedom. Caste system, originated from the work division among the victorious Aryans and the defeated Dravidians and ratified later by (ancient) religious Brahmin scholars, sown the seeds of enmity among the different castes and separated the people permanently. Then, every caste being confined, restricts its love and relations and safeguards its interests and develops separate identity. As a result, common love for the country (patriotism) becomes a distant ideal. When such is the case, how can we expect an unprejudiced and non-partisan person with his ideas to apply universally in a democratic government based on caste system? Therefore, the so-called dynamic leaders can only be double-edged.

R.K. Narayan, being a traditional Brahmin evades to envisage a strong man who may be defined as a man with a sense of equality, freedom and fraternity with his uncompromising attitude to keep his dignity, and high ethical standards, and to volunteer exemplary and self-less service to the needy and the ill-fated, ultimately to pave the way to the consummation of democracy. It's Narayan's chicanery to conceive and parade a tiger-like man but at the same time, to maintain discreet silence over the greatest social evil — the caste system which destroys the very integral fabric of the social structure.

R.K. Narayan is a novelist of values marked by the middle class ethos. His is a vision like a child of mild and reconcilable realities. Like a major part of Indian films depicting the Indian life as if it were an egalitarian society where love is universal, R.K. Narayan does not penetrate the biting actualities. Narayan seeks escapism as the best way with known compromising attitude rather than inviting trouble or opposition by confrontation. Narayan's brain child, Malgudi, identical with Hardy's Wessex, is the symbol of (traditional) India with a restricted outlook, where we do not come across bare facts such as bloodshed resulted out of casteism and political rivalry, atrocities on Dalits, bloody communal violence between Hindus and Muslims, earthquakes, devastative cyclones and so on.

Narayan's *A Tiger For Malgudi* (1983) is an autobiographical novel narrated by the tiger and written with an allegorical texture and tone. Technically, it's impossible for the tiger to peep into the human affairs and interpret them unless it's personified. The tiger, the protagonist named Raja, by its adored Master, the hermit, narrates his past life from the cage placed at the entrance of the new Malgudi circus. Tiger began his life in Memphi forest region. Being led a chequered career, he gradually became a strong, ferocious and seasoned animal called himself, 'the supreme Lord of the Jungle.' Striking terror in the hearts of the weak and dealing death blows to the enemies, tiger turns out to be imperious and supercilious, just to receive great torment on his nose, jaws and paws from the quills of the porcupine when the tiger tries to hurt it. Humiliated, tiger returns into his cave with injuries and does not come out for a few days.

Later, Tiger encounters a lady tiger which is as much big and fierce as himself. In order to decide the supremacy between them a brutal combat ensued in which both were hurt severely and they thought that it would be better to reconcile than to grapple. They began living together and had cubs. Once the mother and the cubs accidentally crossed the borders of the Memphi forest and were caught by the villagers, and shot dead by a huntsman. Their death causes great agony to the tiger and changes him to be more violent. Agitated at the loss of the cattle, tiger had been taken away everyday and defeated to catch the tiger because of his superior tactics, villagers finally approached the collector's office. The collector troubles the villagers with logical questioning and promises them that he would visit their village next month. Villagers surprise what will happen in the meantime. R.K. Narayan shows how corrupt and callous and irresponsible the government officials are and how they exploit the illiterate and naive people. Anyway, the captain of the Malgudi circus, has caught the tiger.

With the arrival of the tiger, Malgudi circus gains momentum. Tiger has been much publicized as large, magestical and fierce one. The captain teaches the tiger his role in the circus. Days later, tiger wins much applause for his remarkable performance of feats. But the tiger himself an individual too, does not move his tail always to the dictates of the captain who tries to coerce him to demonstrate the act of drinking milk along with goat from the same saucer. Captain turns hellbent on enacting the principle of non-violence between the violent and the meek. When the tiger is about to do this feat, he feels unstoppable urge to kill the goat. Captain thwarts him by the whip and makes him starve for days.

Captain understands that tiger is an extraordinary and uncompromising animal. Captain has his own fears that any feat imposed upon the tiger may bring peril to himself. Though unwilling, captain accepts the offer made by Madan, the film producer and director, with a huge amount of money. Accordingly, tiger is to fight with a wrestler called Jaggu, in the film. Unable to withstand his anger precipitated by the application of electric gadget by the captain who tries to draw forcible performance from him, tiger eventually revolts killing the captain.

Tiger enters Malgudi streets. People run for life. Within no time, all the streets remain deserted as if it were a curfew imposed. Walking along the road, tiger enters the school. A hermit, later called Master by tiger, brings him outside with his mesmerizing invocation. This new 'Master' is in fact, a Mr. Gopal retired to Memphi forest to achieve peace and *moksha* (liberation to soul) from the busy, and routine life from as an employee, husband and father. The Master and the tiger settle on the side of a hill situated in the forest. Master helps the tiger attain spiritual transformation.

Tiger, like a man, distinguished itself by ego, stateliness, and independence and by tensile and enormous muscle, wild and terrible depths shining with an exemplary demeanour, and striking dread and awe in the minds of the weak and the depraved and enjoying a unique status among the human world. A king or a rebel who is subdued by a immense force for a time, is destined to revert to his primal and instinctive nature which is supreme to him to stand with a banner of respectability and freedom. Tiger in an ordeal test performance, feels impossible to share the milk along with the goat from the same saucer. And for him, it's revolting to follow the instructions of the captain. When the tiger gives the signal of refusal to obey by trying to kill the goat, captain realizing his mood, says "sorry gentlemen, no encore is practical for this particular act, nor am I in a position to ask Raja to take the bow personally. I'll have to do it on his behalf. But I also hope someday I'll educate him in proper manners to respond to his adoring public."[1]

In his next performance, to meet his natural fill, tiger defies captain's authority and kills the goat which is a befitting food and suited best to its form and body in contrast to the milk — an odd stuff tiger hates most. And at the height of his rebellious attitude arising out of its dignity being at stake by the humiliating treatment given by the captain who compels him to act in the film shooting by applying electric shocks, tiger does not hesitate to eliminate the captain and demonstrates that it cannot or should not be intimidated for monetary gains in a world where values gradually disappear threatening the existence of the good and the innocent. Tiger says, 'If I could have spoken, I would have told him,' "Go away before any harm befalls you, my good man. After all you have fed me and protected me. I shall honour you for it. But, please go away and leave me alone. I won't be your slave any more, I'll never go back to my cage that's all...."[2]

Insincere talk fused with oratorial skill and verbosity appeals more to the credulous people than the simple and the unadorned language. Larger massed who are in the fold of the traditions, do not approve the works that describe life as it is or as it should be. Further, presenting a life imbued with such values — love, integration and patriotism, is a matter of question in a society, marked by disunity. Tiger wonders how man is accustomed to derive pleasure and meaning by meaningless and unnatural acts. He feels contemptuous of the absurd instructions of the captain whom he no longer obeys. Tiger says "...I won't do any of the meaningless turns these foolish men around want me to do.... I like this air and freedom"....[3]

Indian love is restricted by the caste system and sex by the traditional values and the false sense of purity. To gain or keep social prestige by sanctimonious living, they (Indians) are prepared to starve from sex. They betray snobbish but their libidos stir and inflame within making them rigid and self-centred and driving them to treat the idea of sex as taboo in public. Moreover, sex has never been considered a central problem in Indian life. Madan, the producer and director, alluding to the essential depiction of sex and violence and subtleties involved therein in both life and films, aptly says to the captain "Life is created and made possible only through sex and violence, no use fighting against it, shutting one's eyes to the facts of life...."[4] But, this prime truth loses its prominence, when the life of tiger's guru, the master, who has abandoned his wife and children to their grief in the middle and became as acetic is shown as an ideal and universal one. R.K. Narayan further corroborates this view in his earlier novel *The English Teacher* a virtual autobiography of Narayan's own life, wherein, the protagonist, Krishnan, like R.K. Narayan, loses his wife Suseela (Rajam) in his 30s. He remains widower taking joy in carnal and spiritual association with the ghost of his dead wife, which comes in the night and stays with him and goes out in the wee hours.

People accused of crimes and economic scandals, go scot-free because of lack of proper evidence which they can wipe out by muscle power or buying off the witnesses. And by granting anticipatory bails or deferring the trial from time to time, deliberately to keep the grave cases involving country's prestige in abeyance, the Indian Courts being drenched in slush money or motivated by political clout, empower the lawbreakers to perpetuate infringements against the elected governments and to wreak bloodshed on the enemy and commit atrocities on the lower castes. People too have come to honour the rich and power. Tiger indicates that those who are culpable, and haughty, run away from mighty force. Like Jayanta Mahapatra's crocodiles (in Indian Summer) unable to bear the heat of light, getting into deeper waters, upon looking at the tiger, people becoming panicky, run halter shelter. Tiger says, "It was still a busy hour in the city when I entered market road. People ran for their lives at the sight of me. As I progressed through, shutters were pulled down, and people hid themselves, under culverts, on trees, behind pillars. The population was melting out of sight."[5]

Although major part of Hindus were led by Brahminical forces to believe *The Bhagavad Gita* as the most authoritative religious text, yet reformists and major writers like Raja Rama Mohan Roy, Rabindranath Tagore based their writings and life on the essentials of *The Vedanta* and *The Upanishads*. The reason for the latter's deliberate commission of the work *The Bhagavad Gita* in many contexts is that it teaches the philosophy of violence and establishes the inhuman castesystem. Had R.K. Narayan intended to strike a universal note, he ought to restrain himself from quoting *The Bhagavad Gita*. Further, it'll be a miracle in the life of a Brahmin when he risks his life for the sake of others. The master, the hermit, who wants to take control of the tiger that settled in the room of the principal of Malgudi school, argues with the men outside "Why'll you prevent me from going near the tiger?" 'They were at a loss to naswer;' "It's unlawful to commit suicide" ...Master says, "It's after all my life that I'm risking."[6] Advocating Karma principle, which determines the lives of the human beings, master says that no one can die or flee death by his will except by the decision of that great power.

The universal God should never be expected to give a war cry and goads the man to kill the enemy. The question arises here, why do we kill the enemy when he is already dead? Master quotes the very words of God (Krishna) from *The Bhagavad Gita* who declares, "I'm life and death, I'm the killer and the killed.... Those enemies you see Arjuna, are already dead, whether you aim your arrows at them or not!"[7]

Does R.K. Narayan impresses upon the reader that the life of the Master, hermit and his spokesman, called Gopal earlier, is the only way to attain salvation? Master who being sick at heart because of monotonous life, deserts abruptly his wife and children to their own doom. Seeking peace in the forest, he fulfils the duties (four orders) of Brahmin's life. These four orders are, that of the student, the householder, the ascetic and the hermit. He is now in the last phase spending most of the time in the forest. For a modern man, master's action is a completely shirking the responsibility and turning into indolent rather than facing and rising above the problems that perturb the human beings as the order of the day. It appears that he must have experienced the absurdity of existence. Master says to the tiger "I was a man of the world, busy and active and living by the clock, scrutinizing my bank book... one day it seemed all wrong, a senseless repetition of activities...and I abruptly shed everything and fled away from wife, children, home, possessions all of which seemed intolerable...."[8]

Ancient Brahmins inculcated in the minds of Indians that Sanskrit was a divine language as it was designed and used by the angels (*Devatas*). Religious works such as *The Vedas, The Bhagavad Gita, The Upanishads* and other religious and philosophical texts were written in Sanskrit. Because of the (highest caste) privileged status and to perpetuate that eminence, Brahmins did not allow the major part of the people to acquire both the language and Sanskrit Knowledge. Manu, Brahmins' guru says, "By his origin alone a Brahmana (Brahmin) is a deity even for the gods, and (his teaching is authoritative for that."[9] Having been kept with the Brahmins for centuries, Sanskrit comes to be considered Brahminical language. Today, it's spokenly dead.

When the second Honorary Magistrate asks the master to give a written affidavit which absolves the authorities from 'all responsibilities for his life or death', the master, who wants to approach the tiger and get control of him, writes a statement in Sanskrit which the magistrate does not understand.

The chairman looked at the document and said, "stop, wait, tell me what is it that you have written here"?

"Only what you have dictated."

"In a language we don't know, can't accept it...."

"It's in Sanskrit, in which our scriptures are written, language of the gods. I write only Sanskrit although I know ten other languages including Japanese."[10]

Master, tiger's guru, in the garb of a mesmerist, tells the tiger that he has reached the old age, though tiger neither talks nor worries about his age. Teaching the philosophy of the coward, and the crafty, master says that he must shed violent nature and acquire calm and cool temper. In fact, criminal nature lying within can be fought both within oneself and within others. After all, life is a matter of thrill being precipitated by 'the thread of perpetual tension continually mastered by the intelligence'. What Camus says is significant in this regard, "wc all carry within us our places of exile, our crimes, and our ravages. But our task is not to unleash them on the world; it is to fight them in ourselves and inothers."[11]

So a king remains a king when he retains the violent tendency besides benevolence and compassion. He must live a king and die a king. To strip him of this vital nature is to destroy his majesty. The master says, "The demon, the tormentor, or the tyrant in history, if he ever survives to experience senility, becomes helpless and dependent, lacking the strength even to swat a fly. You are now an adult full-grown tiger, and assuming you are fifteen years old, in human terms you would be over seventy years old, and at seventy and onwards one's temper gets toned down through normal decay, and let us be grateful for it. You cannot continue your ferocity forever. You have to change...."[12]

In the olden times, superstitious Hindus led a life of self-imposed prohibitions and condemnations. For instance, venturing into the sea was declared a taboo. In the religious texts, such as *Puranas* and *Ithihasas*, India was treated as if it were the whole world surrounded by the seas and Himalayas which were believed to be the abode of Lord Shiva. Their geographical ignorance was rooted in their denouncement of fathoming the origin of either nature made wonders of artificial barriers existing in the society. So, it was no longer a cause for bewilderment if Vasco da Gama discovered sea route from Europe to India in 1498 and if Tenzing Norgay of Nepal, and Sir Edmund Percival Hillery of New Zealand reached the summit of Mount Everest in 1953 for the first time.

Jayaraj, the photographer, who had taken the pictures of the master earlier, identifies the master who is now going on the street along with the tiger. He narrates about the master to a group of people that the master was formerly called Gopal, worked in a college and led the marital life for many years and had children and suddenly left his family. When the group questions Jayaraj to explain 'why did he leave the family abruptly,' Jayaraj expresses vexation as through it were sin to raise questions about the saints or sorcerers.

"Any reason why he went away?" "I know as much as you do. Why ask me? Enough...talk of something else. Let's forget him and his tiger. Something uncanny about him... unsafe to talk about such men, who may be saints or sorcerers. Who knows what will happen? Remember the ancient saying. Don't probe too far into the origin of a river or a saint? You will never reach the end."[13]

People continue to survive by committing sins or perpetrating crimes escaping law by using money power or political clout or the privilege of the Caste. Further, *pujaris* (Brahmin priests) sweep away their sins everyday by recommending religious antidotes of remedies in the form of rites. They who strike terror into the society themselves carry the greatest fear within. They are morally shattered and unable to stand before a majestic force. Master, observing how people are making way for the tiger and retreating and staring at the tiger in fear, says, "what our country needs most is a tiger for every village and town to keep people disciplined..."[14]

The reason for the lack of common or public responsibility should be sought from the nature of the society, based on Brahminical attitude — looking after one's own welfare, and progress and claiming or striving for one's own status or superiority. Thus, Indian, perceptivity narrowed by the castesystem, is personal and private disowning common or fellow-feeling. But any responsible citizen in a free and casteless society does not fail to notice what's happening around. He reads the mind of everyone and of society as a final target. In Dostoyesky's *The Brothers Karamazov*, Father Zossima writes in his biographical notes "make yourself responsible for all men's sins. As soon as you sincerely make yourself responsible for everything and for all men, your will see at once that you have found salvation."[15] Tiger following the master on the street, could not help taking watch around, which the master denounces and tries to destroy his broader perceptiveness. Tiger says, "we passed on while I stuck close to his heals and moved along without lifting my head or at anyone too long." My master told me, "The eye is the starting point of all evil and mischief. The eye can travel far and pick out objects indiscriminately, mind follows the eye, and rest of the body is conditioned by the mind. Thus starts chain of activity which may lead to trouble and complication. So don't look at anything except the path."[16]

On account of the existence of human love and brotherhood in Christianity and the belief that it is the true religion, Christian believers have a strong sense of seeing the rest of the world as Christian one. So the master vegetarian himself, who leads the tiger into the Memphi forest, starts to change him spiritually. At first, he teaches the tiger to become herbivorous telling him that God has predetermined thus. Master says, "God has decided for you a difficult diet. I can help your mind and soul, but I cannot affect your body or its functions."[17] Master implies that spiritual transformation can only be realized through the adoption of vegetarianism. Being convinced, tiger thinks that God will not accept him if he tastes the flesh of animals. Tiger feels guilty, impure and inferior when he attends to his innate urge killing an animal on the spur of impulse. Tiger says, "Even for drinking water I chose another stream with in the forest, since I did not want to sully the spring in which my Master performed his morning ablutions...I tried to attain some kind of purification by reducing the frequency of seeking food."[18] Tiger inclines to develop aversion to the animal flesh. Tiger says, "I could not bear to recollect this habit : it nauseated."[19] M.N. Srinivas, the sociologist says, "To orthodox Brahmins, the Englishman who ate pork and beef, drank whisky, and smoked a pipe, was the living embodiment of ritual impurity. On the other hand, the English had political and economic power for which he was feared, admired, respected and disliked.".[20]

Ceasing his natural habit, tiger begins to depends upon fruit and leaves. He defends his newly acquired eating practice as great one on par with such animals as elephant and hippotomus who, though huge in size, are herbivorous. Tiger says, "How mighty the hippo and the elephant looked, although they ate no meat."[21] Furthermore, the idea of purification possible only by means of adopting vegetarianism was also propagated by Raja Rao, the metaphysical (Brahmin) novelist, in his work *On The Ganga Ghat* in which his characters — Bholanath and Pandit Viswanath praise Adolf Hitler and pray for his sins as they have heard that Hitler was a celibate and vegetarian and must be considered a devotee of God. Raja Rao's characters are unmindful of the fact that Hitler had a mistress, evan Braun whom he married on 29th April 1945 and the next day, they committed suicide. Further, Hitler was responsible for leading the world to the Second World War and for ordering hundreds and thousands of death sentences and was considered "world's much hated man." Raja Rao writes, "they heard that Hitler was a vegetarian and a celibate : tell me, what more could one need to be called devotee of the Lord"?[22] In another instance, Raja Rao says, "...And no decent person ever eats meat, except the low class people and Europeans who also eat the pig, so the elders say."[23]

Master, quoting from *The Bhagavad Gita*, says to tiger that God exists within every one and we receive spiritual power from Him. "Remember also He is within everyone of us and we derive our strength from Him."[24] But in the same *The Bhagavad Gita*, God (Brahman — the universal soul) declares "the fourfold castes system has been created by me on the basis of qualities and actions."[25] These words of God have strengthen the roots of the castesystem and created enmity permanently among the castes, and negate the very principle of oneness of all souls inseparably related to Him. Further, master teaches about the oneness and the human love. Significantly, Tiger does not know any barrier existing between one tiger and the other. He knows that he can love any other tiger and his love does not see any boundaries unlike in the Hindu society. Brahmins crave to merge with the Brahman (*the Universal Soul*) but they hate to unite with the Brahman of the Dalit (*the Untouchable*).

The question of the sense of suffering and injustice which emerge from the social status of the castesystem, does not arise in the life of Indian (privileged) Caste Hindu who looks at the brighter side of the life and the society. The social environment and the social rank he enjoys, keeps him happy and contented, imaginative and poetic. He describes a world untouched by the ugly side of life. His poetry mixes the imagery of elegance and luxurious scenery entirely disdaining the social realities. Tiger, because of its constant association with the master, becomes lyrical and utters, "...I lifted my gaze to the horizon, the sun shining on the land filled me with joy. The leaves of the mighty, banyan trees sparkling like gems, the bamboos swaying their golden stems with their piligreed leaves — I felt I could ask for nothing more in life."[26] Guessing the mind of the tiger and making a note of transmigration of the soul of the tiger, Master says, "No one would credit a tiger with so much poetic joy, it is inconceivable.... You must have been a poet, perhaps many centuries ago in the court of a King...."[27] It must be recalled that court poets whether in ancient or middle or modern ages are mostly Brahmins.

Moulded by the guidance of the master, Tiger imitates master's way of life. He begins to precipitate his fate to bring an early end to him rather than allowing it (the fate) to take its own course. Thus, tiger gradually becomes a 'dead lion.' Tiger says, "Gradually I realized that I was becoming less inclined to get up and move, preferring to spend long hours in my own corner hidden behind the shrub. I preferred to go without food rather than undergo the strain of chasing game. I could not run fast enough to catch anything. Many creatures eluded me with ease."[28]

Traditionally speaking, there are two definitions that can be given to the idea of Transmigration of the soul. At first, soul has no death. Soul, leaving dead man, enters another at the time of conception. This doctrine of transmigration had been firmly used to strengthen the caste system. Accordingly, lower caste person has to serve the higher caste people to win (good) higher caste birth in the next life. "But let a Sudra (lower caste man) serve Brahmans (Brahmins) either for the sake of heaven, or with a view to both (this life and the next); for he who is called the servant of the Brahmana gains all his ends."[29] Thus lower Caste man was made to believe that it's because of his past actions he is born now to serve the higher castes. Moreover, since the soul has no death and it continues to survive entering one body to another, the question of heaven and hell does not arise as they are non-existent on the basis of this principle.

Secondly, much to the disadvantage of the nation, this idea of transmigration of the soul, resulting in formation of belief of rebirth being sunk deep in the minds, generates the mood of resignation, and submission to the prevailing fate, and indifference to the situation that involves or demands risk and sometimes life. Generally, those who could not realize their wishes, or aims console themselves, that they would fulfil them in the next life. This dangerous philosophical tendency leads to the destruction of dynamism. It's surprising when the master hopes that he and the tiger leaving the present forms, will meet again in the next life. The moot question is, when the master neither serves his family, nor the society, nor he keeps the tiger as tiger but transforms him into a cat which better deserves the attention of the children, what does the modern man or nation expects from such master and his disciple in the next life? Master says, "Both of us will shed our forms soon and perhaps we could meet again, who knows? So good bye for the present."[30]

NOTES

1. R.K. Narayan, *A Tiger for Malgudi*. Indian Thought Publications, Mysore, 1983, pp. 72-73.
2. *Ibid.*, p. 113.
3. *Ibid.*, p. 113.
4. *Ibid.*, p. 81.
5. *Ibid.*, p. 115.
6. *Ibid.*, p. 142.
7. *Ibid.*, p. 142.
8. *Ibid.*, p. 161.
9. G. Buhler, *The Laws of Manu*, Motilal Banarsidas, Delhi, reprint 1988, p. 447.
10. R.K. Narayan, *A Tiger for Malgudi*, Indian Thought Publications, Mysore, 1983, p. 143.

11. Albert Camus, *The Rebel* (*L'Homme Revolte*), Penguin Books, 1971, p. 265.
12. R.K. Narayan, *A Tiger for Malgudi*, Indian Thought Publications, Mysore, 1983, p. 145.
13. *Ibid.*, pp. 153-154.
14. *Ibid.*, p. 155.
15. Fyodor Dostoyevsky : *The Brothers Karamazov*, trans. by Constance Garnett, A Signet Classic, New American Library, 1980, p. 295.
16. R.K. Narayan, *A Tiger for Malgudi*, Indian Thought Publications, Mysore, 1983, p. 155.
17. *Ibid.*, p. 157.
18. *Ibid.*, p. 159.
19. *Ibid.*, p. 159.
20. M.N. Srinivas, *Caste in Modern India*, Media Promoters & Publishers Pvt. Ltd., Bombay, 1962, p. 51.
21. R.K. Narayan, *A Tiger for Malgudi*, Indian Thought Publications, Mysore, 1983, p. 160.
22. Raja Rao, *On The Ganga Ghat*, Vision Books, New Delhi, 1989, p. 78.
23. *Ibid.*, p. 42.
24. R.K. Narayan, *A Tiger for Malgudi*, Indian Thought Publications, Mysore, 1983, p. 158
25. Mahadeva Sastry, Alladi, *The Bhagavad Gita,* trans. from Sanskrit with the commentary of Sri Sankaracharya by Samata Books, Madras, 1991, p. 125.
26. R.K. Narayan, *A Tiger for Malgudi*, Indian Thought Publications, Mysore, 1983, pp. 165-66.
27. *Ibid.*, p. 166.
28. *Ibid.*, p. 173.
29. G. Buhler, *The Laws of Manu*, trans. from Sanskrit by Motilal Banarsidas, Delhi, 1988, pp. 428-29.
30. R.K. Narayan, *A Tiger for Malgudi*, Indian Thought Publications, Mysore, 1983, p. 176.

16

Nirad C. Chaudhury's Critique of Bengal and the 'Bāngāli'

—Rama Kundu

Calcutta being the original stronghold of the British in India, Bengal had to come in early and direct contact with the colonial 'culture' and 'anarchy' alike and naturally the response of the English-educated Bengali elite of the first generation was ambivalent towards the British as evidenced by writers like Dinabandhu Mitra, Bankimchandra, *et al.* around the mid-nineteenth century. They registered their fascination for the European culture, its 'sweetness and light' as well as their rejection of the 'barbarism and philistinism' as manifested in the practice of the colonists. Rabindranath Tagore subsequently came to represent the maturest response to this new wave; he assimilated and transcended both the Western influence and the Indian heritage to offer a new approach of living exchange on equal levels. Nirad C. Chaudhury, born towards the end of the nineteenth century, after twenty-six years of Tagore, exhibits an interesting outlook. He seems to have overcome the contradictions that characterized the early Bengali elite, but not in the Tagorean way. His preference for the British — as people, culture, society — is unambiguous; he shows no oscillations like many writers of his earlier generation between their commitment to the indigenous tradition and their longing for the new ways shipped over from England.

Personally too he has chosen a life of self-exilement in Oxford since 1970. Even before that, since 1942 he has been outside Bengal. But this should not necessarily mean that he has forgotten Bengal altogether. *Ātmaghāti Bāngāli*, published in 1988, on his ninety-first year, bears evidence to the writer's nostalgia for the place where he was born and lived for fifty-five years. However, even nostalgia may not mellow the critic within a man like him. The present volume bears ample proof to the complex response of Niradbabu to his motherland. Chaudhury's English books are widely read. But his few Bengali books are understandably not so well-known or publicized. This book gives intimate glimpses of the Bengalee/ 'Bāngāl' (his own term) hiding within the 'continental' Saheb.

Ātmaghāti Bāngāli is planned to cover the span of the entire nineteenth-century Bengal as also occasional references to the twentieth century. But the focus has been laid on a very limited area/section of the Bengalee society and culture; it is the highly educated section of Bengal who were never too many.

This second Bengali book by Nirad C. Chaudhury (the first one was also about the Bengalee life, *i.e., Bāngāli Jībane Ramanī* (1968) projects a thesis : the Bengalee life had once touched the acme in various fields under the impact of English language and literature; but since the turn of the century, and especially since 1935, Bengal has started on a declining course; symptoms of decadence are appearing everywhere. This saddens the writer. So, in order to remind the Bengalee of his lost glory, and of the forgotten history of his Renaissance that Mr. Nirad C. writes this book with the fond hope that this remembrance may bring them back from their present 'suicidal' (*ātmaghāti*) course and turn towards another Renaissance.

Chaudhury's book is, as it were, Gibbon in miniature in the Bengalee context. It is about the rise, decline and fall of Bengalee, life during a certain period of recent history. In this volume the writer assumes the role of a social historian, — quite entertaining though — as he sums up within the brief span of 200 pages the social-intellectual life of the Bengalee over a phase of more than hundred years. It was a phase which, according to Chaudhury, marked the 'blossoming' of a new consciousness in the social and individual lives of the Bengalee under the impact of Western education. The writer lovingly describes this 'blossoming;' but his ulterior aim is to expose the subsequent tragedy of Bengal compared to its earlier promises and excellence.

The material is arranged into ten chapters. The first chapter — 'Rebirth of the Bengalee' traces the change in the 'Bengalee life' (Chaudhury's 'Bengalee life' applies to a very limited section) to the inauguration of the Hindu College in Calcutta in 1817. With the introduction of as the medium for education, and with the establishment of the University of Calcutta in 1857 this process of change was further strengthened and the new Bengalee consciousness began to take a mature shape and expression. The writer defines this development as a 'mental revolution' or 'Renaissance' of Bengal. In this connection he also alludes to the other Renaissance of Bengal which had been ushered in the sixteenth century by Chaitanyadeb with his new cult of love. Chaitanya too had appeared against a similar backdrop — a society stagnated by unquestioning surrender to irrational/inhuman rites and rituals. The writer also shows that the cleansing effects of Chaitanya's cult of humanism based on devotion and love had already disappeared from the pre-British Bengal, and its place was usurped by coarse vulgarity. Around mid-nineteenth century the educated Bengalee's acquaintance with English literature brought an overall change to the scene. "The new generation of Bengalis saw in the intellectual life of Europe a force to extend their mental horizon" (*AB,* 19). Chaudhury's perceptive mind recaptures the fascination and enthusiasm of the new generation of Bengalees around the time and their joyous response to the surge of new ideas. As the educated Bengalee found his own heritage inadequate he naturally turned toward the vista of Western thoughts and life freshly opened by before him. The new way was so indisputably attractive that there was no difference of response in this respect between the liberal and conservative elites of Bengal as represented by Bankimchandra and Vivekananda. The real difference rose between the Sanskrit-educated pundits and the English-educated elites who did not understand each other's language. The writer reiterates Vivekananda's view that as Europe had once "drawn from the fountains of the Greeks" Young Bengal drew from the fountain of European thought through English language.

Chapter Two — 'On the Eve of the Renaissance' explodes the myth that the Bengalee were the direct inheritors of ancient Hindu civilization and the heritage continued unimpaired till the British advent in our socio-cultural life, and as result their was the glorious synthesis that determined and coloured the new Bengalee life of the nineteenth century. The writer holds that everybody in those days would have spoke in terms of the merging and synthesis of East and West. Even Tagore too had propounded this message of synthesis and exchange in his 'Bharat-tirtha'. All the Bengalees, including the writer himself, had accepted this message with respect and trust. But later, around 1925, the turn of things in Bengal had set him wondering if there was really any clash or synthesis here between Eastern and Western civilization. He argues that actually people were paying lip-service to the programme of upholding some so-called 'Indian tradition,' while blindly following the Western way at the same time. Niradbabu seems to find an explanation in the social situation of Bengal on the eve of the British onslaught. He maintains that the Bengalee daily life during this period had no connection with the pre-Muslim Hindu civilization and its ancient scholarship and culture. As result our life had assumed the easy simple rural way which is defined by the writer as 'folk civilization' : One mature culture had disintegrated and its place was not yet taken by an appropriate substitute. (The British influence had been so eagerly absorbed here because it was expected to fill in this void.) Chaudhury takes care to remind the reader that two mature trends were still present in the eighteenth century Bengal : the Islamic civilization and the Hindu pundit's study of the 'shastras.' But neither of these formed the main current of Bengalee or Indian culture. The Islamic civilization was mainly confined within the cities and among the rulers, and did not spread among the common Hindu or the poor rural Muslim. The pundit's pursuit of knowledge was also confined within a special and necessarily small circle. The greater mass lived in a primitive, juvenile state. Even the memory of a past and the feeling of a continuity and wholeness that is present in all mature societies was lacking here. *The Ramayana* and *The Mahabharata* operated during this period as the only collective memory of the multifaceted achievements of an ancient Indian civilization. The author suggests that the process of this racial oblivion had probably started with the establishment of the Muslim rule. The Hindu ruler and the aristocratic Hindu society which provided a frame for a rich Hindu culture had been either destroyed or too enfeebled to sustain the ancient trends of a rich civilization. But, the author points out that there was also a positive sequel to this development. This was the period when countless folk religions, folk rites, folk literatures and folk songs sprouted. This rural culture was our only treasure on the eve of the British advent. The author thinks that is the reason why after the rediscovery of the glory of the ancient Hindu civilization in the nineteenth century the educated Bengalees (as also other Indians) became indifferent to their immediate past and became fantasized by their remote past which was often distorted by wishful thinking and too coloured by imagination to emerge as a real strong basis for a healthy cultural exchange on an equal level.

The second chapter is a quite perceptive study of the scene, and an appropriate sequel to the first chapter. But the promise created thus is withdrawn in the subsequent chapters which seem to be often too bookish and marred by casual/one-sided and sometimes absurd observations. Chapter Three 'The Spread and Use of the English language' starts by rejecting the very common notion that the British had introduced English education to have clerks and employees at low cost as "pure and shameless lie unparalleled in history." The author shows how actually, when English was adopted as medium of education in 1835, all high-ranking officials British officials residing in India were against the measure.

In this chapter Chaudhury also casts light on a comparatively unexplored area of our social history : how the knowledge of English literature had come to influence the domestic life of an average educated Bengalee. There was an extraordinary harvest of Bengali translations of European classics and Bengali essays on the European literature, arts, history, philosophy, and both women and men of educated families avidly read them. An interesting feature of this period which Niradbabu rightly was that the Bengalee gathered knowledge through English but the newly shaped Bengalee mind found complete and powerful expression of this assimilated knowledge in Bengali literature. The writer contends that the influence of this English-oriented Bengali literature on young minds ran to any extent. He assumes that young men and women tried to shape their lives according to what these writers wrote. Again, the Bengalee writer of the day gathered his material from this new Bengalee life too. Thus the writer and the reader, — literature and life — mutually influenced and involved each other. They also points out that English education also enlisted social prestige and was indispensable for a professional career, — an observation which is still applicable to Bengal in the 1990s.

Chapter Four 'Results of English Education' refers to the initial excesses caused by the new education. Thus immediately after the opening of the Hindu College Westernization came to include not only Shakespeare study but also taking wine and beef. Such excesses were ridiculed by eminent Bengalees like Dinabandhu Mitra, Madhusudan Dutta among others. Bankimchandra, however, had made an objective evaluation of this imitation, conceding the possibility that a conscious imitation of the positive things might also lead to self-improvement.

By means of a few select examples the author tries to show how perpasive the imitation was. In his characteristic entertaining style (and also a bit nostalgically) Niradbabu recounts the introduction of Western-modelled furniture in rich and upper middle class houses including hanging lantern, table lamp, mirrors, pictures of landscape as well as pictures/ sculptures of naked/drapped beautiful women; the extra set of perfect European dress for formal occasions in addition to the indigenous dress for normal occasions; more radical changes took place in the women's dress including use of chemise and shoes. The writer claims that even daily speech used in domestic transactions underwent a change from strong slang to soft sophistication. He also recalls how women of rich families, instead of wasting the entire time in the kitchen, started sewing, knitting, carpet-designing, and, of course novel reading. Sewing was considered a necessary qualification for marriageable girls. Chaudhury alludes to Tagore's *Gora* as an illustration of this new generation of women, and also of the charm they exercised on the young men of the time.

Chapter Five, — 'Marriage, Conjugal Life and Love' shifts focus from external details to the internal life, the deeper subtleties of man-woman relationship. The basis of the argument here is that the impact of English education was apparent in all the aspects of mental activity in Bengal at the time including man-woman relationship. True, the ritualistic details of marriage remained the same (and these are still continuing more or less unchanged). But at the imaginative level there was a shift from ancient eroticism or medieval vulgarity to a romanticized emotion. This observation, though interesting, appears at best naive over-simplification if one only looks up the documentary records regarding the woman's lot in Bengal. Romantic/Platonic love could be the subject of literature, or was to be found in the life of very few individuals, but never the general experience. At least where the woman was concerned, it was and has been more or less the same situation of cynical exploitation through centuries.

Thus, when the writer contends : "But there cannot be any doubt that due to the new education under the British regime the conjugal life of the Bengalee got completely transformed" (67), it seems too naive an assessment. No less naive in his claim that in those days loyalty to one's wife was a norm of the English society, and the English-educated Bengalee also tried to cast himself into that mould; one would like to ask — 'was it so?' and 'how many'?

Again, the writer mentions the occasional conflicts of conscience that arose in the mind of the young Bengalee of the nineteenth century regarding the question of priority between religiosity and love. He explains this moralistic tendency as something anachronistic to the Bengalee tradition and defines it as imported puritanism from England to which was added the old mother cult of Bengal; and the two together made love appear a fascinating as well as an embarrassing emotions.

Chapter Six, — 'Love' continues the attempt to establish that the new concept of love as a romanticized Platonic ideal rather than sex-oriented eroticism was accommodated in the Bengalee life in both marital and extra-marital situations. In this context the writer makes the fantastic claim that due to the influence of *Romeo and Juliet* the age of marriage (for girls) in Bengali novels was raised from eleven to sixteen; also teenaged girls (in the novels of Saratchandra for example) emerged with the unrestrained vigour and expression of their romantic love. A new respect for the body of the loved one was seen which was completely absent in the pre-British tradition-bound Hindu society. Also the careful cultivation of post-marital love stabilised and strengthened the bond between the couple.

Chapter Seven, — 'In Search of the Woman' describes the enlightened Bengalee's (male) search for the ideal woman in his life; it was in a way a search for personal fulfilment through the female partner. This reflected a new respect for and appreciation of the woman as an individual which was non-existent in the tradition of Bengal. Again, the woman was considered a kind of succour (that is also a role) for the inevitable sorrows in the man's life which usually came from two main sources : the injustice, contempt, oppression perpetrated by rich/powerful fellow countrymen; secondly from the subordination to the British and the resultant feeling of humiliation. According to the author, the Bengalee male had only one means of salvaging his self-esteem; it was through the love and kindness of the female partner. That the woman was not just a bedtime partner of the husband and a full-time maid-servant for the husband's family was (and is) of course a new and reassuring perception; but one wonders how far this perception worked (and works) beyond the pages of imaginative fiction.

Chapter Eight, — 'Strength of Character and Love of God' brings out how "During this age the Bengalee had shown extraordinary talent as well as strength of character" thanks to the Western puritanic teachings of new morality, manners and austerity. The author mentions Vidyasagar as a supreme example of this phenomenon, for whose likes, principle was an inward or personal view of right conduct.

This perfectly valid observation is followed by an absured thesis about the Bengali's newly acquired idea of God who came to be looked up to as the saviour in his personal love-life. Here Chaudhury seems to speak without any basis but his personal feelings and family memories. Hence his argument — though the educated Bengalee Hindu observed all traditional rites, at heart they were conditioned by the Brahma concept of God as propounded by Rammohun — might appear rather surprising to scholars in the area. Though the monotheism of the Brahmas has been traced back by Rammohun himself to the *Upanisada,* according to Niradbabu, the God of the Brahmas was the Christian's God : "There was no doubt about it" (171). However, he finely brings out the common Brahma's conscious attempt at the time to distance himself from the Hindu heritage and environment, which brought him closer to the Christian in thought and life-style. In an atmosphere often marked by unconcealed mutual contempt between the two sects, *i.e.,* the Hindus and the Brahmas, the latter tilted — rather heavily — towards the West. In his characteristic charming way Chaudhury describes the Brahmas of this period who never admitted that they were Hindus by origin and heritage; they used to read the *Bible* and the European theological texts rather than the ancient Indian literature and scriptures; the idea of community prayer was also taken from the Christians.

In this context the author makes the arbitrary claim that the God of the Protestants had not only conditioned the Bengalee attitude to God but also indirectly influenced his attitude to marriage; earlier it was considered the safe way to have carnal pleasure and children; now an extra dimension was added to it under the Protestants' influence who were against celibacy and held that marriage was ordained by God. Thus marital love came to be considered God's blessing and ordained by God.

In the same chapter, however, Chaudhury points out a significant historical truth when he says — it was the time when one remarkable and admirable habit of the Bengalee elite was to weigh and assess his own faith and conduct continuously, whether the issue was love of God or pursuit of mortal love. Whatever opinion they arrived at in either public or private matters, whichever course they took or way they behaved, they tried to weigh and consider the arguments on both sides; they did not do anything without this painstaking self-probing, — a practice sadly missing in today's Bengal.

Chapter Nine underscrores the gulf between today's Bengali life and that of the nineteenth century. The two are, according to the author, so different that today's reader in Bengal may find it difficult to visualize the previous century, and may even find his description unbelievable. Chaudhury also admits here : "in fact the life about which I have written was not the folk-life of that age either; ...it had far transcended the mundane family life or community life" (183). But the problem, as rightly perceives, was that even this 'higher' life could not get completely separated from the 'low' or average, and the consequence of the contact was rarely happy. Throughout the nineteenth century the main feature of the history of Bengal was the clash between the prevailing traditions and the new trends. Here the reader gets an anticipation of the on coming depression of the last chapter as Chaudhury points out — with his characteristic boldness and clarity — the negative sides of the situation. He says, where the new trend won in this clash there was happiness, and where it was defeated there was disaster. Here the writer contradicts his earlier enthusiasm to admit that although in the national field the new emerged victorious on the whole, it was not so in the personal sphere. Not only in novels and stories but also in real life there were such characters who had been shattered due to this clash.

However, a glorious aspect of the time, as the writer recalls, was that a large number of people were motivated towards non-materialistic efforts. If one did nothing else, then at least he would have devoted himself to study. Some became writers, some religious missionaries. Since 1905, when the freedom movement started in right earnest many became either Congressmen or terrorists. How to earn money or run the family were not questions that bothered them; they were serious idealists who left their mark in various fields of contemporary history; the writer effectionately calls them 'Apanbhola' (unselfconscious) whose number has strikingly fallen in today's Bengal; with his enjoyable self-confidence Nirodbabu also includes himself in the list of these 'Apanbholas' among whom have appeared all the excellent Bengalees of modern times.

The Tenth or last chapter — 'The Fall of the Bengalee' is more contemplative than descriptive. The writer is saddened at the unrestrained decline of the Bengalee life which turns him a fatalist : "Like the individual," he says, "the life of a community is also conditioned by fate" (197). Here the focus shifts from the past to the present, and the writer makes certain generalizations about the Bengali character, alluding to some of its extraordinary qualities and some serious defects. He holds that in the nineteenth century the Bengalee had tried to rise and had risen in various fields of public as also private life by dint of his own effort. Even then he could not overcome the innate faults and weaknesses of his character. Anyway, those were kept restrained at the time by his urge to create a new way of life. But since 1917-18 the Bengalee spirit had again started flagging and the defects again swelled up to cover the virtues like weeds in a garden. Here Chaudhury makes a volley of attacks on the various weaknesses of the Bengalee character with particular emphasis on his lack of firmness. Thus when he served and sacrificed for his country that was an unconscious instinctive act, and the same instinct now drives him along the route of suicidal self-destruction. The book concludes in a note of deep sadness : "I had been in Delhi from 1942 to 1970, and in England since then. But it is less easy to forget one's own race as it is to forget some persons. Yet this remembrance brings nothing but sorrow." (200)

Regarding the significance of the Western influence on nineteenth century Bengal, and its tremendous impact on the socio-cultural situation here there is no dispute among critics and no dearth of scholarly research. Niradbabu does not add much in the way of scholarship or explorative analysis in this field. But the book derives its special flavour from the author's personal involvement; he passionately tries to understand the reason of the transience of Bengal's brief Renaissance because he is as emotionally moved by its sad termination as he is nostalgically stirred by its happy memory; an intimate personal touch in every page makes the book what it is.

Neither does the author claim to have made a theoretical discourse or a made-to-order thesis. He clearly points out the difference between his portraiture and that of the present-day Bengali writers with their "loud smatterings of all the fashionable Western cliche." He declares : "I am not prepared to impose geometrical 'cubes' on a natural scene" (183).

However, one has got to admit that Nirodbabu's honest personal impressions/responses — though never dull — are sometimes no less puzzling than those made-to-order 'cubes.'

Again, there are too many small and not so small holes in the texture of the argument. Also, the unqualified appreciation of the British on almost all the scores may not seem too savoury to a people who had been so long under the British rule. Many of his observation, — especially those on the woman's situation — are based purely on his own limited personal experience and on contemporary Bengali novels, and consequently show a serious lack of proportion. Moreover, the rambling style of relaxed recollection frequently hinders rather than helps in projecting an argument pointedly. The argumentation is also not always consistent; it is sometimes brilliantly perceptive and persuasive, sometimes wildly fantastic, and surprisingly absurd on occasions. The narration is in the tenor of personal recollection, and does not carry the impression of a painstaking researcher's exploration; rather it is frequently weighed down under the pressure of oversimplifications, generalizations, too many diversions.

These are the obvious blemishes of *Ãtmaghāti Bāngāli;* but the book is much more than these. Nirad C. Chaudhury can never be accused of one folly, *i.e.* parochialism. But his apparently sharp criticism of the Bengalee, his grievance against and pain for them only further underscores his love and nostalgia for the place which he has left for ever. This book, written in Bengali, on the Bengalee, on the writer's ninety-first year bears evidence to this love expressed in the language of passionate criticism. The book combines a touching nostalgia with scathing chastisement; this is also self-criticism, because even when he criticizes, Chaudhury does not forget that he himself is also a Bengalee. And that accounts for the unique effect of his exhortations.

Sometimes the very boldness of Nirad C.'s comments seems fascinating. For example, his critique of the so-called Bengalee Marxists of today : "The new logicians of Bengal boast : we are Marxists. If they had the least insight into their own character they would know that they were but repeating Bankimchandra : 'The Bengalee is controlled by circumstances, circumstances are never controlled by the Bengalee.' Marx had said the same thing about mankind. Such utter lie has never been voiced by any eminent man of talent; because man can control his environment he has risen above animality" (189). The cause of the writer's sorrow is that the Bengalee as a race has failed in this test. Similarly 'outrageous' are his observations on Saratchandra and the weaknesses of the Bengalee character. Nirad C. cannot forgive Saratchandra, in spite of his excellence as a novelist, for his attempt to justify the cowardly, selfish, good-for-nothing characters whose wrongs are typical of the race, and cannot be excused by any means. He also severely castigated what he finds to be the major defects of the Bengalee elite — his contempt for the non-Bengalee, his fondness for pandering his little knowledge, and the inability to see his own past, present and future unbiasedly with reason and intelligence. He thinks that it is this ineptitude that has rendered the Bengalee so vulnerable today.

Indeed, the book as a whole may be considered one long bold exhortation by an "old man with an eagle eye" who has perceived from afar the decadence that has set in here. There can be no dispute among honest, conscientious Bengalees that West Bengal today is going through a steadily declining path of decadence and slow suicide. The *Ātmaghāti Bāngāli* is meant to be an appeal-cum-warning to the 'decadent' Bengalee of our times who has been cut off from his own indigenous springs of creativity; at the same time, caught up in the throes of ape-like imitation he has forgotten his glorious nineteenth century history of learning and assimilation. That is why Chaudhury's volume on Bengal remains highly relevant for us today who are undergoing the direct experience of the agony of 'waste' Bengal.

One last query : why did Nirod C. write this book in Bengali? Was it meant to be a very special and exclusive message for the Bengalees alone?

Anyway, it is evident that the state of Bengal and the Bengalee had continued to worry the author till the last. Even in his last book, *Three Horsemen and the New Apocalypse* (1997), written by a man in his ninety-ninth year, which the author proudly claimed to be much more than "only senile babbling" (Preface), he came back to the theme of the decadence of Bengal.

In this book which is full of quotations from the author's own earlier writings, he recalls that as early as 1947 he wrote about his apprehension of the oncoming decadence. Here he had envisioned the decadence of Bengal as part of a larger process; this decadence involved not only Bengal, but India too, and included Europe and America as well within its area.

In 1987 too, on his ninetieth birthday, he had summed up his anxiety in a quotation from Pope's *Dunciad* :

> "Lo! thy dread Empire, Chaos! is restored;
> Light dies before thy uncreating word;
> Thy hand, great Anarch! Lets the curtain fall.
> And Universal Darkness buries all!"

At that time he had not expected that he would have to add up to his story of the Indian decadence. In 1997 he sadly realises that he has to do it.

Though Chaudhury finds the Indian form of decadence to have been divested of the element of "malignity" which characterises the decadence of Europe, yet that is no consolation for him. "It is only a comatose senility," — a "hollow ghost" (*Three Horsemen* 111); emptiness and lifelessness are its features.

The author notes that there had been two earlier periods of decadence in India, — before the advent of the Moghuls, and before the advent of the British. In the present and the third one, which, according to him, and set in by the mid-forties, he finds the same symptoms coming back. Chaudhury elaborates his thesis by analysing 'aspects and stages of political decadence,' and the 'General character of social and cultural decadence.'

One may not agree with many of the author's assumptions, and may even feel exasperated with a number of his innuendoes. However, he establishes in his incomparable way that the present state of Bengal "has a bearing on the pan-Indian decadence" (*Three Horsemen* 122). What particularly disturbs Chaudhury is the phenomenon which he describes as the passing away of the Bengali '*Bhadrolok*,' the land-owning elite gentile of Bengal, which, according to him, synchronised with the withering of the modern Indian culture.

The nostalgia is understandable considering the brilliant impact of this class on Bengal and India in the 19th and early 20th centuries. But perhaps it is too much to expect such a class to survive in the face of today's complex socio-economic situation. And one feels like sharing Niradbabu's sadness as one sees today how the mores of a consumerist money-minded society have seeped into the mentality of the Bengali middleclass. With the pungent irony Chaudhury points out :

"On their part, the Bengalis who are poor by *status,* even though not for money, nurse unappeasable class hatred and dream of revolution" (*Three Horsemen* 124).

This is sufficient to infuriate the committed "revolutionaries" who would condemn the 'intolerable' flippancy. But in the meantime things have taken an ironical turn. As if to prove the validity of Chaudhury's theory of Bengali decadence, even the "revolutionaries" too, at least a section, appear to have stepped in. Little could the old man divine from his far-away resort in Oxford how a sizable number of them have caught up with the status-targets, — luxury cars, executive-class flights, five-star trips, and the other accessories. The one-time die-hard fighters have been forced to take the back seat. In the process 'Waste' Bengal has slid — perhaps irretrievably — into "an area of darkness."

17

A Carnival from Kerala : *The God of Small Things*

—Suresh Shukla

Anyone familiar with the present-day Scenario of Indian Writings in English knows more about blessings, less about a curse to Ms. Roy. *The God of Small Things* has created a good deal of excitement among careful readers, critics and professional reviewers. In the recent times, a lot of things have happened and continue to happen not only in this part of the global campus but even across the Arabian Seas. All of us are truly surprised and puzzled by Ms. Roy's...the very first stroke, much coveted Booker Prize and fame. It is a big rise of the Indian Star in the West! Ms. Roy has chiselled a niche in the treasure-trove of the Indian Fiction in English.

The gist of the matter seems to lie in this :

Modern Indian technology is a new portent in an old World, yet the Indians in the rural area keep on observing those socio-religious taboos. However, the world has looked and appreciated the very potentium of these creative writers who present realistic description, be it of any particular state or Indian continent. A group of creative writers have put forward acceptable intellectual interpretation, frequently referring to the Hindu scriptures and current problems of the Indian society. Thus, Ms. Roy shows sound acquaintance with the socio-economic as well as the churning political process of the Kerala State. At this stage, one would like to know how Ms. Shirley Chew observed in The TLS : "Much praised and promoted as it has been *The God of Small Things* cleverly crafted, often witty and moving first novel by a talented new Writer. Its weaknesses are the kind one might expect in a first novel; the most glaring being a tendency to overwrite."[1]

In spite of this Spectacular success of *The God of Small Things*, it is very painful to take note of the perfunctory remarks of the most respectable...among doyens, Prof. C.D.N. Probably, rev. Professor C.D.N. seems to be in a fit of anguish calls Ms. Roy 'A trickster,' 'a self-hypnotized Word retailer,' 'the inebriate author.' I think, Hon'ble Professor C.D.N. is in the dire grip of phobia, as he does not seem to be reluctant in cursing 'Hon'ble Five Member Jury' in calling 'the feather-brained.' Pardon, be the word, there was no need to curse...Creativity in the shaping. I earnestly wish, Rev. C.D.N. might have touched *The God of Small Things* with noble anger.[2]

The God of Small Things is fairly longish and quite ambitious in scope. It is a fact that in the due course of time, re-appraisals might evoke a fresh stance or two. Any new critical disagreement might point-out to a certain depth of implication in the novel.

The very format is amorphous, fairly complex; it has wide cast of characters : Kochamma, Mammaji, Ammu, Chacko, Estha, Rahel, Sophie Mol, Kochu Maria, Father Mulligan, Rev. Ipe, Comrade Pillai, Murlidharan, Vellya and Vellutha. From the very inception of the novel, the locale is Ayemenem, a town in Kerala, 'A rare breed of Siamese twins.' Estha and Rahel meet after a very long time. The main force at the back of Ms. Roy's narrative pattern is in search for answers to the fatal events which occurred long back that unforgettable December than a trip of Chacko's ex-wife and his daughter Sophie. Chacko's plan was to give a speical treat to Sophie. Somehow the wheel of fortune turned awfully bad. A mishap leads to misunderstanding. Thus, Ms. Roy launches back into the past. The authorized extract shows the ordering and generalizing powers working on the records of memory, there might be a quick recalling or erasing of the circumstantial, physical and emotional details. Any individual without Catholic outlook might start enlisting pitfalls, be it all about the cellular structure of the novel. To elucidate it clearly as under : Baby Kochamma's Questioning Spirit.

"There's something I wanted to ask you, Father, Baby Kochamma would say. In first Cornithians, Chapter ten, verse twenty-three, it says" :

'All things are lawful for me but all things are not expedient. Father, how can all things be lawful unto Him?

I mean I can understand if some things are lawful for Him but....'[3] (p. 23)

The twins squatted on their haunches, like professional adult gossips in the Ayemenem market.

Time present is extricably bound up with time past and time future and it is the people with a capacity for sensations and feelings of present time who beat out mostly. The past is vividly present with a little squeak of hinges, positively recorded by Ms. Roy. It reads as under :

> They sat in silence for a while.
> Kuttappen mortified, the twins preoccupied with boat thoughts.
> 'Has Chacko Saar's Mol Come!' Kuttapen asked.
> 'Must have,' Rahel said laconically.
> 'Where's She?'
> 'Who knows? Must be around somewhere.' We don't know.
> 'Will you bring her for me to see?'
> 'Caril,' Rahel said.
> 'Why not?'
> 'She has to stay indoors. She's very delicate. If she gets dirty.
> She'll die.'
>
> (pp. 209-10)
>
> 'I see.'

The cells of narrative keep on changing. The imagery is pictorial and even impressionistic.

To justify it clearly it reads as under :

Kari Saipu's house had been renovated and painted. It had become the centrepiece of an elaborate complex, crisscrossed with artificial canals and connecting bridges. Small boats bobbed in the water. The old colonial bungalow with its deep verandah and *Doric* Columns, was surrounded by smaller, older, wooden houses, — ancestral homes — that the hotel chain had brought from old families and transplanted in the Heart of Darkness. Toy Histories for rich to play in. Like the sheaves of rice in Joseph's dream, like a press of eager natives petitioning an English magistrate, the old houses have been arranged around the History House in attitude of deference.

'Heritage' the hotel was called'[4] (p. 126).

At times Ms. Roy probes into physiognomy at length. To illustrate it in all details about Pappachi. It reads :

> "He was a photogenic man, dapper and carefully groomed, with a littleman's largeish head. He had an incipient second chin that would have been emphasized had he look down or nodded. In photograph he had taken care to take hold his head high enough to hide his double chin, yet not so high as to appear haughty. His brown eyes were polite yet maleficent, as though he was making an effort to be civil to the photographer while plotting to murder his wife" (p. 51).

To add a little more in the form of pithy sentences, one might find following sentences of some interest :

(a) "He (Comrade Pillai) walked like a chameleon" (p. 14).

(b) 'She had lost weight on her face and shoulders, which had turned her from being a round person into a conical person' (p. 21).

(c) "Then he (Father Mullijan) would reopen his umbrella and walk away in chocolate robes and comfortable sandals like a high-stepping camel with an appointment to keep" (p. 24).

Ms. Roy's well controlled wit can be traced very clearly from the following illustration :

'She (Baby Kochamma) found that senior sisters monopolized the priest and bishops with biblical doubts more sophisticated than hers would ever be, and that it might be yeats before she got anywhere near Father Mulligan' (pp. 24-25).

Similarly, Ms. Roy takes a lot of pains to give a graphic word picture of physical aspects also. The following illustration would be quite justifying.

'She had forgotten just how damp the monsoon air in Ayemenem could be swollen cupboards creaked. Locked windows burst open. Books got soft and wavy between their covers, strange insects appeared like ideas. In the evenings and burned themselves. On Baby Kochamma's dim 40-watt bulbs. In the day time their crisp incinerated corpses littered the floor and window slits an until Kochhu Maria sweeps them away in the plastic dustpan, the air smelled of something burning.'

An alert reader is bound to inhale this type of smell on tracing the integration of expressions in *The God of Small Things*.

May I argue that the notion of the Indian creative writers writing in English do not have the same strength and parity to appeal general readers on this part of the global campus or abroad. All of us know that the command of a language is to be attained through rigorous practice and any individual's genuine urge for the same. Whenever any creative writer's piece of work is to be in the limelight, one would love to chew a marrow-bone. It often becomes a self-sought exploratory exercise. *The God of Small Things* is good enough for such work. However, I regard...command of a language as the ability of mature and sound grooming in the midst of the native speakers or any such identical set-up at home. It implies both a high level achievement and ability to adapt and develop expressions. Or one's own urgency, as Sir Kipling tried in using words like : 'bhisti' or 'dooli' Ms. Roy impresses readers, as a writer of impulse rather than premeditation. In spite of her strength or spontaneity, she does not command well her material. Apparently, she has operated several off-shoots, be it a Pappachi's wrath beating Mammachi with a vase and timely intervention of Chacko. Chacko makes a humble plea...seeking a promise... 'I never want to happen this again...' (p. 48). Or reference to the workers' problem in Kerala or the conjugal love game of Ammu. Chacko. These lovers do not depict mutual celebration and strength of their fidelity but a reflection of well glided gross sexuality.

Ms. Roy used metaphors in *The God of Small Things*. A few specimens of metaphor are enlisted from humdrum situations.

(a) She spent hours on the riverbank with her plastic transistor shaped like tangerine.

(b) Baby Kochamma balanced like a big bird over a public pot (p. 95).

(c) The blonde Baroness who shone like a diamond (p. 110).

(d) Comrade Pilla's smile broadened as he turned his attention like a searchlight on Rahel (p. 130).

(e) His (Comrade Pillai) mind hummed like the table fan (p. 277).

(f) He looked like an unfriendly jewelled bear.

(g) He had an unshaven, jowly face. His teeth, like yellow piano keys, watched little Elvis the Pelvis (p. 102).

Figures of speech are departures from the direct way of writing or speaking. Every writer or a good public speaker has own style and says in his/her own way. At times a writer conscientiously makes an attempt to say a thing forcefully. In fact, Ms. Roy seems to have overdone it. Therefore, there is a continuous deflection. It might create a very itchy effect for any careful reader. Metaphor is as ultimate speech itself, and speech as ultimate thought. One should use it to a certain limit.

There are extra-fictional pronouncements or the implicit voice of the novelist. It reads as under :

(1) ...Communism represented a fate worse than death (p. 66). Ms. Roy refers to Kerala State.

(2) Going to Oxford didn't necessarily make a person clever.

(3) Cleverness didn't necessarily make a good prime minister.

(4) All Indian mothers are obsessed with their sons and are therefore poor judges of their abilities (p. 56).

(5) ...I never want to hear you discussing people's deaths with them again.

Ms. Roy's digressions are heavy for general readers. Of course, the Syrian Christians' rise and fall, or the role of E.M.S. Namboodiripad might be taken as one of the factual documents of Kerala. Ms. Roy has the courage to wish to show things as she has very closely experienced them or banked upon quite genuine sources. Lastly, whatever may be the memoirs of Ms. Roy, it is to be taken as a deliberate romance. *The God of Small Things* should be read a carteblanche for critics; it offers a new range of data. It is a bold venture and an excellent indication of what the novel can do when it breaks those shackles and constraints of the bygone days.

REFERENCES

1. Ms. Shirley Chew, *The House in Kerala. The TLS, May 30.*
2. Rev. Prof. C.D.N., *The Literary Criterion*, Vol. XXXII, 1997.
3. Ms. Arundhati Roy, *The God of Small Things,* India Ink, New Delhi, 1997, p. 23.
4. *Ibid.*

18

Moral Vision in the Poetry of Krishna Srinivas

—*K.A. Agarwal*

Krishna Srinivas is the most out-standing name among the contemporary poets. He has addressed his poetry to the people of the whole world. His poetry breaks the limits of the boundaries of race, colour, clime and country. It blends the consciousness of the modern age with the ancient sublimity of great rishies. His poetry is read and enjoyed not only in his land but in foreign countries also. His poetry contains the essence of humanity. He is a poet of spiritual unfoldment. It moves from darkness to light.

Krishna Srinivas is an Indo-English poet of distinction. Undoubtedly he is a classic of our times. His poetical works like *Dance of Dust, Everest, Give Elements, Beyond, Maya, Water* and *Sonnets* etc., are poems of "excellences." They contain human culture. His other poetry books are *Sankara, Ramaneya, Vallalar, Madhavs, Christ, Muhamad, Tamil Vedas, Buddha* and *Mahavir* etc. They are inspiring poems devoted to human values and world-unity. They transcends all barriers of religions, castes, creeds, colours and nations. Prof. Syed Ameeruddin rightly observes : "His life is a journey from darkness to illumination; a quest to know the blaze of realities; a tireless exploration to discover newer horizons; a task to lead others to lofty thoughts; to reach the core of the cosmos."

Dr. K.V.S. Murthi, a great critic on Krishna Srinivas, has also praised his poetry in these words :

> "The poetry of Krishna Srinivas, an internationally reputed poet admired as fiery cosmic articulator, is repute with multidimensional sensibility and energetic expression, idealism and cosmic sweep."

In his poem "Water" he says that the present world is a highly mismanaged world. He writes :

> I cry with the river,
> I grow with the river,
> I frolic with the river,
> I age with the river,
> I regenerate with the river.

Here Krishna Srinivas has presented a poetic vision, water has been symbolized. It is the source for life but its purity has been polluted by the ever crowded civilization.

Dance of Dust was published in 1946. This poem is one of his early epical poems which established him as one of the living greatest poets of the contemporary literature. It is an extraordinary poem with the utterances of humanity. It moves from darkness to light. In fact the darkness is because of the ego. Of course our true nature is divine but ignorance and sense of pride cover our divinity. So unless we cross the river of ego we cannot reach the bank of light. This poem reminds us of the Vedic declaration, "Tamso Ma Jyotirgamaya." It means "O Lord lead us form darkness of light." It is a wonder that in spite of the neat floor and clean lamp with full oil there is no light. The human being is not able to get light. The poet tells his readers that through ignorance the common people keep themselves separate from God. Ignorance is a strong rock which does not allow to see the Divine Light. It hides our true nature and through ignorance the true self becomes the fantasy of an age. The poem moves from common and worldly life experiences to uncommon and divine experiences. In this way *Dance of Dust* is a philosophical and symbolical poem. In other words the theme of the poem is "destruction and construction of the world." It reminds us of wars. The poet himself says :

> "The war came — carving cemeteries of cities, planting fevers in the arteries of our world.... And this long poem *Dance of Dust* is the pouring of my agonizing soul.... Past is my born, I hunger for the reign or everlasting peace and Paradise Regained."

The poem has the development of religious sensibility. People are ignorant of their own actions. Their lives are loveless confusion of struggle and light. The whole world is suffering from the disease of ignorance and skepticism helplessly. The modern people are suffering from religious uncertainty because they are on the darkling plain. The poet says :

> "Man kills man is sport,
> And flags dripping with blood;
> Flutter over peaks of flesh;
> And ships loaded with gold and ivory,
> Sweep the seven seas in revelry,
> Babes torn from women's breast,
> Are sold as slaws to silver might;
> And raped to honey dew,
> In silken chalice of juicy crevice,
> In the name of art, religion and rule.

The lines are the cry of agonized soul of the poet. He revolts against the existing culture and social norms of the world :

> Culture sleeps in many beds,
> In vagrant shades and truant times,
> Ravishing connoisseurs,
> Feeding genius with fires from many hearths,
> Snug silent, antediluvian.

The poem exposes the drawbacks of modern society. We are coloured in Western culture which has renaissance spirit and teaches us only to lead a materialistic way of life. But *Dance of Dust* inspires us to embrace Vedantic-Culture of purity. Auden declares "We must love each other or die" while

Arnold's says "Oh love! let us be true to each other." Krishna Srinivas has the message of "World Peace" and "spiritual unfoldment" through this poem. For the immortal preaching it has been liked by the scholars. It has been accepted by a host of readers because it exposes violence against women, children and innocent people. It must be stopped otherwise all culture and social progress will come to an end. It is every inch an Indian poem characterised by the qualities of Beauty, Truth, Goodness, Love and Power.

Here "Dust" has symbolical meaning. It stands for unrest, violence, exploitation and terrorism. The poet prays to God that the people should realize their mistakes and there should be a cultural-revolution. He dreams about the economic, cultural, social and intellectual emancipation of the people.

> A storm of conquest,
> Taming the wrath of seas to ply the oars,
> Accumulating the filth of bloody wars,
> Prinking the bubbles
> Pinning the babes,
> Tearing the rainbows from heavens,
> Fluttering banners of bureaucratic pride,
> India gleams as leaf quite due.

There should be no discrimination between man and man because caste, creed and colour are based on falsehood. All are children of God and, therefore, the ruling class has no right to oppress and exploit the masses. All type of oppressions like physical, economic, social, religious or cultural must be stopped. This poem cultivates Indian values of life, art, literature and culture.

> Christ crooned commandments;
> Buddha dreaded dust
> And counselled caution, Nirvana
> Exhilarating Transcendence.

Both Lord Buddha and Lord Christ had worked for the spiritual gains of humanity. Here gods and human beings play with each other. The poet has full faith in the DIVINE NATURE. He writes :

Despair not :
You and dust anon must
Fix the lease of rigmarole
And hush the wrath of wormy wars
And crack its typhus in an iron tomb.

He advises to take the Journey from dust to divinity. The different type of wars, conflicts quarrels and disputes are in the world because we have forgotten our divine nature. We should realize our divinity and we should follow our goal of human upliftment. It is possible only through national integration and international integration. He gives the gospel of human unity in this poem because "Earth is the best space for love."

In the *Five Elements* the poet deals with the five elements — water, wind, fire, earth and void. These elements are present from time to eternity. Here the poet has energized his spiritual resources for the future generations. Here he criticizes terrorism, violence, horror and nuclear wars because they are mounting upon the humanity. The poet write :

In passion I am born
In passion I live
In passion I perish
So too, you, my Kaveri

*　　*　　*　　*

At Kaveri ghats
Sages and saints chant their beads
And lisp a million Om
Grow million fires
Char million desires.

The poem emphasises upon the need of human unity to solve the tension between different human groups. In this poem the poet wants to convey the philosophy of ONENESS. His approach is bound to be synthetic. The poem bridges the gap among politics, religion, philosophy, science, mythology and theology. The poet is conscious of the fact that anger, greed, passion, arrogance, hatred, terrorism, violence, exploitation of man by man, national and international prejudices, tension, hypertention, cultural ignorance, other ignorances, communalism, pollution, ecological imbalance and other evils are challenging the very existence of mankind. So the poem preaches the solution for all these evils. It can be possible only through *human unity*. This poem is a precious document of humanity. Rapid technological growth has brought moral degeneration. The chilling moral stagnation has eaten the ones of our civilization. The global catastrophe is increasing day by day. The mankind is suffering from a transformational crisis. It takes the reader to the long cultural and poetic journey which will enlight us with self-knowledge, spiritual wisdom and universal message of oneness and it is read and enjoyed as a precious document of humanity. It transforms the hearts and minds of human beings form darkness to light. The references of vedic literature and ancient sages in the poem are the sources as nectar to the morally degenerated world of today. The poem raises its voice loudly against vulgarity and profanity of world culture.

In this poem Krishna Srinivas shows his intelligence, a sound sense of culture, history, philosophy and rare genius of aestheticism. It touches classical heights.

'Maya' is a socio-philosophic poem. It reveals the mystery of all existence. Krishna Srinivas has taken Maya into a new vision. He says that those who denounce Maya are ignorant because Maya can never be seen as distinct from Brahman. Often people call Maya as 'Avidya' but we should keep this fact in mind that both Maya and Vidya are properties of Brahman. Whenever there is failure to see the world as creation of Brahman, there arises Moha, Shoka and Dukh. Poet Srinivas believes that the self and the entire world are nothing but the absolute Brahman.

The poem 'Maya' is an interesting narrative poem which deals with the relationship between man and woman. The poet begins this poem in a socio-philosophic way.

From the Unreal lead me to Real
From languor lead me to light.
From death lead to eternity.

The poet has considered Maya in the Human shape and narrates her story. A mythical character Maya is 19 years old daughter of Geetha who works in an office. She showers her love, affection and kindness on Maya. The teenaged girl also regards the soft sentiments of her mother. But then temple like house is collapsed when one day the girl is informed by her main-servant about the questionable life of her mother. Her mother has illicit relations with her office-boss. Here we are reminded of the typist lady in T.S. Eliot's poem, *The Waste Land*.

Like T.S. Eliot, Krishna Srinivas also discovers the modern myth of corruption. It is a general belief that when the woman becomes corrupt, she produces corrupt children and then the whole civilization becomes corrupt. The purity of human race surely depends upon the purity of the mother. But here Krishna Srinivas does not believe the old rotten belief. He does not agree that corrupt mothers produce corrupt children. There have been many corrupt mothers but their daughters have adopted the path of purity and virtue. The poem, "Maya" deals with the themes of the man-woman and mother-daughter relationships. The poem reminds us Goldsmith's famous lines on Woman-character. He writer :

When lovely woman stoops to folly
And finds too late that men betray
What charm can soothe her melancholy
What art can wash her guilt a way.

The answer is only to repent for her wrong deeds. The poem is a beautiful narration about the character of 19 years old girl Maya who in spite of her mother's corrupt life comes out as a woman of purity and virtue. The poet has emerged here as an experimentalist. He has dealt here man and woman relationship as creative endeavor and co-operative action. It is in their creativity co-operative attitude, confidence and purity that the future of the world community depends. The whole poem has been written in a philosophical mood, vein, tone and language. It is an innovative poem. Dr. R.K. Singh observe :

> "Through Maya, Krishna gives the message of liberty, restraint and truthfulness."

Dr. Syed Ammeruddin's words about 'Maya' are most worthy to be quoted here :

> "The institution of marriage has been created not only to streamline the way of flesh and the hunger of ravishment but also to blow off the last particles of broken dust paving way to serene calm and thrushing man and woman into a dual heaven.... everlasting Eden....perennial paradise."

Krishna Srinivas advocates for conjugal love. Man and woman should lead the life of purity as husband and wife. This poem emphasizes the importance of the divine characters which are possible as an ideal couple — husband and wife. Only then they can see and realize the purity and divinity in their inward parts. Thus, they can find the spirit of truth and realize the kingdom of heaven upon this earth. Such a couple can find peace, harmony, on this earth. In fact man's true nature is divine and the knowledge of the self can make the man and woman illumined. The poet's discovery of Maya in our modern world is praiseworthy. His Maya stands for purity and a symbol of woman-virtues.

His next poem *The Everest* has the theme of the fusion of various elements. The poet develops a theory of human history in the poem. He fuses the human history with that of geographical birth of the Everest. He fuses the image of the past and the present into a unified whole. It is systematic study of both the histories for more than fifty milleniums. The poet closely watches and interprets the links of the Everest and the mankind. It is the witness of many human civilizations of the past. "The poem shows underground connections and seeds of comparative religion, philosophy, culture and anthropology."

> And that day will dawn
> When gods churn again
> An Everest morn

The poet uses in this poem the images of vast abyss, darkness, magic zodiacs, fossilized earth and image of the past and present into a unified whole. For him the Everest is a natural beauty.

> I searching Me
> And Me searching Thee
> And I and Me
> Mirrored in He
> I and Me no different He,

He sings of 'Eternity' with philosophical ideas. He emphasis to alive India's prime principle of equality, liberty, fraternity, universal brotherhood and love for humanity. The poem achieves the aesthetics of impersonality. It emphasizes the need for multi-culturalism. The various religious thinkers, prophetic genius and literary giants bestow the best elements of tradition of multi-cultures :

> Mohameds and Christs
> Dantes and Shakespeares
> Blakes and Eliots
> Bubbled at the brim
>
> * * * *
>
> Vyasas and Badaryanas
> And sagely tribes
> Seeded in Manna icicles
> Drip Vedic Chants

And Upanishads
In words heard and memorised

He thinks the Everest a cup of 'Som Rasa' of wisdom. It is a symbol of the harmonies of heart, mind and soul. It represents Indian's Sublime culture and civilization. It creates as enchanting world of eloquence, harmony and genius. The poem is a store-house of Indian-philosophy. The poet has used befitting references of the Ganges, the Kaveri, the Yamuna, the *Upanishads*, the *Bhagavadgita* and the incarnates of Indian life Lord Krishna and Lord Buddha. He has also referred the great contributions of great contemporary personalities like Mahatma Gandhi and Pt. Jawahar Lal Nehru. The poem pleads for human justice and it is possible only by accepting the principles of equality, liberty, fraternity, love and universal brotherhood.

Present echoing the past
And becoming revised beyond
Fifty milleniums ago
From rage of atoms rose
Cephalized metazoa
Rolled up and enveloped
And god burnt to bone
Rose over fossiled earth

The musical expression and the philosophical ideas of the poem move our hearts as nothing has moved them earlier. It watches the cycles of civilization. It also represents the multi-culturalism which is the need of the time. It is a classical poem having sublime thoughts of world-unity, world-peace and world-order.

His poem *Tamil Vedas* shows his great mastery over Tamil literature and language. In Tamil the four thousand lyrics are very famous and the Tamils all over the world sing them as a part of their prayer. They are the soul of Vaishnavism. Krishna Srinivas has presented the gist of the Tamil Vedas in beautiful poetic form. Dr. Syed Ameeruddin has rightly observed :

> "Since all the four Vedas are sung in Sanskrit, these Apostles, called Alwars, have transported into Tamil all the countries where Tamils live, these immortal lyrics of Alwars are sung with great devotion every morning. Especially in East, descendants of Tamil, who migrated into these countries milleniums ago, sing with gusto these soul stirring verses."

The poet has used very simple but harmonious style in composing verses in his poem *Tamil Vedas*. Like a Sadhaka he has devoted his true sublimity to this poem. He has followed the Vedic dictum 'Charaiveti, Charaiveti.' Some of the lines in the poem may be read like mantras.

Krishna Srinivas is not only lover of India but he is also a staunch lover of the entire universe and mankind and so the scope of his poetry is not a prison-house of one ideology or nation or culture but it is as vast as the open sky. He believes in 'Vasudev Kutumbhkam.'

His poetry achieves the power of the mantra to register and master experience. He often repeats words phrases and sentences to emphasize his view point and depicts his experiences. He has done to a lot of translations from Sanskrit, Tamil, Arabic and other languages. But he is not a mere translator or borrower he has the Shakespearean quality. Whatever he borrows from other sources, he totally absorbs it and makes it as his own. We can say in bold words that Krishna Srinivas is a great modern poet. In the end I quote the words of Dr. Syed Arneeruddin which are the true appreciation of this great Indo-Anglian poet :

> "Krishna's Divine Blaze illumines the most universal theme — KNOW THYSELF. It is to discover one's archetypal being through complexity of imagery and thought, uniting life and pursuit. His imagination transcends the permutation of paradoxes used to uncover the mysteries of existence."

REFERENCES

1. Krishna Srinivas, 'Poetical Works,' Madras World Poetry Society International, Raja Street, 1979.
2. Dr. K.V.S. Murthi, Professor of English, Andhra University from his article "Krishna Srinivas — A Poet," World Poetry Society International, Raja Street, Madras, 1980.
3. Syed Ammeeruddin, *Krishna Srinivas : A Colossus in World Pannassus* (World Poetry Society, Madras, 1995).
4. K.R.S. Iyengar, *Indian Writing in English* : Bombay, Asia Publishing House 1973.
5. T.M.P. Mahadevan : "Western Vedant" in "Vedant for Modern Man" (George Allen and Unwin Limited, London, 1952).
6. Swami Yatishwarnand, "Spiritual Unfoldment in Vedant for Modern Man" (George Allen and Unwin Limited London, 1952).
7. M.E. Shields : "Krishna Srinivas and his Poetical Works" (Oxford University Press, Delhi, 1987).
8. V.K. Gokak : "The Concept of Indianness with Reference of Indian Writing," *Indian Writing in English* ed. by Ramesh Mohan, 1994.
9. "Ten Twentieth Century Indian Poet," edited by R. Parthasaraty (Oxford University Press, Delhi, 1984).
10. Buckminster Fuller : 'Modern Poetry' (Oxford University Press, Delhi, 1985).
11. Som Benegal's essay "A Bold Peace Approach" — *The Hindustan Times*, Friday, August 2, 1996.
12. Dr. Suresh Chand Dwivedi : *Krishna Srinivas — A Poet of Total Experience* : World Poetry Society International, Madras 1997.
13. R.K. Singh : An article on "Krishna Srinivas," the lines quoted in S.C. Dwivedi's book "Krishna Srinivas — "A Poet of Total Experience."

19

Woman's Striving for a Meaningful Life in Anita Desai's *Cry, the Peacock*

—*Vinod Kumar Maheshwari*

Mostly, the novel *Cry, the Peacock*[1] has been written through the stream of consciousness method with conversational episodes very little. Maya, the heroine of the novel, records the memory of her life with her father, and with her husband Gautam and his family. Being a sensitive daughter of a well-to-do father, her impressions are impulses-borne, reacting to human reality and environment according to her likes and dislikes. The novel is essentially a dream-stuff of the doom-haunted Maya. There is also an element of tragic pathos in her expressions, varying from one moment to another according to her anxiety-ridden moods. Thus, there is dreaminess in what she expresses and to what she reacts.

In Shakespeare's *The Tempest* (1611), one gets aware of the dreaminess of life : '...We are such stuff/As dreams are made on, and our little life/Is rounded with a sleep.'[2] Prospero spoke these words out of his mellowed wisdom. In *Cry, the Peacock,* the anxiety-ridden heroine, Maya also intones herself in dreaminess with the only difference, she is helpless and is haunted by the impending doom.

Even as there may be minor shortcomings here and there in the novel-structure, the portrayal of Maya is projected in a sympathetic vein. Maya needs the benefit of sympathy and understanding from readers. Her life is shadowed by the three-fold effect of death-doom and destiny. Even as, her mind is at times highly chaotic and anxiety-ridden, she does not lose her discriminating sense. In this way, one is able to appreciate her womanly impulses. In assessing Maya's agonising struggle to wrestle within herself for a meaningful life, Virginia Woolfe's suggestion has been very helpful :

> The greater part of any library is nothing but the record of (noticeable) fleeting moments in the lives of men, women and (other creatures). Every literature, as it grows old, has its rubbish-heap, the records of vanished moments and forgotten lives told in faltering and feeble accents that have perished. But if you give yourself up to the delight of rubbish-reading, you will be surprised, indeed you will be overcome, by the relics of human life that have been cast out to moulder. It may be one letter — but what a vision it gives! It may be a few sentences — but what vistas they suggest![3]

In the cultural firmament of India which is undergoing vast changes now one finds that there are good, bad, monstrous and erratic specimens of women — ranging from film-actresses, models, house-wives to the fallen sisters of Gandhiji; and in this background, a woman like Maya occupies a unique place. Being sensitive and having spent her childhood in comfortable conditions of parental care, it was expected that her marital life should be wholesome and happy; but, it could not come about, mainly, on account of her extra-sensitiveness, and also on account of the death of her pet dog, Toto with whom she had come to establish motherly circuit. Besides, it is equally reasonable to say that had she not gone with her *ayah* to an astrologer with albino eyes, she would not have been doom haunted; for this gnome-like astrologer had prophesied to Maya in her girlhood phase an unatural death four years after marriage to either husband or wife. Suddenly, she undergoes a hallucinatory experience of 'remembrance of things of the past' and gets terrified and panic-ridden — which is an important component of female psyche.[4] Maya was conscious of this sinister impact on her mind : It is vividly expressed. The allusion is to astrologer :

> A persistent sense of some disaster I had known, and forgotten, or perhaps never known, only, at one time, feared, and now rediscovered. ...Not merely a foreboding, but a distant apprehension of a presence. Like an under-current beneath the throbbing of drums, a foreign odour amidst the scent of lemon blossoms, a struggle of despair that continued beyond the sleep of death. ...I searched the stars, unhappily, fearsomely even. ...It was as though I were faced with an important message in a language I could not read. Thinking now of Toto (the dead pet dog), then of a growing desire to call Gautama, and ultimately of whatever I knew of the constellations, I sifted through the hieroglyphs. It was a language I had once known. ...God! God! I cried, and sat up in terror. There was no clash and clamour after that. I was aware of a great, dead silence in which my eyes opened to a vision that appeared through the curtains of the years, one by one falling back till I saw again that shadow. A black and evil shadow. Its name was not that of a demon in a Kathakali dance drama, nor was it one of the limpid appellations of the moon. It was, I remembered it now, Fate (27-28).

It is the unbearable turmoil in a haunted woman who suffers more than man in a similar condition. It is primarily because woman is more emotional than man. While man can counter-balance the emotional surge by reason woman finds it well-nigh impossible to tame the uncontrollable emotions on the strength of her psychic resources. And when the surge of emotions has to pass under the shadow of an ominous prophecy, then, a woman like Maya is left with no other alternative but to heave a maddening sigh — oh God! oh God!, as in the above extract; and now to continue with the same, one finds :

> He had been large or small? I cannot remember, but his eyes I do : they were pale, opaque, and gave him an appearance of morbidity, as though he had lived, like a sluggish white worm, indoors always, in his dark room at the temple gates, where the central lingam was painted a bright, vicious red as though plunged in sacrificial blood, and light burned in a single lamp from which oil spilled into a large, spreading pool. Just as his shadow spread and spread, a stain edging towards me who stood, clutching my ayah's hand, in paralysed terror and even fiercer fascination, my toes curling away from the oil, from his shadow. 'Not only here, but in your horoscope also,' he said, tapping the long chart the *ayah* had had made for me, 'and there, on your forehead too,' he smiled, and laying down the paper, he raised his hand, a plump, oiled hand with dyed nails, bringing it close to my face so that I felt as though a bat were caught in the same room with me, and shrank involuntarily (28-29).

Maya, the affrighted woman, recapitulates the shadowy presence of the albino-eyed astrologer. She is terrified of him and feels the repulsiveness. Had Maya been a woman given to turbidity of mind[5] she would have allowed herself to become docilely a victim of the unregenerate astrologer. This is how the uneducated and ignorant women cater to the whims and fancies of the 'religious-minded' people like the astrologer, from whom Maya shrank back in terror. From the novel, one can make out that Maya was not an orthodox Hindu woman. All the same she was acquainted with Hindu philosophy and mythology. Above all, she had a sense of dignity and a silent belief in her womanly grace. It is true that in spite of her being caught in the web of mischievous circumstances she tries to recapitulate feelingly her affectionate relationship with her father. In contrast, the atmosphere at her father-in-law's house was more social and political than being personal and familial, to which a married woman like Maya would be more responsive. However, the fate had not decreed to Maya this much of womanly need. It contributed a great deal in making Maya unhinged within herself. What is known as the meaninglessness in life is essentially a product of the impersonal tenor of family life. In her married life, Maya could get everything possible within the parameters of formal dignity from her husband, Gautam, and also from her other relatives at the Father-in-law's house; but she failed to get an adequate balmy response to her distracted mind at her in-law's place. Precisely, in her moments of temporary relief from her doom-haunted distractions she could remember with gratitude her father's affection in her pre-marital stage. This difference in the attitude of her father and that of her husband and other relatives at her-in-law's place would be touched upon shortly hereafter.

In the meanwhile, as one tries to analyse her response to the evil-minded astrologer in the underlined portion of the extract, cited above, one has a feeling that Maya was an extremely sensitive woman who started twitching with horror at the approaching sight of the astrologer as if he was a liquified image of obscenity from which her toes started curling away. It implies Maya's instinctive repulsion against the perverted astrologer exuding the oil of unregenerate passions within him. Maya's instantaneous reaction to his presence is a sign of her purity and sensitiveness, which in explicit term means Maya's struggle to be her own self. It is a sign of the grit of human character to resist the external pressures of circumstances in getting tainted. So long as one remains unpolluted in mind, he or she would not go adrift in the chaotic sea of confusion. In Latin, it has been stated that when the daemonic agencies want to destroy man, they first pervert his mind. When the perversion starts, there is no end to human perdition. Human beings then are displaced from their true moorings when they lose the track of true values and clarity of vision.

It goes to the credit of Maya that she maintained her womanly equilibrium even when the daemonic astrologer tried to browbeat Maya by his heroic posturings, sometimes showing himself as the messenger of Lord Krishna :

> He chuckled, gnomishly. 'Now we can go back to our very important conversation,' he said. 'Of course, you are still so young, so very young' — flicking the fold of his robe over his loins, flicking it — 'there is still so much time. Or have arrangements already been made — for a marriage?' 'No!' I shouted. 'I will never marry,' and at the same time the *ayah* screamed, 'Give me that horoscope you have made — lies, all lies. Give it to me so we can leave now.' And he raised his hands, rolled his eyes, crying, 'Calm yourselves! Calm yourselves! But we were in a frenzy now — I rushed to the door, the *ayah* seized the scroll. He grew perturbed, peremptory. 'Sit down,' he said, sternly, in a voice of steel. 'Listen to me, woman,' he snapped, like a whip, For there is only a chance, a faint possibility that her life should take this path. The sign is there. The stars prophesy it. But we are in the hands of God, and here his voice dropped, softened, began to quiver with emotion. 'God guides us all. He may guide you onto another path, if you pray for it to be so, offer sacrifices in order that it may be so! He had a rosary....' 'God guides you, child,' he murmured, close to my ear, and chanted a prayer opening his eyes wide and rolling them so that the iris formed white circles that gleamed aroud the pale pupils. 'Four years after your marriage, so the stars prophesy, and the space between your eyes, the mark there supports this prophesy. I have warned you,

> performed my duty. Be wary, child, be wary and fear God. Worship Him, make sacrifices. Pray. Do we not know, all of us here, the story of Prahlad? Of how Krishna saved him again, and again, countless times, through love and mercy? (31-32).

The astrologer, or the magician as Maya called him, played roguish tactics to insinuate himself as the saviour of this woman, before her marriage with Gautam. It was a traumatic experience for Maya to have suffered the evil presence of 'this fearsome magician.' She heaved a sigh of relief when 'he ushered us out, flicking the garment that slipped about his hips, flicking it as a lizard flicks its tongue at a petrified victim, and then hastily drew back into the shadows before a stray of light could strike him with its purifying glare of whiteness (32).

In Gandhian thought, to acquiesce with the evil, is a form of capitulation before it; and as Maya all along remained at a distance from the fearsome, manipulating magician (astrologer), she showed her mettle as a graceful and respectable woman. If a woman surrenders herself before a wily character, she compromises with the essential dignity of her womanhood. Oscar Wilde has a point when he says that in the face of the hostile force from outside, the truth of one's being is revealed only at the subjective level. It is in this context Maya's ceaseless effort to defend her womanhood needs to be lauded.

But, as they say, the human destiny is inscrutable and that its decree just cannot be evaded. Through one's conscious striving one may try to alter its course; but a human being is bound to fail. Somehow, at a particular time, the hour of reckoning came about Gautam's death to befall in strange sequence of events. It was no fault of Maya nor of anybody else; the end of Gautam came so suddenly without anybody's conscious guessing. Maya was already deluged with ill-starred and haunting images.

As far as Maya was concerned, her husband Gautam's practice of entering into his own thoughts exclusively without any note of communicabillity was disconnecting to her. This made her fidgety; and her feelings in an abridged form are here quoted to show how she suffered in loneliness :

> "Poor Gautama. Not to be able to notice the odour of limes, not to hear the melancholy voice singing somewhere behind the plantains, not to have time to count the stars as they came out one by one — poor Gautama, my poor, poor husband. 'They practise the scales every evening.' I told him, feeling so sorry for his lack of knowledge, his inability to take interest, for it was this that made him a grey shadow stalking, ...stumbling a little clumsily, a little lost in a world so full of very real things. 'And I have never heard them play another thing.'"
>
> 'Slow, are they?' he murmured, stamping out one cigarette after having lit another with it. This dancing jet of light at the end of the little white cylinder seemed the only thing about him that was alive, a fine antennae with which he kept in touch with the world, however shakily. ...'Listen,' I said, stopping at a sound. 'Do you hear that? It's an owl!'
>
> He stopped because my interruption held him, but he merely shook his head and paced on, a somnambulist's figure in opium white. ...But when Gautam held his silence too long, detached himself too completely into his exclusive mind. I drew him out again, finding it unbearable to lost touch of him. 'You are so very silent again.'
>
> He was startled at my touch and voice. 'Am I? Am I?' he said, and threw his cigarette over the parapet in repentance (206-207).

Maya's husband was a smoker; and so by this habit of smoking, Gautam had carved a niche exclusively for himself in the home where his wife also lived. Like Gautam, she dwelt in her own world of make-believe. What is known as *Svabhava* in Sanskrit and Hindi determined the directional pattern of their existence. Even as husband and wife, they sailed in their own ships of destiny. It does not mean that they had some animus, subtle or conscious between them. It was nothing like this. Both of them lived at a sublimatory process of life in which the ritual of blood ceremony played a negligible role. Her husband, Gautam was a busy, prosperous, middle-aged lawyer; and necessarily, he had to deal with the country's complicated laws, and the socio-economic ideas associated with them.

The sublimatory parameters also hold true for Maya, who was extremely sensitive, educated having been brought up with care and understanding of her father whom she remembers with gratitude; so a few lines may be cited to show that Maya was more spiritually indebted to her father than anybody else including her gentle husband. The way she off and on spoke of her father's kindly acts shows that her father had an elevated sense of life and wisdom; and that Maya as daughter was grateful to him. In Shakespeare's view, thanklessness is the worst form of sin as has been fittingly expressed by King Lear to his thankless daughter, Goneril :

> How sharper than a serpent's tooth it is
> To have a thankless child! Away! away![6]

Maya stood on a different plank altogether. She had a positive approach towards human life and its values. One can have faith in a meaningful life only when one defends the values underlying human existence. Maya affirms her existence with womanly dignity. As a sensitive woman, she could see through the sinister game of the unregenerate astrologer and castigate him for his slobbery conduct towards Maya and her *ayah* when they had gone to him in days long back. Here, it may be borne in mind that as this is the 'stream-of-consciousness' novel, may be in which every happening of the past passes through the discriminating sieve of Maya's mind, one gets to know the true worth of her character as woman. She is conscious of her womanly dignity and susceptibility. She weighs different values of life; and stands on the side of humanity and true morality. There is no hesitancy as far as this is concerned. In this way she is life-affirmative. As a married woman, her motherly instincts remain unfulfilled; and so she saw in her pet dog, Toto — a transferred love-object. Since love is an overwhelmingly powerful element of life in woman, it must get instinctual outlet. As the novel begins, the scavenging arrangements are being made to carry away Maya's pet dog; and then, she began to cry — a sign of her motherly attachment for the dead pet dog.

She bore within herself the finer elements of life — love, devotion, gentility, sensuous contact with the world around herself and hated with elemental feeling the gnomic presence of the magician-astrologer when she recalled her encounter with this highly unregenerate character in the company of her *ayah*. It is to the credit of Maya that she could maintain her girlish innocence even as a married woman. She intoned her sense of devotion to her affectionate father in a tragic vein : — 'No one, no one else,' I sobbed into my pillow as Gautam went into the bathroom, 'loves me as my father does.' The curtain fell to behind him, in tragic folds. He did not hear me — the tap was running. The vacuum into which I spoke made me more frantic, and yet he was not really meant to hear' (46).

From this extract, it is apparent that Maya, after her marriage with Gautam, missed something elemental of her life she was having from her childhood. It was the affection-filled love she got from her father. Maya, the affection-filled girl was observant enough to note about her father's life pattern that just 'as the streams in a Moghul garden flow musically through channels of carved marble and sandstone, so his thought, his life flow, broken into small, exquisite patterns by the carving, played upon by altering nuances of light and shade, but never over stepping their limitations, never breaking their bounds, always moving onwards with the same graceful cadence' (45). The delicately poised Maya avidly fond of affection and love found herself in a comparatively arid atmosphere after marriage. 'In Gautama's family one did not speak of love, far less of affection. One spoke — they spoke — of discussions in parliament, of cases of bribery and corruption revealed in government, of newspaper editors accused of libel, and the trials that followed, of trade pacts made with countries across the seas, of political treaties with those across the mountains, of distant revolutions, of rice scarcity and grain harvests.... They had innumerable subjects to speak on, and they spoke incessantly' (46). It was a painful realisation for her to find : 'Poor Gautam, poor near Gautam who was so intense and yet had never lived, and never would' (208). All this made Maya disenchanted with her married life. So the fatal hour of reckoning came at the parapet edge of the roof when in the presence of the affection-starved Maya, the husband fell precipitously down. Thus, one can say that Maya's struggle for a meaningful life is a part of the subimatory drama in rare specimens of womankind enacted all over the world in one form or another. One has to feel for their tragic ordeal! It is a fine story of a woman as Virginia Woolfe would also say.

NOTES AND REFERENCES

1. Anita Desia, *Cry, the Peacock* (Delhi : Orient Paperbacks, 1980). All further references are to this edition and are shown in parentheses within the text.
2. William Shakespeare, *The Tempest* (London : Collins Publishers, 1974), 161.
3. Virginia Woolfe in her famous essay, *How should one read a book.*
4. A front-page news feature in *The Hindustan Times,* March 12, 2001 reports women in Jammu under psychological stress of nightmarish terror-owing to the presence of foreign terrorists in J.K.
5. Turbidity of mind means the avidity for sex-oriented feelings.
6. William Shakespeare, *King Lear* (London : Collins Publishers, 1974), 110-11.

CONTRIBUTORS

P.N. Sinha, Professor of English, J.P. University, Rajendra College Campus, Chapra, Bihar.

Rama Kundu, Professor, Department of English, Burdwan University, Burdwan, West Bengal.

Ashok Kumar Bachchan, Reader in English, University Department of English, L.N. Mithila University, Darbhanga, Bihar.

Ranjit Singh (Mrs.), Reader in English, Sarah Tucker College, Tirunelveli, Tamil Nadu.

B. Yadava Raju, Associate Professor of English, Osmania University, Hyderabad, Andhra Pradesh.

B. Mishra, Department of Language, BITS, Pilani, Rajasthan.

C. Anna Latha Devi (Mrs.), Department of English, Scott Christian College, Nagercoil, Tamil Nadu.

Fed Mathew, Lecturer in English, St. Pius X College, Rajapuram Post Office, Kasaragod District, Kerala.

O.P. Budholia, Department of English, K.R.G. Government (Autonomous) College, Gwalior, Madhya Pradesh.

Vinod Kumar Maheshwari, Reader, Department of English, Agra College, Agra, Uttar Pradesh.

Shiv Kumar Yadav, Lecturer, Department of English, G.D. College, Begusarai, Bihar.

Chhote Lal Khatri, Department of English, S.S. College, Jehanabad, Bihar.

J.K. Nair, Assistant Professor (English), Government College, Khairagarh, Rajnandgaon District, Chhattisgarh.

P. Rajendra Karmarkar, Assistant Professor of English, Andhra University P.G. Centre, Kakinada, Andhra Pradesh.

Suresh Shukla, 6/B Chandrajyot Society, Vejalpur Road, Ahmedabad, Gujarat.

K.A. Agarwal, Reader in English, Gurukul Kangri University, Hardwar, Uttaranchal.